£20

THE HIZBUL

LINA KHATIB AND DINA MATAR AND
ATEF ALSHAER

The Hizbullah Phenomenon

Politics and Communication

HURST & COMPANY, LONDON

First published in the United Kingdom in paperback in 2014 by
C. Hurst & Co. (Publishers) Ltd.,
41 Great Russell Street, London, WC1B 3PL
© Lina Khatib, Dina Matar and Atef Alshaer, 2014
All rights reserved.
Printed in India

A Cataloguing-in-Publication data record for this book
is available from the British Library.

ISBN: 978-1-84904-335-9

www.hurstpublishers.com

This book is printed on paper from registered sustainable
and managed sources.

CONTENTS

Acknowledgements   *vii*

Introduction: Hizbullah's Communication and Political Evolution
                           Dina Matar and Lina Khatib   1

1. Hizbullah's Political Strategy
                                          Lina Khatib   13

2. From the Invasion to the Liberation: Communicating Hizbullah's
    Political Repertoire, 1982–2000
                  Dina Matar and Atef Alshaer with Lina Khatib   39

3. Hizbullah in the Twenty-First Century: The Struggle for Political
    Survival, 2000–12
                                          Lina Khatib   71

4. The Poetry of Hizbullah
                                        Atef Alshaer   119

5. Hassan Nasrallah: The Central Actor in Hizbullah's Political
    Communication Strategies
                                          Dina Matar   153

Conclusion: Hizbullah at a Crossroads
                           Lina Khatib and Dina Matar   181

Notes   *191*

Index   *221*

ACKNOWLEDGEMENTS

The authors would like to thank the Leverhulme Trust in the UK for generously supporting the research for this book through a Research Project Grant.

Thanks are due to the following people who have assisted with research: Jacqueline Barkett, Mona El-Hamdani, Elizabeth Buckner, Hikmat El-Khatib, Hisham Issa, Maha Issa, Zahera Harb, Tarik Harb, the Harb family in Lebanon, Amal Saad-Ghorayeb, Yousef Chweiri, Sophia Sa'adeh, Muna Sukkariyeh and Kay Dickinson; Khalil Ahmad Issa for reciting some of the poems quoted in Chapter 4; and Hizbullah's Media Relations Department personnel.

Thanks to Elias Muhanna for providing valuable comments on parts of this book and to Nadim Shehadi for his support.

An early version of Chapter 1 appeared in *Survival*, 53, 2 (April/May 2011), pp. 61–76, and Chapter 3 is based on a shorter version that appeared in Lina Khatib's book *Image Politics in the Middle East: The Role of the Visual in Political Struggle*, London: I.B. Tauris, 2013, as well as a working paper published in January 2012 under the title 'Hizbullah's Image Management Strategy' in *CPD Perspectives on Public Diplomacy*; thanks to Philip Seib and the Center on Public Diplomacy at the University of Southern California for supporting Lina Khatib's research in 2010–12 through a research fellowship at the centre.

INTRODUCTION:
HIZBULLAH'S COMMUNICATION AND
POLITICAL EVOLUTION

Dina Matar and Lina Khatib

Hizbullah, the Lebanese 'Party of God', is a late twentieth-century phenomenon, the outcome of a series of socio-historical and political junctures marked by domestic political upheaval and regional conflicts.[1] Hizbullah is a by-product of regional geostrategic alignments: the group is ideologically and politically connected to Iran, and its capabilities, weaponry and operations are influenced by Iranian patronage.[2] It also has long-term strategic links with Syria, which has acted as a conduit for the supply of arms and personnel from Iran and serves as an important ally in domestic politics. In the space of thirty years, Hizbullah has established itself as the most powerful political force in Lebanon and as a dynamic actor in the broader region through its use of a sophisticated political communication strategy which blends military, social, economic and religious elements while remaining adaptive to changing socio-political contexts. This strategy, as this book will show, has been a central tool that the group has used to disseminate its image and ideology.

Hizbullah's emergence as an Islamic jihadi group in 1982 came at a new nadir in Lebanon's prolonged and complex history of domestic

1

political turmoil. The armed Palestinian presence in the country and the Lebanese civil war, which began in 1975, exacerbated the country's political and social fragmentation. The 1982 Israeli invasion, in which thousands of people died, further compounded this situation by seriously damaging Lebanese infrastructure and forcing the break-up of old alliances and the forging of new ones—it also led to the return of Western troops to Beirut. Yet while the Israeli invasion is often cited as the most important factor in the creation of Hizbullah as an Islamist resistance force in the 1980s, other historical conjunctures also contributed to its formation. Among these are the 1979 Islamic Revolution in Iran; the emergence of various Islamist movements in parts of the Arab and Muslim worlds; and the increasing politicisation of Lebanon's Shiite population, a process that began in the 1960s through the efforts of prominent Shiite clerics such as Imam Musa al-Sadr, who sought to become the paramount leader of the Shiite community.[3] Al-Sadr believed that his fellow Shiites could overcome their marginalisation if they were able to speak and act according to their beliefs and religion.[4] In 1969 he became head of the Lebanese Supreme Shiite Council and in 1974 he founded the Movement of the Deprived to help the poor and dispossessed in Lebanon regardless of their sectarian or ethnic affiliations, although the movement came to be strongly associated with the Shiite community. A year later he established the paramilitary group Afwaj al-muqawama al-lubnaniya (the Brigades of the Lebanese Resistance), known by its acronym Amal, an activist movement involved in social and political reform and the liberation of South Lebanon.

Hizbullah bears many similarities to the other Islamist parties that emerged in the twentieth century. But unlike other regional Islamist movements, such as the Egyptian Muslim Brotherhood, whose principal raison d'être was to oppose authoritarian regimes, Hizbullah emerged in a country with a long history of open struggles, where power[5] was contested by a range of confessional and ideological groups. Indeed, the internal dynamics of Lebanon's multiparty, multi-confessional political system—institutionalised by the 1943 National Pact paving the way for the country's independence from France[6]—allowed Hizbullah to set and cultivate roots in popular culture, particularly in Shiite-populated areas in Lebanon. This in turn allowed the group to expand its political power, to set up diverse media outlets, to establish its own socio-political activities and outreach programmes and to engage in a real and symbolic 'war of position'[7] with other political forces in Lebanon.

Hizbullah's ideological aims and political intentions were not made public until the publication of its 1985 manifesto, the 'Open Letter'. This document detailed the group's ideology and presented an image of Hizbullah as a grassroots Islamist jihadi movement that sought to establish an Islamic state in Lebanon on a similar basis to Iran's *wilayat al-faqih* (the guardianship of the jurisprudence)[8] once a consensus for such a system had been realised within Lebanon itself.[9] The manifesto also emphasised Hizbullah's commitment to fighting colonialism and imperialism as well as the provision of social services to its supporters. Although the manifesto included a thinly veiled attack on the Lebanese political system, which was described as infidel in nature, it stopped short of endorsing its immediate replacement with the rule of Islam, providing the first signal of a pragmatic and gradualist approach[10] that would define Hizbullah's image and language in subsequent years. In fact, replacing the Lebanese government with an Islamic republic along the lines of the Iranian revolutionary model had never been a preoccupation of Hizbullah's leadership, despite the implicit emphasis placed on this long-term goal in its manifesto and in other declarations by Hizbullah's elites.[11] Instead, the intention was to change the Lebanese political system into a majoritarian democracy, which would allow the party to reach a position of leadership from where it would be able to impose ideological hegemony.[12]

To this end, when competing Lebanese factions signed the Tai'f Accord (which ended the country's fifteen-year civil war in 1989), Hizbullah began a concerted policy of *infitah*, or 'opening up', which was designed to integrate the movement into the Lebanese political and social spheres and to ease its transformation into a distinct Lebanese political party. This goal was to be achieved largely by playing according to—though also by manipulating—the rules set by the existing political regime. Thus in 1992, headed by the charismatic Sheikh Hassan Nasrallah as its Secretary General, the group participated in Lebanon's first post-civil war elections, a move that marked a distinct phase in its gradual integration into Lebanon's multi-confessional system. Throughout the 1990s, Hizbullah consistently presented a public image that was intended to show that its transformation from an Islamist movement into a mainstream political party was authentic and legitimate. It also sought to demonstrate that it was a nationalist rather than a purely Islamic movement, a tactic that allowed it to maintain its Islamic identity while accommodating Lebanon's Christian population and liberal components of Lebanese society. In May 2000 Hizbullah increased its share of seats in the new parliamentary elections held after the Israeli withdrawal from southern Lebanon, an event in which the group had played a major role, thereby strengthening its identity as a national party and heralding a new phase of political jihad to enhance its domestic position as a civilian political party accommodated by the Lebanese political system. The liberation of southern Lebanon, Hizbullah's support for the second Palestinian intifada (uprising) from 2000 onwards and its public condemnation of the US-led 'war on terror' and invasion of Iraq further increased its bargaining power in the domestic sphere and enhanced its regional reputation.

Within five years, Hizbullah's 'war of position' with Lebanese political parties and civilians opposed to its insistence on maintaining arms and its relationship with Syria turned into open political confrontation in the 2005 Cedar Revolution following the assassination of the former Lebanese Prime Minister Rafic Hariri on 14 February 2005. The July 2006 war with Israel, however, helped change the balance of power in Hizbullah's favour by furnishing the group with an opportunity to re-indigenise its image as a national Lebanese party. The 2006 war began when Israel responded with a disproportionate display of force to a provocation by Hizbullah in the South—the subsequent armed conflict killed more than 1,000 people, mostly Lebanese nationals, and displaced 1 million others. Although Israel managed to destroy most of Hizbullah's strategic missile arsenal and a large number of its rocket launchers, the movement's endurance in the face of the attacks allowed it to present itself as the victor. While the outcome of the war was ultimately inconclusive, this did not prevent Hizbullah's charismatic and powerful leader Hassan Nasrallah from describing it as a 'Divine Victory', thus strengthening Hizbullah's image as an Arab national force within Lebanon and beyond.

However, in the two years that followed, Hizbullah's credibility as a Lebanese party was brought into question when several of its armed militia took control of West Beirut in May 2008, a move that helped to re-establish long-standing sectarian tensions and divisions along Sunni–Shiite lines. Its credibility in Lebanon was also weakened following reports that some of its personnel had been involved in the assassination of Hariri in 2005, while its support and image in the wider Arab world suffered deeply as a result of its support for the Assad regime's brutal repression of opponents during the Syrian uprising from March 2011 onwards.

Communication and Politics

This book argues that Hizbullah's communication strategy has served as the foundation for its political evolution and endurance as a movement. Ever since its inception, Hizbullah has paid constant attention to its image, seeking to manage and institutionalise it in order to achieve legitimacy, to reach out to different constituents[13] and to implement its political goals. The starting point for this book is that Hizbullah's political evolution and its success[14] within particular contexts cannot be appreciated without understanding the methods, tools and practices it has employed since its formation in 1982, and the relationship between agency and structure—i.e. the activism of its elites and ideologues functioning within organised and deeply rooted structural arrangements, and the relationship between this activism and political contexts. Indeed, it is Hizbullah's highly organised structure that has allowed it to develop and reproduce authority in popular culture, and to devise and implement communication strategies in line with changing political, economic and social contexts. As Ahmad Nizar Hamzeh writes, this structure assumes:

the shape of a hierarchical pyramid coinciding with the territorial division of Lebanon's governorates, in particular the ones that have a majority of Shiites— that is, Beirut, Biqaa, and South Lebanon. Structurally, the party consists of leadership, political and administrative, and military and security organs, along with a number of service subunits within each apparatus.[15]

This book argues that Hizbullah's political, economic, military and cultural mobilisation and activism cannot be seen as natural or taken-for-granted responses to accumulated grievances (as suggested in some of the literature on political Islam[16]) or as a reactionary product of a cultural essence (Islam). Rather, Hizbullah's activism and mobilisation have resulted from the agency of its elites and ideologues and their implementation of a political communication strategy designed to widen its support base and increase its influence. From the outset, the group's clerical and ideological leaders, along with some key figures in the Lebanese Shiite community, such as the Sheikh Mohammed Hussain Fadlallah, began organising popular and cultural activities aimed at mobilising targeted publics through traditional socio-religious networks. These networks not only consisted of formal religious institutions, such as mosques, but also included an intricate layer of religiously based rituals and ceremonies that the leaders would attend (thus lending them religious legitimacy) as well as a variety of popular cultural practices that comprise the core of social life. Hizbullah's Secretary General Hassan Nasrallah later took on the task of public mobilisation and became the central actor in Hizbullah's decision-making process, yet he still continued to function within the constraints of the group's institutional structures.[17]

The literature on social movements, including studies of various Islamist movements, emphasises the importance of formal and informal networks[18] for mobilisation and the new contexts afforded by expanded communication technologies. The latter, as Castells has argued, have led to a shift from an 'industrial paradigm' to an 'information paradigm'[19] in which the real power is the power of instrumental flows and cultural codes embedded in networks. The literature, particularly within sociology, has also emphasised the importance of collective action frames for understanding the evolution and character of social movements, and the role of frames in producing meaning and mobilising support. According to this perspective, social movements are not mere carriers of extant ideas and meanings that grow automatically out of structural arrangements, unanticipated events or existing ideologies. Rather, movement actors are viewed as signifying agents actively engaged in the production and maintenance of meaning.[20] Collective action framing refers to both social movements and media as it involves 'public discourse that is, the interface of media discourse and interpersonal interaction; persuasive communication during mobilisation campaigns by movement organisations, their opponents and counter-movement organisations and consciousness raising during episodes of collective action'.[21] In recent years a large number of studies have examined the dynamic relationship between media and social movements and the interdependency between them. Two dominant strands exist: the first advocates a close relationship between social movements and the media so that movements can achieve their aim, and the second argues that mass media bias and apathy often force movement elites to abandon mainstream media and rely on radical media.[22]

This scholarship, and particularly the use of collective action framing to shape public opinion or mobilise support, is certainly useful for explaining aspects of Hizbullah's organisation and mobilisation. But it does not fully explain how such groups develop their own communication strategies to attract support and shape public opinion; nor does it account for the ways in which actors and groups shift and change their image, language and rhetorical frames during cycles of protest or socio-political crises, and how they manage to hold on to their perceived image even outside periods of protests and crises. As a close reading of its history reveals, Hizbullah has adapted its image and language to suit particular contexts, thereby increasing its power and reach while simultaneously retaining some credibility within its main constituency—the Shiites of Lebanon—even though its popularity in the larger Lebanese sphere and the Arab world has suffered in different historical periods, particularly because of its support for the Syrian regime's brutal crackdown on opponents. Finally, social movement theory tends to underestimate the extent to which movements, political forces and actors are increasingly defined by their public face, or image, particularly in the age of globalised, digital media. As the different chapters in this book show, Hizbullah's attention to its public image, including perceptions of its leader Hassan Nasrallah, has been a defining feature of its political communication strategy since its inception in 1982.

To put the chapters in context, and drawing on a diversity of conceptual approaches, the evolution of Hizbullah's image can be understood with reference to two interrelated dynamics. The first is the relationship between organisations and the environment, or political opportunity structures,[23] which movements use to mobilise supporters and achieve hegemony. In Lebanon, several political opportunity structures were already available: a historically weak Lebanese state; Lebanon's complex, yet fluid, social, political and cultural dynamics; and a fragmented but diverse Lebanese media space—all of which are a legacy of the fragile power-sharing system among the country's many confessional groups that was established when Lebanon gained independence from France in 1943. Other factors included the repeated incursions by Israel into Lebanon, the armed Palestinian presence in the country in the 1960s and 1970s, Lebanon's fifteen-year civil war and

Syria's and Iran's interests and role in supporting Hizbullah. Furthermore, Hizbullah emerged in the context of the continued marginalisation of the Shiites in Lebanon, which the party used in order to justify, on a social and moral level, its concentration on improving the Shiites' situation in terms of politics, development and defence,[24] presenting this as a natural and inevitable framework for progress.

The second dynamic is the relationship between language and culture,[25] both of which are important resources for the implementation of various strategies and calculations. In this sense, we see both language and culture, in the anthropological sense, as malleable and fluid, and therefore as offering spaces and terrains for contestation over image and ideologies.[26] As this book reveals, Hizbullah has used culture and language as a dialectical relationship between system and practice. It used culture as an instrument in achieving its objectives, and it used language, imagery and symbols not only to articulate its own identity but also to excavate and respond to pre-existing socio-historically accumulated values and practices that define ordinary people's lives on many levels. In other words, Hizbullah used language in different forms and ways to create and sustain a 'hegemonic ideological space' through which it managed to define people's lives according to plans, schemes and political calculations. In this way, to borrow from Gramsci, hegemony by consent is not induced through different state apparatuses but through associational, everyday and cultural spaces, including mosques, religious centres, popular ceremonies, parades, rallies, public spaces, poetry recitals and festivals, as well as formal media channels and platforms. It is in all these spaces that Hizbullah managed to build and sustain an image of itself as a 'rationality, a way of thinking and existence (episteme)' that, as Amal Saad-Ghorayeb argues,[27] ordinary people are able to relate to in their everyday lives.

Hizbullah's Communication Strategy

Since its inception in 1982 Hizbullah has used a sophisticated communication strategy that has run parallel to the group's political evolution. This strategy combines elements of the professionalised political and marketing strategies that are popular in Western election campaigns with a culturally sensitive communicative model of mobilisation that actively selects, appropriates and disseminates meaningful symbols, images and language to construct and sustain a constant interchange of communally relevant knowledge.

This strategy operates simultaneously and continuously at different levels, in formal and informal spaces of social interaction, in the private and the public, the political and the cultural spheres. At the same time, it consistently relies on, and uses, traditional networks of sociability embedded in popular culture. In contrast to secular, liberal and leftist groups already competing for power and influence in Lebanon, Hizbullah managed to build on, and expand, pre-existing national and transnational 'thick networks' of religious and social relations set up by Shiite clerics in the second half of the nineteenth century. Informal[28] and indirect ways of contesting authority have a long history in the Middle East and North Africa.[29] Religious networks, in particular, have often functioned as sites for oppositional public spheres in which religious rhetoric is reconstituted as political rhetoric and religious leaders emerge as political leaders. As its organisational structures became more formalised and its political communication strategy more institutionalised, Hizbullah would establish and expand formal media outlets and platforms to reach out to a larger audience outside of the Shiite constituency of Lebanon, its original target group. By the beginning of the twenty-first century, Hizbullah's communication strategy had developed into a constant process of strategic communication or a permanent discursive and visual campaign that used professionalised political campaigns characterised by 'excessive personalisation, a political star system, mass media impression management and an increasing negativity'.[30]

Hizbullah began developing formal media institutions in 1982 when it published an obscure newsletter called *al-Mujtahid* (The Struggler), which had a distinctive Iranian-inspired rhetoric and style. The newsletter carried reports about Iran and local developments related to Iran, such as celebrations of the Iranian Islamic Revolution in Iran and in Lebanon, as well as the activities of Islamic committees and speeches by Iranian and Lebanese clerical leaders. However, the publication of *al-Mujtahid* came to an abrupt halt with the onset of the Israeli invasion of Lebanon in June 1982, when it was replaced with a four-page leaflet called *Ahl al-thugour* (The People of the Outpost) which continued to focus on Iranian affairs and the battle between the Islamic nation and the Israeli enemy.[31] In 1984, Hizbullah launched its weekly newspaper *al-'Ahd* (The Pledge), which was to become its most influential formal communication tool for disseminating messages and reaching out to target audiences until the al-Manar television station was established in 1991. In 1989, Hizbullah formalised its communication strategies with the establishment of its Executive Council (*al-majlis al-tanfithi*) which was charged with overseeing several institutional structures, including the day-to-day activities of the Central Information Unit[32] which was responsible for developing formal media institutions.

The institutionalisation and centralisation of Hizbullah's political communication strategy meant that all visual and discursive forms of cultural output would carry the same messages in order to appeal to the target audience during a particular historical juncture. At that time, Hizbullah had begun its *infitah* (opening up) policy, which sought to integrate the group into the Lebanese political system and to transform its image from an Islamist party of 'faithful Lebanese who believe in Islam, resistance, and liberation of the land' to 'one of the most prominent Lebanese political parties'.[33] By 2013 it was publishing its own newspaper, *al-Intiqad* (formerly, *al-'Ahd*), which is available online, and it also had its own satellite television station (al-Manar), several websites, including one for al-Manar offered in multiple languages (Arabic, English, French), and its own radio station (al-Nour). Hizbullah also produces children's games, merchandise, books and computer games, as well as posters and billboards, in addition to mass rallies, to communicate with its multiple audiences.[34] Its leader Hassan Nasrallah has established a reputation for delivering attention-grabbing speeches. Hizbullah additionally relies on a wealth of public relations resources and personnel, as well as marketing companies such as Idea Creation which helped in the design of the victory campaign following the 2006 war with Israel, in order to reach out to its audiences.

The success of Hizbullah's strategy requires it to keep a close eye on political developments in the local Lebanese scene, and it has proved highly skilful in turning them to its advantage. The group also relies on cultivating an image of popular support for itself in order to enhance its credibility. Hizbullah branded the withdrawal of Israel from southern Lebanon in 2000 and the movement's survival following the 2006 war as great victories, portraying itself as the liberator and protector of Lebanon. This type of branding has been helped by the charismatic authority and popularity of its leader Hassan Nasrallah, who tailors his speeches to appeal to different audiences within and outside Lebanon, while emphasising anti-sectarian rhetoric. Hizbullah has proved remarkably adept at using visual and public displays of its power, from billboards depicting the Israeli defeat in 2006 to the Spider's Web exhibition in 2007 to the exhibition of its success against Israeli forces at the Mleeta visitor centre in southern Lebanon. The group uses images of its leaders and martyrs with strong Islamic references in public spaces in Lebanon. The visual and public display serves to enhance the image of its power and to reassure its supporters of the group's strength, continuity and rootedness in culture.

This book begins with a chapter contextualising Hizbullah's political communication strategy within its short- and long-term political aims. Chapter 2 explores the methods, features, tools and rhetorical framework used in Hizbullah's communication strategy, focusing on the period between 1982 and 2000 (i.e. from the year of the Israeli invasion to the Israeli withdrawal from southern Lebanon), and relates them to the historical and political contexts within which Hizbullah operates. Chapter 3 follows the same structure but discusses the period between 2000 and 2012. Chapter 4 examines Hizbullah's poetry as a form of communication, providing a contextualised historical analysis of the use of poetry to appeal to different constituents. Chapter 5 traces the rise of Hassan Nasrallah in power and the shift in his image from a devout, relatively unknown cleric into Hizbullah's first charismatic leader in the media age. It explores how his image and charismatic authority are the main components of Hizbullah's centralised political communication strategy, which aims to widen the group's support base and influence in Lebanon and beyond. The book ends with a conclusion that brings the discussion to the present by reflecting on the challenges that Hizbullah is facing as a result of the Syrian uprising.

Any conceptual model or analytical approach cannot fully explain the complexities of a phenomenon such as Hizbullah. The authors of this book acknowledge that the approach which is followed could be viewed as privileging a communication-based model of organisation and mobilisation, which could in turn serve to detract attention from other issues that have influenced Hizbullah's activism, not least the military struggle with Israel, its ideological conflict with global powers and its organic roots with Iran. However, the main contention of the book is that the relationship between politics, activism and communication is a symbiotic one, and thus any analysis of politics cannot exclude a communicative approach. Furthermore, in adopting this approach, the book aims to avoid the pitfalls of portraying Hizbullah as a reactionary force whose emergence is explained as the result of favourable conditions or the outcome of a problematic cultural essence, Islam. Rather, the approach provides the means to address Hizbullah as a political force and a 'rational' political actor that, like other political actors, has engaged in a game of political survival. The following chapter discusses this game of political survival in detail.

1

HIZBULLAH'S POLITICAL STRATEGY

Lina Khatib

Despite its relatively humble beginnings in the 1980s, Hizbullah has today emerged as the leading political and military actor in Lebanon. The upward trajectory of the group's political influence is due, at least in part, to its sophisticated political and communication strategy, which combines military, social, economic and religious elements while remaining adaptive to changes in Hizbullah's political surroundings. Any study of Hizbullah's communication strategy must consequently place it within the broader context of the group's political strategy.

This chapter provides an overview of Hizbullah's strategy, examining it within the context of the barriers and enablers that affect it in the political environment. The chapter starts with an analysis of Hizbullah's long-term political aims and the factors affecting the group's ability to achieve these, before moving on to address the main components of Hizbullah's political strategy.

THE HIZBULLAH PHENOMENON

Hizbullah's long-term political aims

Hizbullah's involvement in local, regional and international politics at specific milestones in Lebanese history—including periods of external intervention and Hizbullah's participation in Lebanese elections, as well as international developments such as the UN Special Tribunal for Lebanon (STL), established to investigate the 2005 assassination of Rafic Hariri—has drawn media and scholarly attention to these events and Hizbullah's policy towards them. Yet a narrow focus on its policy towards these issues runs the risk of overlooking the group's long-term political aims and their role in informing Hizbullah's decision-making process in specific contexts.

From its 1985 Open Letter to its 2009 manifesto, Hizbullah has consistently presented its vision as one that transcends Lebanon—the Open Letter was primarily addressed to Muslims worldwide, and the 2009 manifesto similarly frames Hizbullah's outlook as global in scope.[1] The manifesto declares that 'The Resistance in Lebanon has evolved from a Lebanese national value to an Arab and Islamic value and has become today an international value that's taught all over the world.'[2] While Hizbullah's day-to-day activities are focused on intra-Lebanese issues, such as securing more representation within the Lebanese parliament or increasing its influence within the Cabinet, the group's long-term political aim is to assume a position of leadership in the global Islamic world. In order to achieve this goal, Hizbullah willingly participates in the current Lebanese political confessional system with the aim of becoming the leading political power in Lebanon. But the group's ultimate aim is to reach a position of leadership by changing the system itself. In the words of Hizbullah's Deputy Secretary General Naim Qassem, 'The Party's final objective, in its political jihadist vision and program of work, is not to reach ultimate ruling power within the current sectarian system.'[3] Hizbullah MP Mohammad Raad reiterated this objective in December 2004 by stating that most Lebanese would support the continuation of the 'resistance' if a referendum were conducted in Lebanon—and if such a referendum were to take place, one 'should ask whether the presidency should still be reserved for the Maronites'.[4]

Such a statement, with its allusion to 'fairness' of representation, is reflected in Hizbullah's 2009 manifesto, in which the group is presented as a reformist, nationalist movement working towards the creation of a 'fair' state:

> To conclude, it should be mentioned that one of the most important conditions for the establishment of a home of this type is having a fair state, a state which is capable and strong, as well as a political system that truly represents the will of the people and their aspirations for justice, freedom and security, stability and well-being and dignity. This is what all the Lebanese people want and work to achieve and we are a part of them.[5]

In arguing its case for political reform, Hizbullah has consequently sought to reassure its rivals by emphasising its ostensibly moderate intentions.[6] The latter are presented in democratic terms, with the 2009 manifesto confirming the group's commitment to the creation of a majoritarian democracy:

> The main problem in the Lebanese political system, which prevents its reform, development and constant updating is political sectarianism … The fact that the Lebanese political system was established on a sectarian basis constitutes in itself a strong constraint to the achievement of true democracy where an elected majority can govern and an elected minority can oppose, opening the door for a proper circulation of power between the loyalty and the opposition or the various political coalitions. Thus, abolishing sectarianism is a basic condition for the implementation of the majority–minority rule.[7]

Although the wording of the manifesto is deliberately vague regarding the exact nature of the majoritarian democracy that Hizbullah proposes, the group's declarations since 1985 suggest that it aspires to an Islamic democracy under the *wilayat al-faqih* model (i.e. the political structure adopted in post-1979 Iran). This aspiration has been explicitly referred to on a number of occasions, including the 1985 Open Letter, which called on people in Lebanon to accept an Islamic state, in an article in *al-'Ahd* on 26 March 1999, which argued for the establishment of a 'pure' Islamic state,[8] and in Hizbullah's August 2004 'Identity and Goals' declaration, which states that '[a]nother of its ideals is the establishment of Islamic Republic'.[9] In a speech and question-and-answer session on 26 May 2008, Secretary General Hassan Nasrallah declared his sense of pride in belonging to the party of *wilayat al-faqih*, before going on to emphasise that commitment to *wilayat al-faqih* is an unchangeable value for Hizbullah, rather than a pragmatic political objective. In a book published in the same year, Naim Qassem presents a framework for *wilayat al-faqih* that legitimises the Iranian model: 'It is a mistake to imagine the role of the *wali faqih* [the clerical authority] in the executive positions, because he [the *wali faqih*] draws the general outlines and bestows legitimacy on that direction; then the authorities and leaderships in question uphold the responsibilities completely in accordance with its detailed systems and its administration which is congruent with its conditions and reality.'[10] This framework reconciles the existence of *wilayat al-faqih* with the institutions of a 'modern' state, but only on the condition that the state is under the jurisdiction of the *wali faqih*. The concept of *wilayat al-faqih* allows for the existence of a variety of political systems, yet state decisions must ultimately be taken by the *wali al-faqih* regardless of who is the head of state. In this sense, *wilayat al-faqih* implies a need to create not several distinct Islamic states with their own *wali*s, but one state/meta-state, with one *wali*—in Iran. As Hizbullah has established itself as the strongest political party in Lebanon, it could be argued that Hizbullah has moved closer to making the Lebanese state answerable to the *wali al-faqih*. However, the diversity and complexity of Lebanese society, which prevent any single group from completely dominating another, serve as a barrier to realising this vision in full.

In public, Hizbullah has been careful to play down its commitment to establishing an Islamic state in Lebanon because the group has realised that this is not an attractive prospect for at least half of the Lebanese population. Some even interpreted the absence of any reference to *wilayat al-faqih* in Hizbullah's 2009 manifesto as a sign that the group had abandoned this political aim. But this omission is not a sign of abandonment—it is an indication of the group's political pragmatism. Sceptics may of course argue that the opposite is also true, namely that Hizbullah's public references to *wilayat al-faqih* do not necessarily represent a definite commitment to this ideal. However, Hizbullah's overtly religious persona in its outreach to the Shiite community and its cultivation of religious practices—including its emphasis on the martyrdom trope, its creation of religious schools and youth centres, the religious programming in its media and the growing conservatism in its stronghold areas in southern Lebanon (where Hizbullah is increasingly restricting the public consumption of alcohol, for example)—clearly suggest that the first interpretation is the more accurate of the two, particularly as Hizbullah is partly a product of Iran, the headquarters of the pan-Islamic *wilayat al-faqih*.

The interplay between agency and structure

As with all political groups, Hizbullah's decision-making and political strategy result from interactions between agency and structure. Gideon Rose states that decision-making can be explained by examining the interaction between agency (i.e. the 'freedom of action to choose one course over another') and structures, or 'aspects of the environment' that steer actors in a particular direction and not another.[11] When viewed through this analytical framework, Hizbullah's internal structure clearly grants the group significant agency, which is in turn supported by a number of enablers from the group's external environment. Yet throughout its history the group has also faced and sought to overcome a number of external barriers to its political strategy.

Hizbullah's organisational structure follows a top-down model where the highest level of leadership exerts ultimate authority. Although attempts were made to reform this structure in the mid-1990s, with newer members proposing the adoption of a local Lebanese agenda and a dialogue-based approach towards other political entities in Lebanon,[12] these efforts failed owing to the marginalisation of the newer membership by those who were closer to the Iranian clerical leadership. However, irrespective of his own power and appeal, Hizbullah's secretary general is still accountable to the organisation. In 1992, Subhi Tufaili, Hizbullah's first Secretary General, was effectively removed from his post because of opposition from the group's diverse institutional organisations to his policy of boycotting the Lebanese parliamentary elections.[13] The intricate workings of Hizbullah and its decision-making processes remain largely absent from the public eye. Yet as this book's subsequent chapters demonstrate, Hizbullah has successfully managed, partly through its use of diverse forms of communication, to project an image of itself as a practitioner of participatory politics. The rallying of communities in southern Lebanon against the Israeli occupation, for example, is often presented (and interpreted) as a grassroots movement. While it is true that such a movement existed in the South, the reality is that key anti-Israeli operations in southern Lebanon, particularly in the

1990s, were largely orchestrated by Hizbullah in a strategic fashion. Hizbullah succeeded in giving the people of the South a sense of ownership over such operations, but this does not mean that they have any say in the political, military and other decision-making processes within the group. A potentially mitigating factor in this regard is Hizbullah's reliance on the large constituency of Shiite migrants for funding and for forming regional networks for the group. However, Hizbullah has created a self-sustaining system in its engagement with this constituency that mirrors its relationship with constituencies within Lebanon, in also providing it with a sense of empowerment through being part of an influential regional network, yet without actually delegating power to its members. Having a top-down structure means that Hizbullah has the freedom to choose courses of action without being accountable to its constituents.[14]

A number of external enablers and barriers have an impact on Hizbullah's political strategy, while some factors also serve a dual role. The first enabler is the Lebanese system of managing conflict, which is a model that aspires to political consensus (albeit with varying degrees of success). Hizbullah has successfully used this system to its advantage by securing progressively larger gains each time the model has been put to the test. One example is the 2008 Doha Accord, which provided Hizbullah and its allies with a veto over Cabinet decisions despite the fact that the group lacked a parliamentary majority. The Doha Accord was an agreement brokered by Qatar between Lebanon's political factions that ended the country's eighteen-month political vacuum following Hizbullah's decision to protest against the government's proposed removal of its communication network (the government had viewed the network as parallel to its own, but Hizbullah relies on it for its security). Hizbullah's protest originally began with a sit-in in downtown Beirut in December 2006 before evolving into a political stalemate that left the country without an elected president. In May 2008 the protest escalated into a violent confrontation when the group's militia stormed areas of Beirut affiliated with the rival Future Movement led by Rafic Hariri's son, Saad. Thus while the Accord was supposed to have resulted from consensus, it was in fact a political decision imposed by Hizbullah and its March 8 allies, mainly the Free Patriotic Movement led by Michel Aoun, on the rival March 14 camp led by Hariri.[15] The Doha Accord consequently demonstrates that Hizbullah's threat and use of internal violence were sufficient to force political concessions, including the Cabinet veto that was granted to March 8. It also illustrates Hizbullah's shrewd ability to take advantage of the consensual nature of the Lebanese political system.

The second enabler in Hizbullah's strategy is the Lebanese state itself. Owing to the weakness of the Lebanese state and its inability to defend itself against Israel, Hizbullah believes that its role as a Lebanese resistance force is both inevitable and necessary. It also links its weapons with the presence of Israel, arguing that it will continue to bear arms as long as Israel exists, regardless of the latter's presence on Lebanese soil.[16] On the economic level, Hizbullah criticised Rafic Hariri's Beirut-focused economic revitalisation plan following the end of the Lebanese civil war in the early 1990s. Yet at the same time, Hizbullah actively prevented Lebanese state services from reaching the people of southern Lebanon and those in Beirut's southern suburbs.[17] This suggests that it is not in Hizbullah's interest for the Lebanese state to grow in strength unless the state is under its direct control. Hizbullah is only likely to agree to the presence of a strong Lebanese state if Hizbullah itself is the army and the economic provider—in other words, if Hizbullah is the state. This stance has broad support among Lebanon's Shiites who, prior to the rise of Amal and Hizbullah, had been subjected to political, economic and social marginalisation. Hizbullah has stepped in to present itself as the sole legitimate representative of the Shiite community's interests. As Vali Nasr argues: 'Restoration of power to the Lebanese government without a plan to give the Shia more say in running the country will likely alienate them. If the Shia believe that Hezbollah alone can defend their rights and promote their interests, then they will continue to support its brand of politics.'[18] Hizbullah has established a de facto monopoly over the Lebanese Shiites, and thus it is not in Hizbullah's interest for another entity to make a claim to the defence of this religious community.

The third enabler for Hizbullah's strategy is its relative power in Lebanon. Hizbullah's political opponents, the March 14 coalition, have proved unable to impose restraint on the group's actions. As will be discussed later in the chapter, Hizbullah has successfully quelled or co-opted its Shiite opponents, which in turn means that the group also lacks any internal forms of restraint. As Gideon Rose argues, when a political entity is able to act without any constraints, whether internal or external, its doctrine can 'pass from an idea into policy' without being challenged.[19] In an analysis of American war decision-making, Rose concludes that the political and military actions of the United States over recent decades are not simply about pursuing power—they also reflect power. A similar argument can be made with regard to Hizbullah, whose growing relative power has allowed it to exercise its political will more widely.

The next set of enablers comprises Iran and Syria. Iranian and Syrian support for Hizbullah is well documented, although Hizbullah is far from being an Iranian or Syrian puppet; rather, it would be more instructive to view Hizbullah as a product of the Iranian Revolution, but one that has assumed a life and identity of its own. While Iran certainly acts as a funder and a facilitator, Hizbullah enjoys a large degree of autonomy from Tehran, whereas the group's relationship with Assad's Syria has historically been a mutually beneficial partnership.[20] The benefits of the latter have, however, been seriously questioned as a result of the Syrian uprising from 2011 onwards.

The United States and Israel play a dual role in Hizbullah's strategy, acting as both barriers and enablers. Thus whereas the United States characterises Hizbullah as a terrorist organisation, and while Israel poses a potential existential threat, both countries have nevertheless been instrumental in Hizbullah's political rise—Israel, after all, provides the group with a raison d'être, which is in turn strengthened by the US–Israeli alliance. The 2006 war that followed Hizbullah's kidnapping of two Israeli soldiers across the border is a very clear example of this. The war, in which the United States supported Israeli attacks on Hizbullah, catalysed unprecedented support for Hizbullah not only among the Lebanese at large but also among Arab and Muslim communities worldwide, and paved the way for Hizbullah to claim a greater degree of control in the local Lebanese scene. The war marked the pinnacle of Hizbullah's communication and public relations strategy, as will be discussed in detail in Chapter 3.

But Hizbullah also faces challenges, including a number of barriers that it has tried to overcome in more recent years. One of these was Rafic Hariri. According to Nicholas Blanford, Hariri gambled 'his entire economic and political programme for Lebanon on a successful outcome of the Middle East peace process', and thus, from Hizbullah's perspective, he 'held dangerous views regarding accommodation with Israel'.[21] As early as 1993, Hizbullah's newspaper *al-'Ahd* had condemned a reported statement by Hariri that 'peace between Lebanon and Israel would greatly benefit Lebanon'—in an article published by the paper on 10 September 1993, the statement was described as 'dangerous' and blind to 'the dangers of an "Israeli" peace to Lebanon and the various catastrophes it would bring'.[22] Hariri was furthermore supportive of the Syrian withdrawal from Lebanon following UN Resolution 1559, which was adopted on 4 September 2004. The Resolution is in itself another barrier for Hizbullah because, in addition to the Syrian withdrawal (which eventually took place in 2005), it also calls for all Lebanese militias to be disarmed. As Hizbullah regards the status of its weapons as non-negotiable, it views the Resolution and those who seek to implement it as existential threats. A more recent challenge for Hizbullah, the UN Special Tribunal for Lebanon (STL), which was set up in 2009 to investigate Hariri's 2005 assassination, can be seen as a product of these two barriers. The tribunal was created following calls from the March 14 coalition for an international investigation of Hariri's death. Initial reports hinted at Hizbullah's involvement in the assassination, leading to the indictment of four of the movement's members. This had a significant impact on Hizbullah's regional reputation, one which the group's public relations arm has struggled to manage.

Although Hizbullah has learned to negotiate its way through the Lebanese political confessional system, this system is ultimately a barrier for Hizbullah because it sets a quantitative and qualitative limit to its political power. As a result, Hizbullah has actively sought to change the system. In the interim, the group has lobbied for a change in the Lebanese electoral system, with calls for proportional representation to replace the existing first-past-the-post system. Studies have shown that the former system would be more favourable to Hizbullah owing to the geographic and demographic distribution of voters in Lebanon.[23] Hizbullah has benefited from the fact that proportional representation is perceived as 'fairer' by electoral law experts, thus enabling the group to present its calls for electoral reform as being about citizenship rights rather than an aspiration for further political power. In the spring of 2013, this dispute between different political factions in Lebanon stalled discussions about electoral reform, with a deadlock reached between those who promoted proportional representation and those who sought to arrive at a hybrid system that, it was supposed, would satisfy all stakeholders. In this sense, the consociational confessional system has served to prevent Hizbullah from dominating Lebanon entirely.

The final barrier for Hizbullah is that it needs Sunni approval on the Arab level in order to achieve its aim of becoming a regional (if not a global) political leader in the Muslim world. Hizbullah has always recognised the need to appeal to non-Shiites. Its 1985 Open Letter, for example, states that 'It's not important that a party controls a street. What's important is that the people engage with this party',[24] while its August 2004 'Identity and Goals' declaration asserts that 'Hezbollah does not wish to implement Islam forcibly but in a peaceful and political manner, that gives the chance to the majority to either accept or refuse. If Islam becomes the choice of the majority only then will it be implemented.'[25] The Arab uprisings that began in Tunisia before gaining momentum in 2011 and beyond provided Hizbullah with the perfect opportunity to appeal to Sunni populations across the Arab world and to reiterate its discourse of resistance. The group quickly embraced the revolutions in Tunisia, Egypt and Libya, while it was careful to speak against sectarian rhetoric in relation to the uprising in Bahrain, which was widely seen as having been spearheaded by the Shiite majority in the country. The uprising and subsequent conflict in Syria, however, which witnessed significant military involvement by Hizbullah, have seriously damaged Hizbullah's efforts to reach out to Arab Sunnis.

Hizbullah's attempts to appeal to Sunni Muslims extend to the way in which it sells its political projects, including the idea of an Islamic state (which is presented as a choice rather than an imposition), its weapons (presented as defensive arms) and its relationship with Iran. In the case of the latter, David Hirst argues that part of Iran's motivation for sponsoring Hizbullah as an anti-Israeli resistance movement was to allay Arab and Sunni suspicions of the Shiite hegemony perceived as being at the heart of Khomeini's efforts towards 'exporting the revolution', especially as the Palestine Liberation Organisation—the main paramilitary organisation engaged in anti-Israeli resistance at the time—had been forced to leave Lebanon following the 1982 Israeli invasion.[26] Hizbullah is currently trying to downplay Iran's influence (though not its role as a partner) as it seeks to appeal to the wider Arab and Sunni world as well as the group's Christian allies. Hizbullah's 2009 manifesto declares:

In this context, Hezbollah considers Iran as a central state in the Muslim world, since it is the State that dropped through its revolution the Shah's regime and its American–Israeli projects, and it's also the state that supported the resistance movements in our region, and stood with courage and determination at the side of the Arab and Islamic causes and especially the Palestinian one.[27]

As for the case of Hizbullah's weapons, 'Hezbollah deftly learned to say one thing and do another ... Hezbollah mastered the art of doing so without appearing to lie or betray its Islamic heart.'[28] This was clearly illustrated following Hizbullah's takeover of West Beirut in May 2008, when its weapons were used against other Lebanese despite Nasrallah's earlier promise that they would never be used inside Lebanon. Nasrallah's promise regarding this issue presented an image of Hizbullah as a group that does not shed Lebanese blood as a matter of principle, thereby overlooking the group's previous military confrontation with Amal, a rival militia, during the War of the Camps. The War of the Camps was a series of battles between Amal and the Palestinian factions in the southern suburb of Beirut between 1985 and 1988. Hizbullah joined the war in 1987 in support of the Palestinians, and managed to dominate Amal, thereby declaring its political and military superiority within the Shiite community—a position it has since sustained. In 2008, Hizbullah not only ignored this past use of weapons, but it also sought to frame the events of May 2008 in its media as a case of 'self-defence' against 'victimisation', as will be illustrated in Chapter 3.

When structures obstruct agency, actors will generally seek to change the structures in question, and this is precisely what Hizbullah has tried to achieve: in the case of Hariri and UN Resolution 1559 the decision was to fight back, whereas in the case of the Sunnis, Hizbullah has tried to present itself through a non-threatening framework centred on the idea of victimization in order to garner Sunni support. In the case of the Lebanese political system, the group is actively working towards reshaping it to its advantage.

A useful analogy for understanding Hizbullah's decision-making and ambitions is to imagine Hizbullah as a state. Fareed Zakaria[29] measures state power along four lines:

the degree of cohesion in central institutions ... the degree of autonomy from society; the ability to generate revenue; and the scope of governmental responsibilities. Strong states have higher scores on each of these dimensions. Weaker states, by contrast, suffer from fragmentation, penetration by interest groups, lack of revenue, and minimal responsibilities. All else being equal, stronger states have greater access to economic resources and are therefore more likely to adopt ambitious foreign policies.[30]

If Hizbullah is viewed through the prism of a 'state' competing with the Lebanese state, then it becomes clear that it has the upper hand in all of the areas Zakaria defines. According to such an analogy, Hizbullah's 'foreign policies' are those directed at other political entities in Lebanon. As states have historically 'tended to seek more rather than less influence … [and] to shape their external environment',[31] it is logical to propose that Hizbullah's political ambitions will become even greater as it seeks, and gains, more influence in Lebanese politics. One of the most important factors enabling Hizbullah in this regard is the weakness of the Lebanese state and the existence of 'hybrid sovereignties' within it, led by competing political and sectarian leaders.[32]

Components of Hizbullah's political strategy

Engaging in pragmatism

Hizbullah is often described as being pragmatic. The need to be pragmatic is a lesson that Hizbullah learned early on. After declaring that the creation of an Islamic state was its primary objective in its 1985 Open Letter, in which it also asserted that it did not recognise the legitimacy of the Lebanese state, Hizbullah began to change its tone by selling its objectives in more patriotic terms and branding itself as a national resistance movement. Ahmad Nizar Hamzeh[33] and David Hirst refer to Hizbullah's approach as 'gradualist pragmatism'.[34]

Gradualist pragmatism means that Hizbullah is far from dogmatic in terms of ideology. Certain values like *wilayat al-faqih* have remained constant, but ideology is as much a political tool for Hizbullah as it is a driving force. In 1992, for example, Hizbullah realised that its participation in the Lebanese parliament following the civil war would be more useful than staying outside—the group eventually received permission from the Iranian Supreme Leader Ayatollah Ali Khamenei to do so through an *istifta'* (referendum), thereby harmonising ideology and politics. Following the 2005 withdrawal of Syrian troops from Lebanon, Naim Qassem stated that Syria's withdrawal 'made us directly responsible for providing domestic protection in a better way than before'.[35] Direct responsibility meant taking the decision to participate in the Lebanese Cabinet. Nicholas Blanford explains that the 'participation of Hizbullah in the government of Fouad Siniora also represented an opportunity to defend its armed wing against proponents of Resolution 1559'.[36] As such, Hizbullah can be seen as performing within the classic parameters of political opportunity structures.

Pragmatism also applies to the way in which Hizbullah deals with Lebanon's Christians, whereby they are no longer *ahl al-dhimma* (*dhimmis*, i.e. non-Muslims excluded from certain rights enjoyed by Muslims, according to the Open Letter) but are now framed as 'partners'.[37] This partnership, which is most prominently manifested in the memorandum of understanding signed between Hizbullah and Michel Aoun's Free Patriotic Movement, stems from Hizbullah's recognition of the need to collaborate with other groups in order to claim that it is supported by a majority within Lebanon. In 2008, when commenting on the consociational political system in Lebanon, the Hizbullah MP and foreign affairs official Nawaf Musawi stated: 'We understand the political reality of Lebanon very well ... No single group can rule by itself. The Lebanese can't be governed except by consensus, and we want a democratic and consensual country.'[38]

But this pragmatic approach implies dealing with the current political system in Lebanon only until it can be changed. In the 2008 edition of his book on Hizbullah's ideology, Naim Qassem claimed that the group would continue to accept 'consensual democracy till we can reach majoritarian democracy'.[39] The same position is reiterated in Hizbullah's 2009 manifesto:

Yet, and until the Lebanese could reach through their national dialogue this historic and sensitive achievement, which is the abolishment of political sectarianism, and since the political system in Lebanon is based on sectarian foundations, the consensual democracy will remain the fundamental basis for governance in Lebanon, because it is the actual embodiment of the spirit of the constitution and the essence of the Charter of the co-existence.[40]

This highlights a need to rethink the characterisation of Hizbullah's increasing participation in Lebanese state institutions as 'Lebanonisation'. There are two conflicting views on this. The first, optimistic view sees it as a consequence of Hizbullah's growing domestic political role, and a mechanism that will ultimately make Hizbullah less ideological as it becomes more accountable to its constituents.[41] The second view is that Lebanonisation is a facade which Hizbullah uses to hide its Islamist agenda.[42] However, the reality is somewhere in between: Lebanonisation is neither a process of full integration into the current system nor a facade, but a pragmatic strategy to enable Hizbullah to implement its political agenda.

Pragmatism allows Hizbullah to operate on two parallel tracks, within and outside the state system. In seeking to maintain its weapons in the face of Resolution 1559, for example, Shiite ministers who supported Hizbullah engaged in a boycott of the Cabinet in December 2005. This lasted for six weeks and only came to an end when Hizbullah was granted an 'exemption' from the Resolution in which the government designated the group as a 'national resistance' force rather than a militia.[43] This status was reiterated in the Doha Accord of May 2008, with the army and the resistance being characterised as mutually exclusive yet complementary entities. But as the events of May 2008 demonstrated, Hizbullah had also resorted to an outside-the-system track in its efforts to retain its weapons. The same applies in terms of Hizbullah's policy towards the STL. Hizbullah has sought to challenge the tribunal through the state system by pushing the Lebanese government to revoke it formally. However, it has also used unilateral means to counter the STL, including an attack on tribunal investigators who were seeking to obtain medical files at a gynaecological clinic in Beirut's southern suburbs in November 2010. Hizbullah presented the attack as resulting from the 'moral outrage' of local citizens at the insult to women's honour caused by the visit, as women (and, it was reported, men dressed as women) mobbed the male investigators, beating them and stealing the laptop they were carrying.

Within this framework, Hizbullah's 2009 manifesto can be understood as simply reflecting the group's political pragmatism. The group does not plan its political strategy solely on a short-term basis. It recognises that it may need decades and generations for it to achieve its ultimate goals—and it is willing to wait. This pragmatism has resulted in an upward trajectory in terms of its relative power, with Hizbullah gaining a growing number of seats in parliament and the municipalities,[44] as well as representation in the Cabinet and military dominance within Lebanon. It is unlikely that the group will abandon its broader plans on the basis of having achieved these gains alone.

Hizbullah is able to act in a pragmatic way because pragmatism is justified within its ideology. Hizbullah relies on pragmatic principles in Islamic jurisprudence that provide it with flexibility in terms of behaviour: it follows the principles of 'necessity permits what is prohibited' and '[w]hat cannot be accomplished in its whole ... [should] not be left [abandoned] in its whole'.[45] It also seeks to justify its actions according to the following derivatives of sharia:

(a) the protection of reason (hifz al-'aql); (b) the protection of the self (hifz al-nafs); (c) the protection of family and descent (hifz al-nasl); (d) the protection of religion (hifz al-din); and (e) the protection of property (hifz al-mal).[46]

These provide religious justification for Hizbullah's actions against any entity or development deemed to be a threat to these derivatives.

Hizbullah therefore embraces its own version of realpolitik. While realpolitik refers to choosing practicality over ideology in the pursuit of power, Hizbullah has managed to find a balance between the two. As Naim Qassem explains: 'The dominance of interest over principles is unacceptable, but considering interests to be in the framework of maintaining principles is acceptable.'[47] In this sense, Hizbullah's ideology offers a significant amount of flexibility in that it provides the group with a considerable degree of leeway in choosing its political actions while maintaining credibility in the eyes of its supporters.

Cultivating an image of credibility and exaltation

Hizbullah's messages and strategies appear credible because the group itself has successfully cultivated an image of credibility among its supporters as a result of its actions on the ground. This has been achieved by providing promises of measurable aims, thereby linking words and deeds. Examples include the 2006 'defeat' of Israel and the release of Lebanese political prisoners from Israeli jails in 2008, both of which had earlier been promised by Nasrallah.[48] Hizbullah has been able to sustain this image of credibility even though it has not always abided by its promises, as in May 2008, when its weapons were used inside Lebanon. David Hirst comments that the statement that

Hizbullah's weapons would never be used against other Lebanese was 'only a promise, not a guarantee'.[49] Media outlets close to Hizbullah also justify the use of weapons as a sign of 'comfort'. On 8 November 2010, for example, the news site Elnashra, which is sympathetic to Hizbullah, published an article stating that Hizbullah supporters are 'comforted' by the visibility of Hizbullah's weapons in Lebanon because 'it is a sign that the Party will continue as long as it possesses weapons that allow it to defend its existence, no matter the source of threat: Israeli, Lebanese, or foreign'.[50]

Hizbullah's 'proof' of delivering on its promises have enabled the group to present itself in exalted terms. In his speeches, Nasrallah creates an image of Hizbullah leaders as dogmatically infallible and thus untouchable. This exaltation was persistently communicated in Nasrallah's speeches regarding the STL, in which he presented Hizbullah as beyond any accusation of wrongdoing.

Using Israel as a benchmark

The strategy that Hizbullah has used against the STL has sought to frame the tribunal in terms similar to those which the group uses to describe Israel. This is the most credible accusation that the group can hurl at others, owing to Hizbullah's reputation as the only serious regional resistance force against Israel. Since 2005, Hizbullah has tried to frame those who oppose it as traitors and Israeli collaborators. Nasrallah repeatedly uses the phrase 'cutting the hand' to refer to the punishment awaiting those who stand in Hizbullah's way. In his speech of 25 May 2005, for instance, he stated that 'If anyone tries to disarm the resistance, we will fight him the way the martyrs fought in Karbala [and] ... consider any hand that tries to seize our weapons an Israeli hand, and cut it off.'[51] In a subsequent speech on 8 May 2008, Nasrallah described the internal domestic crisis as 'a declaration of war ... against the resistance and its weapons for the benefit of America and Israel. The communications network is the significant part of the weapons of the resistance. I said that we will cut off the hand that targets the weapons of the resistance ... Today is the day to carry out this decision.'[52] This was followed on 3 August 2010 by a speech in which Nasrallah directly threatened Israel, saying that the hand of anyone who touches the Lebanese army would be cut,[53] and another speech on 11 November 2010 in which he stated that the hands of anyone who tries to get to members of Hizbullah (in reference to STL indictments) would also be cut.

In so doing, Hizbullah has been able to place its Lebanese political opponents on the same level as Israel, or, more precisely, as an extension of the Israeli threat. In 2006, after the summer war and just before the resignation of six pro-Hizbullah ministers from the Fouad Siniora Cabinet in an effort to bring about the collapse of the government, Nasrallah stated that 'What has happened since the end of the war ... is an extension of Israel's war against Lebanon. And just as we fought in July and August, so we will fight today, but with other weapons and other rules.'[54] The MP Ali Fayyad, the director of Hizbullah's think tank, the Consultative Centre for Studies and Documentation, echoes this, claiming that 'Hezbollah ... has managed during the [2006] war to crack Israel's deterrent power. However ... that alone wouldn't assure a Hezbollah victory in the regional context unless the Party of God could manage to fend off internal threats to its authority.'[55] While the use of the term 'internal threats' is an allusion to Hizbullah's political rivals, the group has also faced internal threats within its own ranks, including the discovery of a number of Israeli collaborators in 2009. However, Hizbullah has marketed these incidents in a way that has sought to assure its supporters that the spies were only low-ranking members, while stressing the need to bring them to justice. In a speech on 23 May 2009 in the southern town of Nabatiyyeh marking the anniversary of the liberation of the South, which followed the arrests of a network of spies by the Lebanese security forces, Nasrallah responded to the revelation that the spies were Hizbullah members by stressing, 'begin to execute Shiite collaborators first'.[56] Through this statement, Nasrallah asserted Hizbullah's strict adherence to a justice framework that ensured continued trust from its constituents. Yet at the same time, the statement completely ignored Hizbullah's earlier claims that its members were beyond any wrongdoing (the label 'Israeli collaborators' had earlier been reserved exclusively for others).

Cultivating Shiite loyalty

Throughout its existence Hizbullah has systematically worked to cultivate loyalty from the Shiite community, both within and outside Lebanon.[57] From its inception, Hizbullah has relied on members of the worldwide

Shiite diaspora for funding, recruitment and military operations. Members of the substantial Shiite migrant community in Africa and Latin America, in particular, have played a vital role in Hizbullah's overt and clandestine methods of fundraising. This engagement is facilitated by the community's close ties to the homeland, which have enabled money, goods, people and weapons to flow in both directions.[58] The large presence of this diaspora in other Arab countries, such as Egypt and the Gulf states, has also helped to widen Hizbullah's appeal, particularly after the liberation of the South in 2000 and during the 2006 war. In Bahrain, a Shiite-majority country, Hizbullah has used members of the migrant community to help establish a regional network.

Hizbullah has of course also worked hard to cultivate the loyalty of the Shiites in southern Lebanon. Hizbullah's provision of social, medical and educational services to Lebanese Shiites, particularly in the South, is well documented, as is the group's role in granting the community a sense of political and economic empowerment and of security, particularly with regard to Israel.[59] Since 1982, Hizbullah has used a strategy in the South that approximates the 'clear, hold, build' political–military analogy often used in the contexts of foreign intervention: 'clear' refers to 'defeating the nation's enemies and then destroying them or at least driving them back to whence they came'.[60] 'Hold' refers to 'protecting the cleared areas by garrisoning them with … [one's] own and friendly forces, so that the nation's enemies stay down or at least back'. Rose argues that such a strategy 'only tends to work well enough on a temporary basis but it can be dangerous, costly, and politically problematic. So the only truly satisfactory long-term solution … is the "building" of stable … indigenous political orders in the areas in question, ones that allow local populations to thrive.'[61] Hizbullah has applied this strategy in southern Lebanon by clearing the area of Israeli troops in 2000 (the disputed Shebaa farms notwithstanding), then holding the area militarily, and then entering the building stage—building an indigenous physical, social, political, economic and military infrastructure from within the South focused on the region's Shiite community. The 2006 war and the devastation it caused led to a new stage with large-scale reconstruction in the area and in southern Beirut. Hizbullah's reconstruction of the infrastructure in these areas (which is mainly funded by Iran) was not just about restoring the built environment but was also politically motivated in that it was designed to sustain the loyalty of the Shiites who had paid a high material and human price during the war.[62]

In the wake of the political tensions that followed Hariri's assassination in 2005, Hizbullah became more reliant on sectarian loyalty and formed an alliance with the other main Shiite party, Amal, in that year's parliamentary election. This alliance has caused 'any move against itself to be interpreted as one against the Shiites as a whole'.[63] Indeed, in the absence of other significant political representatives, and with the policies and lack of outreach of the March 14 camp serving to alienate Lebanon's Shiites, the Shiite community has largely remained loyal to Hizbullah. This loyalty is maintained by the group's monetary hand-outs and the provision of other services to its constituents. After the 2006 war, these increased beyond the supply of essential goods and extended into the provision of luxuries like entertainment (e.g. amusement parks and cafes) as Hizbullah's supporters began expecting larger returns for their sacrifices during the war.[64] The opening of Shiite-focused public spaces has further ghettoised the Shiite community. This is not only because of the reduced need to go 'outside' core Shiite areas for entertainment, but also because of the exclusionary policies of March 14 and the heightened sense of Shiite alienation that Hizbullah has cultivated through its emphasis on the community's victimisation.

Sustaining political power through coercion

Although largely undocumented, one of Hizbullah's strategies that runs parallel to the persuasion of its allies is the coercion of political supporters and the group's constituents.[65] Hizbullah has extremely wide support among the Shiites, but it would be incorrect to assume that all Shiites blindly follow the group. Shiites rally around Hizbullah partly because of conviction and partly because of fear.[66] Hizbullah successfully silenced Amal in 1988 after a military victory in the South and during the War of the Camps.[67] No other Shiite faction has since been able to challenge this position, although the group faces contention from feudal Shiite families in southern Lebanon, such as the al-Ass'ad and al-Khalil families, whose traditional authority has been challenged by the rise of Hizbullah. Hizbullah has occasionally responded to this through intimidation. In 2007, Ahmad al-Ass'ad, a prominent feudal leader and former MP, created the Lebanese Option Gathering (later,

Option Party) as an independent Shiite political movement opposing Hizbullah. He and his party members have since been subjected to a campaign of violence, including the burning of Ahmad al-Ass'ad's car in 2009 and the fatal shooting of the head of the party's student wing in 2013 as he took part in a protest against Hizbullah's involvement in the Syrian crisis outside the Iranian embassy in Beirut.[68] Throughout its existence, Hizbullah has demonstrated low tolerance of dissent, whether within its ranks or within the Shiite community more widely. Not only has Hizbullah imposed a spiral of silence whereby the voices of dissidents are simply not heard, it has also consistently engaged in the intimidation of its own constituents in order to achieve compliance.[69] Sheikh Mohammad Hussein Fadlallah, one of the most respected Shiite clerics and *marjaiyah* (religious reference) in Lebanon, was sidelined by Hizbullah in 2005 after he expressed concerns about the rise of an isolationist Shiite current in Lebanon. Shiite 'dissidents' like Sheikh Ali al-Amin or the former Hizbullah leader Subhi al-Tufaili have effectively been subjected to house arrest, while Shiite intellectuals who speak out against Hizbullah often face social isolation or smearing campaigns accusing them of being pro-Israeli, or have been subjected to threats ranging from verbal warnings to assassination attempts.[70] Actions such as these normally go unreported owing to a fear of escalation, reinforcing the spiral of silence that has aided in the construction of an 'honourable' image for Hizbullah in Lebanon and beyond.

Creating a framework of necessity and self-defence

The fact that Hizbullah presents itself as a natural and inevitable product of its environment, and as a group that acts out of necessity, has helped quell any dissent among the Shiite community. Hizbullah partly emerged as a reaction to the marginalisation of the Shiites in terms of politics, development and defence,[71] and the group has sought to capitalise on these issues ever since. The 'natural and inevitable' framework is found in its 2004 'Identity and Goals' declaration, particularly with reference to Israel. It is also reiterated in its 2009 manifesto, which extends the issue of necessity into one of self-defence:

The Resistance role is a national necessity as long as the Israeli threats and ambitions continue. Therefore, and in the absence of strategic balance between the state and the enemy, the Israeli threat obliges Lebanon to endorse a defensive strategy that depends on a popular resistance participating in defending the country and an army that preserves the security of the country, in a complementarity [*sic*] process that proved to be successful through the previous phase.[72]

However, as demonstrated in the cases of Shiite dissent discussed above, Hizbullah has extended the necessity and defence framework to activities beyond the Israeli context. Hizbullah's 1985 Open Letter warned others not to block Hizbullah's objectives. Since then, it has justified its engagement in violence outside of the context of resistance to Israel on the basis of extenuating circumstances. David Hirst argues that Hizbullah justified its engagement in hostage-taking in the 1980s and 1990s on the grounds of 'extenuating circumstances' that required measures to protect the Shiite community against Western/Israeli onslaught;[73] in other words, acts such as these were carried out as a form of self-defence. The same framework applies to the violence of 8 May 2008, which Nasrallah sought to justify by stating that the weapons had been used to defend Hizbullah's weapons. And it also applies to the rhetoric used in reference to Hizbullah's policy towards the STL, which is continuously framed in terms of opposing a conspiracy against the 'resistance'. As Thanassis Cambanis argues, Hizbullah thus seeks to frame acts of violence 'as a reluctant use of force in self-defense'.[74] In this sense, quelling Shiite dissent also becomes a matter of preserving a Shiite 'core' in the face of external 'threats'.

The necessity framework also means that Hizbullah's gains are presented as incidental, whereby Hizbullah seeks to create an image of a group that is reluctant to gain power, with power as 'an incidental gain' in its pursuit of justice.[75] The political influence that Hizbullah has gained as a result of its provision of social services and its defence of southern Lebanon is thus downplayed. The same strategy is applied in Hizbullah's stance towards the STL, in which Hizbullah presents its campaign against the tribunal as being about justice for the group as the wrongly accused, as will be demonstrated in Chapter 3.

The defence framework additionally serves to allow Hizbullah to use war as an element of its political strategy. Carl von Clausewitz wrote that 'Small states cannot wage wars of conquest in our times. But in defensive warfare even the means of small states are infinitely great.'[76] In a decentralised war of defence, the combination of a regular army with a 'people War', where there is a 'nation in arms', is more effective.[77] Hizbullah has engaged in several such defensive wars over the past three decades. There are two reasons why this strategy of defensive war has proved effective for Hizbullah: (1) following Clausewitz, it has a higher chance of military success in the face of a much bigger enemy; and (2) in terms of Hizbullah's image, given that it is consistent with the necessity and self-defence discursive framework.

In 2006, as Hizbullah felt cornered by growing support for the STL and for March 14, it provoked a war with Israel by kidnapping two Israeli soldiers in a move it described as an 'act of resistance'.[78] Hizbullah emerged from the war politically and militarily more powerful than before and with wider popularity across the Middle East.

As von Clausewitz put it: 'War is a mere continuation of policy by other means. War is not merely a political act, but also a real political instrument, a continuation of political commerce, a carrying out of the same by other means ... for the political view is the object, war is the means, and the means must always include the object in our conception.'[79]

Staying one step ahead in the PR game

Hizbullah closely follows political developments in the local Lebanese scene and has proved adept in turning them to its advantage. When the 1989 Ta'if agreement called for the dissolution of all militias in Lebanon, for example, Hizbullah launched a PR campaign to present itself as a resistance force rather than a militia, thereby providing a rationale for the group to retain its weapons.[80] Hizbullah also relies on an image that it has cultivated of itself as having a large degree of popular support. In November 2004, for instance, Hizbullah organised the 'million man march'[81] in support of Syria and the rejection of Resolution 1559— although the event was in fact a direct challenge to Rafic Hariri's camp, it was marketed as a popular protest against foreign interference in Lebanese affairs.[82] The masses were similarly drawn upon on 8 March 2005 in a pro-Syrian demonstration in downtown Beirut orchestrated by Syria and Hizbullah, and in the protest camps in downtown Beirut in 2006–7 calling for the government's resignation.

One of the three main objects of warfare, according to Clausewitz, is public opinion: '[p]ublic opinion is won through great victories'.[83] Hizbullah has branded the withdrawal of Israel from southern Lebanon in 2000 and its survival following the 2006 war as great victories in an effort to appeal to Lebanese, Arab and Muslim public opinion. This was helped by the fact that Hassan Nasrallah, at least until the Syrian uprising of 2011, was seen to embody the aspirations of ordinary people in the Arab and Muslim worlds and was able to tailor his speeches to appeal to those audiences, while emphasising anti-sectarianism to appeal to Sunnis in the Arab world. Hizbullah also emphasises consensus in its rhetoric. Yet while this may appeal to its audience, it glosses over the fact that consensus can be reached through both violent and non-violent means, as Hizbullah demonstrated in the May 2008 events and in its relationship with its own constituents.

Nasrallah is a master of spin and propaganda who has endeavoured to market Hizbullah activities that challenge the sovereignty of the Lebanese state in justifiable terms. In a speech following the 2006 war, and in the wake of criticism regarding Hizbullah's decision to kidnap Israeli soldiers without the Lebanese government's knowledge, Nasrallah sought to justify the action by asking: 'Should I tell the government that I'm going to conduct a kidnap operation? I'd be giving it a huge responsibility.'[84] This attempt to justify the kidnapping also relates to the necessity framework: 'when the state fails in carrying out some of its functions, society must help the state in carrying them out—even if the state doesn't ask'.[85]

While Hizbullah's opponents in Lebanon also have access to public relations resources, Nasrallah's public performances have given the group a distinct advantage over its rivals. Saad Hariri, the March 14 leader, lacks Nasrallah's persona and public-speaking experience, and is often forced to react to Hizbullah's activities rather than taking the initiative. Hizbullah, on the other hand, successfully uses pre-emptive attacks in its PR campaigns, as can be seen in the campaigns against the STL. Saad Hariri has also failed to communicate his message via the most prominent media platforms. His efforts in 2009 to rejuvenate relations with the Assad regime—which he had earlier accused of being responsible for assassinating his father—for example, were conducted via an article in the Saudi-owned newspaper *Alsharq Alawsat*, while his attempts to calm the Sunni street after violence erupted in the summer of 2012 largely took place via Twitter. Nasrallah, conversely, conducts his battles with a domineering screen presence that increasingly utilises communication technologies in spectacular PR shows, such as a multimedia speech in 2010 which attempted to prove that Israel was behind Hariri's assassination.

Hizbullah increasingly relies on visual displays of power in public speeches and other PR campaigns. From the graphic billboards depicting Israeli defeat in 2006 to the 2007 Spider's Web exhibition with its display of ransacked Israeli military vehicles to the permanent display of those vehicles at the Mleeta visitor centre in southern Lebanon, this visual display of power serves as a challenge to Israel and local political opponents. It is also a display of prowess that serves to boost the morale of Hizbullah's supporters while reassuring them of the group's strength.

Conclusion

Though largely successful, Hizbullah's political strategy is not without its weaknesses. One of the most notable of these is Hizbullah's tendency to overstate the extent of its own achievements. For a number of years, Hizbullah rode on the success of its 2006 confrontation with Israel in order to appeal to the Arab world, which in turn granted the group a degree of leeway when it engaged in violence, as was the case in May 2008. However, the efficacy of the 2006 'Divine Victory' in garnering popular support began to fade as other challenges loomed and the dangers of Hizbullah's reliance on force clearly manifested themselves. Gideon Rose argues that lessons drawn from previous experiences influence decision-making. Decisions regarding whether to engage in war, for example, are often based on lessons drawn from the past. But he warns that 'lessons from previous wars can serve as cognitive blunders, narrowing the way officials think about the situations they face, and power can be a trap, underwriting hubris and folly'.[86] In the case of Hizbullah, the fact that it emerged from the May 2008 attack largely unscathed—coupled with the lack of restraint on its power—may encourage the group to engage in a similar, possibly more ambitious action in the future, risking the loss of popular support for Hizbullah in the Arab and Muslim worlds (especially if it is seen as an unprovoked attack on Lebanon's Sunni community). Hizbullah's growing confidence could prove to be its own undoing vis-à-vis the Sunnis in the broader Arab world.

Hizbullah's support for the Bashar al-Assad regime during the Syrian uprising from 2011 onwards could well be the catalyst in this. Iran's response to the 2009 Green Movement and its support for the Syrian regime's stance towards the uprising are likely to serve as examples for Hizbullah's leadership to follow when faced with popular protests in the future. Hizbullah, meanwhile, resorted once more to the familiar framework of victimisation to justify its own intervention in support of the Assad regime as a case of self-defence—in contrast to the past, however, Arab audiences are no longer convinced by this narrative.

What the future holds for Hizbullah will depend on the interrelationship between agency and structure and the way in which this dynamic affects its political strategy. There are a number of certainties for the group: Hizbullah will no doubt hold on to its weapons as a tool against Israel and its Lebanese opponents alike because they act as guarantors of Hizbullah's political influence. It will also continue pursuing its goal of inducing change in the Lebanese political system using gradualist pragmatism. Ahmad Nizar Hamzeh argues that Hizbullah's call for a majoritarian democracy is driven by its aim of establishing an Islamic order and is based on a calculation, according to which Hizbullah will eventually have majority support in Lebanon: 'It is this connection between majority rule and demography that makes Hizbullah hopeful that Islamic order can be established by "peaceful and democratic means" rather than force.' But Hamzeh warns that majoritarianism 'implies a low level of pluralism and encourages a process of homogenization of the society'.[87] Lebanon, long used to a sectarian and pluralistic power-sharing agreement, may prove more resistant to change than Hizbullah anticipates, necessitating the group's prolonged use of force.

A recognition of Hizbullah's complexity (characterised as a terrorist group, a militia, a popular resistance movement, a political party or a state within a state, depending on who is doing the characterisation) is important for understanding the group and its ambitions. This complexity means that Hizbullah should not be viewed as being primarily driven by a will to engage in an endless war with Israel. Ultimately, Hizbullah aims to be recognised as a legitimate political actor on the global level, and its political trajectory thus far suggests that its political survival is highly probable. This also means that Hizbullah will not be satisfied with compromises within the current Lebanese sectarian political system, such as extra seats in parliament or a three-way division of power between Christians, Sunnis and Shiites.

In the interests of Lebanon and the region as a whole, international and domestic actors need to adopt a pragmatic approach towards Hizbullah. Any such approach will necessitate returning to the points listed earlier in the chapter as Hizbullah enablers. It will not be easy to change Hizbullah's agency because this change can only happen from within Hizbullah itself; however, it is possible to aim for a change in the political structure in which Hizbullah acts. A strong, sovereign Lebanese state is needed that represents all its constituents without quelling the voice of minorities, and with strong institutions that uphold the rule of law and provide the required social and economic services. But Lebanon's problems and conflicts are always part and parcel of a regional and international situation that can either facilitate the resolution of internal conflicts or further complicate them. The trajectory of the Israeli–Palestinian conflict, Iran's political future and Syria's recovery from civil war will have a critical impact on Lebanon and on Hizbullah. For the time being, Hizbullah faces one of the most serious challenges in its history as the Syrian conflict tests the limits of its pragmatism and adaptation, and in turn, the skilfulness of its communication strategy.

2

FROM THE INVASION TO THE LIBERATION: COMMUNICATING HIZBULLAH'S POLITICAL REPERTOIRE, 1982–2000

Dina Matar and Atef Alshaer with Lina Khatib

A mediated political evolution

Between 1982 and 2000 Hizbullah transformed itself from an exclusivist Islamist jihadi movement working outside the Lebanese state into a more inclusive political party working within the Lebanese system. During this period, the unique nature of the group's mobilisation and activism had a wide-ranging impact on Lebanese society, an outcome due in part to Hizbullah's use of a sophisticated political communication strategy which developed in tandem with its political evolution and transformation. In its early days Hizbullah focused on rallying support among the Lebanese Shiite community. Mobilisation was initially coordinated by clerical leaders and vanguard Hizbullah activists who believed that any imported party structure of the Western or Leninist type was inconvenient and alien to Islam.[1] These leaders took command in the preparatory and formative stages of Hizbullah's political evolution, devising and implementing Hizbullah's objectives and early political communication strategy in order to legitimise its role in Lebanon and reach out to this target audience.[2] They initially relied largely on informal 'infrastructures of action'[3]—the traditional and submerged networks of action, such as mosques, sermons, speeches and rallies, as well as other spaces of social relations—to elaborate and construct an 'episteme', a way of being, thinking and acting that would allow the group to maintain itself over time. The use of such infrastructures is not unique to Hizbullah. Indeed, other Islamist movements in the Middle East have turned to similar associational aspects of civil society to create and sustain 'enduring collective identities and networked action'.[4] However, what was remarkable about Hizbullah was its attention to the different spaces of cultural production through which it sustained a constant interchange of communally held knowledge that was borrowed or adapted from everyday situations and other discourses and claimed them as its own.

In parallel to these practices, Hizbullah began to develop formal visual and print media platforms as additional tools for mobilisation and influence in public space. In 1982, even before it had officially announced its existence, Hizbullah's core activists began distributing a rather crude publication called *al-Mujtahid* (The Struggler), which mainly reported on the progress and success of the Iranian Revolution, as well as events related to Iran that had been held in Lebanon. The publication of *al-Mujtahid* came to an abrupt halt when Israel invaded Lebanon in June 1982, whereupon it was replaced by another amateurish four-page leaflet with the symbolically charged title *Ahl al-thughour*, roughly translated as 'the people of the outposts subject to invasion and attack'. The leaflet continued to focus on Iranian affairs and the battle between the Islamic world and the Israeli enemy.[5] In 1984, Hizbullah established its weekly newspaper *al-'Ahd* (The Pledge), which became its most important formal political communicative tool until the television station al-Manar (The Beacon) began operating in 1991—while the station initially transmitted its material for only three hours a day, its broadcast time has since expanded considerably.[6]

By the mid-1980s Hizbullah had started to look beyond its traditional constituents for support and consequently began marketing its image and worldview through well-established Lebanese print media in order to reach out to Lebanese nationals at large. Although Hizbullah remained firm in its adherence to the principles of the Iranian Revolution, the group was also keen to present itself as indigenous to Lebanon and thus with a legitimate stake in the Lebanese political and social system. One of the most important, early examples of this practice was the publication of a letter on 25 February 1985 that the group sent to the Lebanese newspaper *as-Safir*, in which Hizbullah sought to reassure those, particularly within the Christian community, who had expressed fears about its Islamic orientation.[7] This letter was the media-disseminated version of the group's first political and ideological manifesto (often referred to as the 'Open Letter') which was published nine days earlier, on 16 February 1985. The Open Letter formally announced Hizbullah's existence and detailed its worldview, including its position on the establishment of Islamic rule in Lebanon, which was described as an important goal in deterring imperialist and colonialist intentions, and the group's ideological adherence to Iran's *wilayat al-faqih* [8] (the guardianship of the jurisprudence).[9] The timing of the publication was significant for two reasons: first, it followed soon after Israel's announcement that it was redeploying its forces in southern Lebanon, which Hizbullah claimed was a result of its resistance operations; and second, it coincided with the first anniversary of the assassination of Sheikh Ragheb Harb, who was killed in an Israeli attack on 16 February 1984. Harb was a prominent leader of the early Shiite resistance against Israel in southern Lebanon whose martyrdom Hizbullah has consistently used as an empowering symbol of activism, sacrifice and personal regeneration.

In the following year, as part of its efforts to emphasise its roots in Lebanese rather than Iranian soil and to enhance its self-image as a resistance group, Hizbullah began sending video recordings of its military operations to Lebanese television stations,[10] with the broadcasts providing visual 'evidence' of its involvement in resistance acts in the South. Although the recordings were amateurish in style, they retained the original sound of battles and thus served as an authentic and dramatic representation of events, a mode of communication that Hizbullah would consistently use to establish a mediated 'regime of truth'. It is unclear precisely when the practice of recording operations began. However, Hizbullah's Deputy Secretary General, Naim Qassem, hinted that the practice started in 1982 with the recording of an operation carried out by Hizbullah's first martyr, Ahmad Qassir, on 11 November, which was shown 'at a popular rally at the end of April 1985'.[11]

THE HIZBULLAH PHENOMENON

In 1989 Hizbullah established its Executive Council (*al-majlis al-tanfithi*), which was charged with overseeing several institutional structures, including the day-to-day activities of the Central Information Unit[12] which is responsible for developing formal media institutions.[13] It was around this period that Hizbullah launched its *infitah* (opening up) policy through which the group began to participate publicly in the Lebanese political system and which heralded a more inclusive and public phase in its political identity. In 1991, the group established its television station, al-Manar, in order to reach out to audiences beyond the core Shiite community in Lebanon. In 2000, al-Manar became a transnational satellite channel, which, along with the website muqawama.org, helped Hizbullah reach audiences outside Lebanon. By the beginning of the twenty-first century, Hizbullah had expanded its newspaper and magazine outlets to include *al-Bilad, al-Wihda al-Ismailiya* and the monthly *al-Sabil*, some of which focus on private matters, while others focus on political and religious affairs.[14]

As will be shown in this chapter and Chapter 3, as Hizbullah's institutions and media spaces expanded, it became more skilful in using diverse communicative spaces creatively. In doing so, Hizbullah has been able to link its discourse to preceding discourses in order to acquire authenticity and continuity, thereby forming a seamless communicated 'repertoire of politics' (i.e. its particular modes of politics and worldview) that has helped it mobilise different groups at different junctures in its history. In what follows, the chapter explores some of the communicative methods, features, tools and rhetorical frameworks of Hizbullah's communication strategy between 1982 and 2000, and relates them to the historical and political contexts within which Hizbullah operates. The following chapter discusses the period between 2000 and 2012.

The pillars of Hizbullah's image

Hizbullah has always sought to market itself as an Islamist party of resistance and struggle against oppression and the oppressors (i.e. Israel and its Western allies). This populist image was attuned to the mood in a country that had been subject to several Israeli invasions, as well as a protracted civil war (1975–90) that further exacerbated sectarian and political divisions and opened the door for intervention from regional and other actors. This was also an image that contrasted markedly with the international label the group had acquired as a 'terrorist organisation' whose involvement in kidnapping and bombing operations in the early 1980s made headlines around the world. Hizbullah's self-image as a Lebanese Islamist party is based on four interrelated pillars that have remained constant throughout its history: (1) Hizbullah as an ally of Iran; (2) Hizbullah as a resistance group to Israel; (3) Hizbullah's commitment to the liberation of Palestine; and (4) the notion that Hizbullah is a religious party representative of the Shiite community in Lebanon.

The alliance with Iran

Hizbullah, the 'Party of God', originally described itself as the 'Islamic Revolution in Lebanon', thus emphasising its organic and strategic bonds with Iran. At the same time, Hizbullah sought to legitimise Iran's symbolic leadership through the use of evocative and historically meaningful language and symbols with the aim of naturalising and legitimising Iran's guidance and role among a local public already familiar with its religious–political discourses. In so doing, Hizbullah borrowed the main tropes and themes that the Iranian revolutionary leaders had themselves used in mobilising the masses, but appropriated them as its own. To emphasise the links with Iran and its leadership as role models, *al-'Ahd*, Hizbullah's first formal media outlet, began to disseminate the writings and speeches of Iran's spiritual and revolutionary leader Ayatollah Ruhollah Khomeini, describing him as the guiding spiritual role model and force behind Hizbullah's self-image as a group fighting injustice and the *mustakbireen* (arrogant forces). *Al-'Ahd* displayed portraits of Khomeini and (later) Khameini on the masthead, coupled with citations from the Quran. Alongside his veneration in Hizbullah media, Khomeini occupied a quotidian existence in the lives of people in Hizbullah-controlled areas of Lebanon, mainly in the southern suburbs of Beirut, as large posters of the leader dominated public space in much the same way as they do in Tehran. *Al-'Ahd* continued to refer to Khomeini's writings even after his death, reminding its readers of his significance, and by association, the significance of Iran to Hizbullah. Khomeini's writings were periodically published throughout the 1980s in order to support Hizbullah's goal of establishing an Islamic state. For example, a special issue of *al-'Ahd*, published after Khomeini's death in 1989, reprinted the following words of the late Iranian leader:

O the deprived of the world, O the Islamic countries, O the Muslims of the world, wake up and obtain your rights, and do not fear the media uproar of the grand powers and their ugly methods, do not submit to your enemies and the enemies of the great Islam, and unite under the banner of Islam and defend the deprived in the world, and march towards the establishment of an Islamic government.[15]

Through the use of these practices, Hizbullah sought to promote Khomeini as the new leader of the Islamic *umma* while asserting his political and religious role in guiding the Islamic world along the lines of the Islamic revolution, as well as the concept of *wilayat al-faqih*. This latter system asserts the supremacy of the clerical leadership and is consequently one which Khomeini himself presented and represented as the ultimate point of authority. Following his death on 3 June 1989, *al-'Ahd* devoted an entire edition to commemorating his death and lamenting his departure.[16] The front page of the issue shows Khomeini along with phrases bestowing divine references on him: 'Farewell to the Imam of Allah, we vowed to you to continue on your steps and stand by Allah.' The Imam is described in divine language, such as 'Khomeni is a sun that radiates light',[17] giving him the status of an all-out redeemer. The paper also reported rallies commemorating his death in different countries, including those held in Palestine. Khomeini is described as the supreme embodiment of human life in the modern age, with his religious role being invoked through the use of statements such as 'O the guide to God' and the appellation 'the chosen one', which is usually reserved for the Prophet Muhammad.[18] Similarly, Khomeini's final address is described as the 'farewell speech', an expression which evokes the Islamic phrase used to describe the last sermon of the Prophet Muhammad prior to his death in AD 632. Subsequent issues of *al-'Ahd* continued to praise revered Iranian leaders, extolling their heroic deeds and their symbolic leadership in order to reach a local public that was already familiar with their religious–political discourses and their symbolic significance.

Iranian influence was also apparent in the content and aesthetic style of the posters that Hizbullah used in order to disseminate its ideological and military messages in public spaces in the group's strongholds in the southern suburbs of Beirut and southern Lebanon. The purpose of these posters was to commemorate Hizbullah fighters who had died in 'martyrdom operations' against Israel, as well as to venerate Hizbullah and Iranian leaders and mobilise people through religious, social, political and military statements. One poster that was used frequently in the 1980s and early 1990s displayed the image of Khomeini and Hizbullah's leaders (Abbas al-Musawi, and later Hassan Nasrallah) with the slogan *hayhat minna al-dholla* (humiliation is far from us), thus sending a message of empowerment that linked this status with Iran's role. Posters of Hizbullah institutions also used the same logos as those employed by the Iranian state organisations that had opened branches in Lebanon, like the Bonyad-e shahid which Hizbullah launched in Lebanon under the Arabic name Mo'assasat al-shahid (Martyrs' Foundation), with its distinct logo of a white bird landing on a red tulip, symbolising martyrs in heaven and on earth. Early posters even adopted the same style as that used in Iran, including the use of graphic images of martyrs' mutilated bodies juxtaposed with headshots of the martyrs while alive, a practice used in Iran in the context of its war with Iraq. Such posters featured verses from the Quran as well as strongly worded captions like 'the fingerprints of Zionist attacks on the martyrs of Islam in the Ansar detention camp'. This naturalised introduction of Iranian aesthetics into Lebanon can be interpreted as an attempt to normalise Hizbullah's Iranian links with the aim of blending aspects of Iranian revolutionary cultural expression into the Lebanese context. In fact, many of the artists who designed the posters were often themselves Iranian or Iranian-trained.[19] Although Hizbullah began to reduce its use of Iranian aesthetics (including the graphic images of corpses) following the group's *infitah* in the late 1980s, it continued to depict its leaders alongside the Iranian supreme leader in posters displayed across the South and the southern suburbs of Beirut.

Commitment to Palestine

Hizbullah's proclaimed commitment to Palestine and the struggle against Israel is another vital pillar in the construction of the group's identity,[20] one which manifests itself in different ways, but particularly by invoking Palestine's liberation as a duty incumbent upon all Muslims. Hizbullah's commitment to Palestine was, and continues to be, publicly communicated through visual outputs and spectacles, including posters and elaborate annual Jerusalem Day parades, as well as by invoking the liberation of Palestine as the main aim of Hizbullah's existence. Hizbullah's posters feature frequent references to Palestine, especially the al-Aqsa mosque, the image of which often forms the background for martyr posters commemorating the group's suicide bombers in southern Lebanon with the slogan 'Jerusalem, we are coming', signifying that Hizbullah's ultimate aim is the liberation of Palestine. In order to emphasise this commitment, Hizbullah's media outlets consistently underline Israel's hostile actions in Palestine and particularly in the al-Aqsa mosque, referring to them as acts that demand urgent responses from all Muslims. An *al-'Ahd* report on 12 October 1990, for example, depicted a blood-spattered wall against a black background with a banner that read: 'Massacre of al-Aqsa ... the siege of the resistance ... O where are the Muslims?'[21] In its first issue published to coincide with Jerusalem Day, *al-'Ahd* described the event as *yawm al-umma* (the day of the *umma* (Islamic nation)),[22] with the aim of summoning its intended audiences to take part in the celebrations. The paper also published articles regarding the significance of Jerusalem Day, an event described as the 'day of return to authenticity ... it is an invitation for distinction at the levels of personality, values and aspirations ... it is on this basis that it was called "The Jerusalem Day," not the day of Palestine ... it is not the day of Palestine only, but it is the day of Islam, the day of the Islamic government'[23]—in reference to Iran as the legitimate guarantor of Islamic power.

Ever since the creation of the State of Israel in 1948, Palestine has served as a symbol and a cause around which Arab rulers and political parties have often rallied in order to gain popular support. Palestine, its liberation and the symbolic meaning of Jerusalem have consistently been used as part of the nation-building discourse in post-colonial Arab states as well as national liberation movements in the Arab world and beyond. This is hardly surprising given the significance of the Arab–Israeli conflict and the Palestinian struggle for self-determination in the pan-Arab imagination. The populist Egyptian pan-Arab leader Gamal Abdel-Nasser evoked Palestine in several of his speeches, in which he also used the symbolism of the al-Aqsa mosque in Jerusalem, regarded as the third holiest mosque in Islam. The Palestinian leadership similarly drew on Jerusalem and al-Aqsa by referring to it in evocative terms through the use of Quranic verses, such as 'and they will enter the [al-Aqsa] mosque as they entered it for the first time'.[24] The symbolism and discourse used in the invocation of Jerusalem by regional resistance groups, and particularly those such as Hamas and the Islamic Jihad, is derived from their constant confrontations with Israel, including those that have taken place in Jerusalem itself. However, it was Hizbullah that appropriated Jerusalem as the *qibla* of the *mujahideen* (the centre-point or direction of the Muslim strugglers) and described its liberation as the ultimate jihad, thus providing alternative pan-Islamist imagery to the various competing imageries of what Jerusalem had signified to many Arabs and Muslims up to the mid-1980s. The appropriation of Jerusalem Day as a centrepiece in Hizbullah's self-narrative and image is designed to allow the group to transcend its Shiite constituency and present itself as a movement that is able to represent the interests of the entire Muslim world. As Jerusalem is considered the third holiest site in Islam after the two mosques in Mecca and Medina, it has thus become the focus of Hizbullah's efforts to appeal to fellow Muslims in light of its occupation by Israel—and it is this occupation that Hizbullah ultimately uses to construct its narrative of resistance. Consequently, while Hizbullah's activities and discourses use the same Islamic heritage as those of the Palestinian movements, the group's principal aim with regard to Jerusalem Day differs in that it is not derived from any direct involvement in Jerusalem itself; instead, it is designed to emphasise the group's inclusiveness and its role as a defender of Islamic narratives, thereby acquiring a sense of legitimacy. Jerusalem Day has become a vital fixture in Hizbullah's calendar, one which is marked by orchestrated rallies designed to show its strength and power, but also to project an image of Hizbullah as an Arab nationalist party and as the legitimate protector of Jerusalem. Resistance against Israel is also inscribed within a pan-Islamic imagery. In this way, Hizbullah's overarching discourse of resistance is not only reserved to armed struggle against Israel but is also intended to serve as a more inclusive, culturally grounded, religiously sanctioned and legitimate discourse that is 'oppositional and political' in its essence.

Alongside its ideological links to the Palestinian cause, Hizbullah's communication strategies were also influenced by those that the Palestinian resistance had used. Hizbullah was one of the first Islamist groups to record its 'martyrdom operations' on video. Beyond the mere recording of personal testimonies by would-be martyrs (which were pioneered in Lebanon by anti-Israeli occupation National Resistance Front groups like the Communist Party and the Syrian Social Nationalist Party in the early 1980s), Hizbullah's videos contained footage of actual anti-Israeli operations.[25] Hizbullah realised very early on that the aim of establishing credibility, popularity and a lasting legacy would be supported by video 'evidence'. The group learned this lesson from the Palestinian Liberation Organisation, which had been a keen producer of 'resistance' propaganda films in the 1970s that drew inspiration from the idea of Third Cinema and the camera as a weapon emerging from Latin American revolutionary contexts.[26] The videos are an example of Hizbullah's efforts to gain control over how its operations will be remembered. As Boris Groys argues, contemporary warriors no longer need artists to represent their heroic acts; warriors themselves have started to act as artists by creating videos with recognisable aesthetics.[27] In this sense, they themselves become the mediators between reality and memory, often creating iconic images that become part of the collective imagination.

Hizbullah hoped that its resistance acts and 'martyrdom operations' against Israeli forces in southern Lebanon, as well as against US and French contingents in Beirut, would be viewed in the collective imagination as acts aimed at achieving justice for the oppressed, thereby bestowing on Hizbullah the lead role in the military struggle against Israel in the 1980s. Israel was portrayed as an aggressive, racist, expansionist and anti-humanist entity that had been established by global forces of power. The slogan 'Today Iran, tomorrow Palestine' consistently appeared in Hizbullah's discourse to convey the image that the liberation of Iran—in other words, the success of the Islamic revolution—would be followed by Palestine's liberation from Zionist control.

Resistance as identity and image

The third pillar in Hizbullah's political communication strategy is its self-image as the legitimate party of resistance to oppression. In writings, communiqués, speeches and slogans, jihad (struggle), a term with Islamic symbolism later replaced by the more nationalistic term *muqawama* (resistance), was constructed as an individual and collective cause in which every Muslim believer had a role to play. Hizbullah's rhetoric is designed to 'empower the people as the first stage towards achieving justice'[28] in a similar way to the rhetoric used by the secular and socialist forces of the 1960s and 1970s. But empowerment is not about handing power to the people. As Amal Saad-Ghorayeb argues, 'Hizbullah's discourse is all about the people and empowering the people, but the ultimate goal is not to empower the people ... Their way is to control and shape the people through justice as a key value.'[29]

According to Hizbullah, justice can only be achieved by appropriating *muqawama* (resistance) as a discourse and as a practice to confront deprivation and oppression, as well as to fight Israel and the global powers. This discourse was constructed in response to the rhetoric of *al-kifah al-mussallah* (armed struggle) that had been adopted by Lebanese (and previously Palestinian) leftist and secular forces to fight Israel—forces, however, which had in practice ended up spending their resources fighting among themselves.[30] These forces, which predated Hizbullah and were popularly known as the 'National Resistance', used the slogan *muqawama bil-nar, la musawamah* (resistance by fire, not compromise), popularising resistance to Israel, particularly in connection with the Palestinian cause.[31] Hizbullah, however, appropriated the discourse of resistance and imbued it with Islamic rather than nationalist values and meanings in order to distinguish itself from other ideologies of resistance. When describing itself in its posters and the early editions of *al-'Ahd*,[32] Hizbullah adopted the phrase *al-muqawamah al-Islamiyya*, which helped strengthen Hizbullah's image as the party of resistance. The discourse of resistance, along with narratives of suffering, heroism, defiance and victory, was disseminated and reinforced daily through various media outlets affiliated to Hizbullah and in the leaflets and communiqués that Hizbullah first began to circulate in the 1980s.

Hizbullah's communiqués operate in tandem with its other printed material, but they provide more detailed information on activities and operations against the Israeli occupation—including the names and details of individual actors and places—thus serving to validate the authenticity of the reports and cultivating credibility for Hizbullah as a resistance group. These communiqués continued to be circulated until the liberation of southern Lebanon in 2000 and provided extensive details of fighting operations, the names of fighters, the weapons used and the outcome of the operations. The communiqués highlight the importance Hizbullah attaches to archiving the events in which it has played a part. One example of this is a communiqué issued in 1996 at the height of attacks against Israeli targets in the South:

With a firm and rooted belief in the necessity of continuity in jihad ... and on the basis of our belief that the enemy does not understand except the language of the iron fist and fire, and that liberation cannot be made except by the jihad of fighters ... The brigade of the Martyrs of Jerusalem in the Islamic resistance headed by the group of the two martyrs Na'mah Hasika and Khadir 'Ubid launched an attack on a security convoy composed of five civilian cars and a van containing a number of the military and security leaders of the Zionist occupation. Fire was exchanged with members of the convoy on which automatic machineguns and rockets were used. At the same time, the group of the two martyrs Hassan Tarhini and Mohammad al-Hadi launched an attack against the military fortress of al-'ishiya [then an occupied area in southern Lebanon] while the group of the martyr Nasir Nasar rocketed the *lahdi* fortress of al-*Raiyhan*, the group of the martyr Abdu Fahdu rocketed the Zionist fortress in the *kasārat al-'Urūsh*, while the two groups of the martyrs Mohammad Wahab and Majed al-Qubisi were shelling the site of Sajad and Khallat Khāzen.[33]

The language used in communiqués such as these serves as evidence for Hizbullah's central rhetorical and political motifs—sacrifice and martyrdom—while the naming of the individuals and martyrs empowers ordinary people in the battle of 'absolute violence', a term which Franz Fanon uses to describe various struggles against colonialism[34] and which brings into focus the need for sacrifice to achieve aims. The remembrance of martyrs substantiates their value and meaning, particularly as the remembering is made through repeated iterative practices and references that reinforce meanings.[35]

Hizbullah as the legitimate Shiite leader

Ever since its inception in the early 1980s, Hizbullah has consistently deployed a discourse that emphasises its roots in Shiite and Lebanese history, as well as its commitment to improving the position of the Shiite community in the face of its forced marginalisation in Lebanese society. In doing so, Hizbullah systematically borrowed and appropriated language that was already being used by the Iranian Islamic revolutionaries and important Shiite clerical leaders, such as the iconic Shiite leader Imam Musa al-Sadr, as well as by Amal, the movement that al-Sadr had founded to represent Lebanon's Shiites.[36] Early Hizbullah posters, for example, often featured the group's logo alongside the image of Sadr with quotes from the latter such as 'Israel is pure evil' or 'weapons are the decorations of men'. Similarly, the early editions of *al-'Ahd* prominently displayed commentaries and statements issued by Sayyed Mohammad Hussein Fadlallah, the influential Shiite cleric who already had a symbolic role in Lebanon and a substantial following as an Islamic *marja'iya* (reference) among Lebanon's Shiites. Although Fadlallah, one of the most important intellectuals in the Islamic world,[37] was never formally associated with Hizbullah, his regular statements, speeches and interviews were systematically used to appeal to the Shiites to mobilise behind Hizbullah and support its resistance acts in the South. In one report Fadlallah described the resistance acts as 'ninety per cent Islamic. So when Israel chases up people, it starts with the believers first. We are not about undermining the nationalism of others, but it is Islam that resists Israel in the south'[38]—a statement that lent a significant degree of legitimacy to Hizbullah's Islamist identity.

In describing themselves and their aims, Hizbullah's media institutions also sought to claim a space in the imagination of Lebanon's Shiite population. This trend began with *Al-'Ahd*, which described itself as the first weekly 'political Islamic paper' that spoke for the marginalised and oppressed whose voices had been suppressed in the mainstream media and in political discourse. Its first editorial on 18 June 1984 stated: 'There is a need for the true word and for clearly defined political visions.'[39] The political–religious discourse of the 'oppressed and the oppressor' was one of polar opposites—the meaning and value attached to each pole was clear, and the rhetoric highly normative, based on a traditional value system that Shiites in Lebanon would understand. The language used was clearly intended to appeal to Lebanon's Shiites as it spoke to their double abjection: as a community denied political, social and economic support by the Lebanese state and a group that had been subject to several Israeli attacks and occupations (most of Lebanon's Shiites come from the South).[40] In one article, for example, Shiites were described as living in abject conditions, with the Lebanese state failing to provide even the most basic of services. The article criticises the lack of 'sanitary care ... the recent events [i.e. the consequences of the fighting in the South] caused diseases such as chest infections and measles'.[41] The clear inference to be drawn from discourse such as this is that the Lebanese state has chosen to ignore the plight of the Shiites and the victims of the Israeli occupation, which in turn justifies the need for Hizbullah's resistance.

THE HIZBULLAH PHENOMENON

The Lebanese state's apparent absence in the South also served to legitimise Hizbullah's role as the service provider to the Shiite community. Hizbullah has established an extremely wide range of institutions and social services, including: Jihad al-bina' (Struggle for Construction), which deals with the construction, rehabilitation and provision of vital services in war-zone areas; Mu'assassat al-shaheed (Martyrs' Foundation), which is dedicated to the provision of support for the families of martyrs; Mu'assassat al-jarha (Wounded Foundation), which aims to help those who have been wounded and disabled as a result of Israeli attacks; Lajnat imdad al-Khomeini (the Khomeini Support Committee), which offers general welfare to needy families; Al-qard al-hassan, which offers small loans; and Al-ta'bia' al-tarbawiya (the Educational Enforcement Office), which coordinates a network of schools, technical institutes and religious study centres throughout Lebanon.[42] Hizbullah uses these institutions to mobilise the Shiite community and to recruit new members, a process which starts at an early age through initiatives like the al-Mahdi scouts and afterschool children's camps that help instil the values of the 'resistance' in new generations of Shiites. The community is further brought together through periodic processions and rallies featuring Hizbullah and religious leaders, as well as other events in which Hizbullah representatives address the gatherings or distribute printed or audiovisual material. The daily life of Lebanon's Shiites has thus become infused with symbolism emanating from Hizbullah—the group has even created prayer books that feature photographs of its leaders and those of Iran on one page with prayer text on the other.

Hizbullah's mediated landscape of martyrdom and sacrifice

In seeking to mobilise and gain the support of Lebanon's Shiites as a collective political group, Hizbullah has formulated a religious–historical narrative of Shiism as a social, cultural and political force that can serve as the basis for individual empowerment, with the aim of creating an 'imagined community'[43] of Shiite resistance in Lebanon. According to this discourse the participation of Lebanon's Shiite community in the development of state and society, and in the resistance against Israel, is a collective religious and civic obligation.

This discourse was not only constructed through Hizbullah's media, but also through religious and symbolic practice.

Following the distribution of its first live recording of fighters storming the Sujud fortress in 1986 to Lebanese television stations,[44] the group's Deputy Secretary General Naim Qassem described the camera as an 'essential element in all resistance operations'.[45] These recordings represent just one manifestation of Hizbullah's mediated 'spectacle of resistance and martyrdom', which is intended to convey a rich, culturally resonant counter-narrative of collective memories and the struggle against oppression[46] while emphasising Hizbullah's central rhetorical and political motifs. The spectacle was played out in different spaces and media. Hizbullah's radio station, al-Nour, would list the names of those who died in suicide operations for several years in order to keep their memory alive in the popular imagination.[47] Al -Manar television would also interview martyrs' families and broadcast video messages from martyrs that had been filmed prior to their death. Exhibits displayed writings and other artefacts collected by a special unit in the Martyrs' Association (the exhibits will eventually be housed in a museum).[48] *Al-'Ahd* began the practice of telling the life histories of Hizbullah martyrs, giving the name, age, attributes and the occasion of the martyr's passing, thereby providing a potent personal and individual narrative of empowerment. Images of the martyrs wearing military fatigues and the Hizbullah headband with the words 'we are coming' written on them were published along with stories conveying their heroism, providing a powerful dialectic between language and image. The dead were honoured as exceptional human beings, empowering ordinary people while also asserting martyrdom as a Shiite cultural paradigm with roots in the martyrdom of Imam Hussein in the Battle of Karbala.

The Battle of Karbala on 10 October AD 680 has served as a pivot around which Shiite practices of mourning and commemoration revolve. The message that the Shiites in particular, and the Muslim world in general, drew from the Battle of Karbala was that injustice should be resisted wherever it exists, even if the means available to the just are far exceeded by those of the unjust. Imam Hussein and his followers constituted a small number who realised before the battle that they were facing the danger of defeat; yet this did not prevent them from resisting the tyranny of the majority, as represented in Yazid's army.[49] Such commemorative practices serve to maintain the important link with history through the death of Hussein, who is commemorated annually on 'Ashoura, when political messages of fighting injustice and defiance usually prevail, creating a Foucauldian sense of 'political spiritualism', as al-Agha describes the event in the context of the Iranian Revolution.[50]

The commemoration of 'Ashoura in Lebanon traditionally involves holding and attending public and private *majalis*, or mourning gatherings, in which the story of the martyrdom of Hussein is retold, with processions held to express public grief and lamentation over the death. As Lara Deeb has evocatively shown in her study of pious practices in Shiite spaces in Lebanon, the structure and meaning of 'Ashoura are fluid in that it incorporates different elements in different locales and reflects the changing social and political status of Lebanon's Shiites. However, while the importance of 'Ashoura has remained constant, the processions themselves have gradually become more ordered and serve to provide a spectacle of Hizbullah's power in the public sphere. In Deeb's words:

> The processions (*masiras*) have evolved, becoming more organised, with people carrying the portraits of Khomeini, Khameini, Hassan Nasrallah and Musa al-Sadr. These are followed by many groups of boys, scouts, youth, and men, organised by increasing age. They were dressed uniformly as scouts or entirely in black, 'Hussain' written on their coloured arm- or headbands. ... The organised groups were followed by a large group of men marching in solidarity, some hitting their chests lightly, and by a group of *shaiks* and *sayyids*, surrounded by security guards. Then the women's part of the *masira* began, with coloured panels of *Ashura* scenes. These were followed by female scouts and students, again in orderly rows organised by age ... As the *masira* arrived at the field designated as its end point, men went to one side, and women to the other. Nasrallah spoke, then everyone prayed together behind him ...[51]

The *majalis*, or *majalis 'aza* (mourning gatherings), were used to narrate the events of Karbala and were often held in mosques or *husayniyas*, buildings dedicated to Shiite commemoration practices. Since the mid-1990s, *majalis* began to be held in tents that Hizbullah had set up in parking lots and other empty spaces in Beirut. Hizbullah's first public *majlis* was held in its main 'tent' in the southern suburbs of Beirut in 1993, with subsequent *majalis* being televised from this site each year where Nasrallah would speak on alternate nights, until a new hall[52] was constructed in 2002. *Al-'Ahd* acknowledged the use of *majalis* in Hizbullah's outreach activities in an article on 23 April 1993, entitled

'Following the Path of the Resistance is a Connection with the *Jihad* of Imam Hussein', which asserted that 'the mourning gatherings that Hizbullah has held across Lebanon to commemorate the nights of *'Ashoura* have transformed into an occasion to emphasise the fixed path of the Islamic resistance in its facing the Zionist occupation'.[53] Practices such as these are central to Hizbullah's strategy of mobilising and reaching out to its main constituency, the Shiites of Lebanon. They serve to summon the Shiite community as a collective while simultaneously bestowing a supreme value on any individual who chooses to sacrifice themselves to the cause.

The martyrdom trope has additionally been employed by Hizbullah as a central organisational theme in its political communication strategy. This trope was most effectively rendered in martyr posters and in commemorative articles, commentaries and stories published by Hizbullah's print media. One notable example is the commemoration of the first anniversary of the martyrdom of Sheikh Ragheb Harb. *Al-'Ahd* devoted most of its 16 February 1985 issue to the slain leader, providing a potent historical narrative of sacrifice and leadership. Harb is depicted in *al-'Ahd* as having played a historic role in the mobilisation of the Shiites in southern Lebanon, as well as having taken part in what were known as the solidarity committees with the Iranian Revolution. Harb was a leading member of the Movement of the Deprived, which Musa al-Sadr founded in 1974,[54] and he participated in the first conference of the movement in Tehran in June 1982. When Israel raided Lebanon in the same month, Harb was active in mobilising the resistance against the Israeli occupation and its networks of collaboration, incurring the wrath of the Israeli occupation forces—he was eventually assassinated by Israeli Special Forces in 1984.[55] In order to engage the emotions of its target audience and reduce the distance between the leader and the led, *al-'Ahd* published an account of Harb's personal traits and life told by his wife, identified as Hajjeh Um Ahmad. In the article Um Ahmad recalled Harb's sacrifices, as well as his kind and gentle character, and congratulated him on his martyrdom, thereby emphasising the role of women as complementary to men in the duties of jihad.[56] The article also contained personal testimonies regarding the role Harb had played in people's lives which described their personal loyalty and attachment to him—all of which are typical practices in the commemoration of martyrs.

Other commemorative articles were dedicated to Ahmad Qassir, who died while carrying out the first Hizbullah suicide bombing (known as the *Jal al-Bahr* operation) in southern Lebanon at the headquarters of the Israeli military in the Lebanese city of Sur (Tyre) on 11 November 1982. Hizbullah refers to him as its first martyr, a status of symbolic significance in the group's mediated history of sacrifice and commemoration. On 9 November 1990 *al-'Ahd* wrote that Qassir's death offered visions of a brighter future to all oppressed:

Prior to 1982, the image was becoming darker and life was getting harder until 11th November 1982, as if there was no history before, even with the existence of Palestinian and Lebanese forces. It was also frightening … until the dawn of November 1982 which came with a bright light … (lo to such brightness). The face of Ahmed Qassir shone and the knight appeared.[57]

The mediation of Qassir's image continues in the present day through the annual celebration of the Day of the Martyr on 11 November, which is held to mark his martyrdom as well as that of other Hizbullah leaders and fighters who are celebrated with speeches and rallies.[58]Mediated commemorative practices were to become constant features in subsequent issues of the paper, serving to emphasise the central rhetorical and political motifs of Hizbullah and providing a counter-historical narrative of struggle against oppression and occupation. This history was expansive and symbolic—all Hizbullah fighters who die in action are elevated to martyrdom. Martyrs' names were announced and published in different spaces and forms, while their images were memorialised in portraits hung in public spaces in Beirut's southern suburb and in southern Lebanon. A 'mediated landscape of martyrdom' was consequently formed that was symbolic in its representation, but nevertheless fundamentally constituted a communicative political act that aimed to mobilise supporters and intimidate opponents, particularly by communicating the fearlessness of Hizbullah fighters in embracing death.

Hizbullah's political and communication evolution

The end of the Lebanese civil war and the signing of the Ta'if Accord in 1989 ushered in a new era in Lebanon with the onset of national efforts to revitalise the economy, to rebuild the country after years of strife and to reinvigorate state institutions. Hizbullah's political and communication strategies began to change in response to this political context, leading the group towards greater integration within Lebanon. While the pillars of Hizbullah's image remained constant—and still do—they were accompanied by other communication methods and tools that Hizbullah started producing in order to appeal to a wider audience.

Presenting Hizbullah's expanded political repertoire

Hizbullah initially regarded the Ta'if Accord as a flawed reform that merely consecrated the fault-lines of the 1943 National Pact—which Hizbullah viewed as contributing to the Shiites' continued marginalisation, despite its provision for a system of power-sharing among Lebanon's three main confessional groups—while the group also criticised the superficiality of the accord's proposed political reforms. In reiterating this position, al-'Ahd emphasised what it described as the sectarian and anti-nationalist features of the accord: 'Ta'if maintains the Maronite system and reinforces the [Israeli] occupation, while the Islamic resistance confirms its steadfastness,'[59] underlining Hizbullah's claim to resistance as a national force.

The Ta'if Accord and the end of hostilities presented a political challenge for Hizbullah. Following the war, the Lebanese government called for the dissolution of all militias and ordered them to hand in their weapons to the Lebanese army. Hizbullah responded with a public relations campaign in which it emphasised its role as a resistance movement defending the whole of Lebanon, and adapted its image to allow for its gradual integration into the Lebanese political system to ensure that it would not be marginalised in the new civil structures of post-war Lebanon. The group eventually agreed to sign the accord once it had received permission from the Iranian government to do so, with Hizbullah agreeing to its security stipulations—according to which the Lebanese army would take over issues related to security—on the condition that it would still be able to retain its weapons and conduct acts of resistance. Indeed, the discourse of resistance and of Hizbullah as the party of resistance effectively undermines the Ta'if Accord, conferring on Hizbullah the 'material power' (in the sense that it kept its arms) which made it the strongest military force and the most cohesive socio-political movement within Lebanon throughout the 1990s and into the twenty-first century.

As attaining political legitimacy and a broader popular base started to become its prime concern, Hizbullah decided to enter the first parliamentary elections in post-war Lebanon. This move necessitated the adoption of a more nationalistic stance in order to appeal to a wider constituency. At every opportunity the group's leaders tried to prove that its transformation into a mainstream party was authentic rather than opportunistic and that Hizbullah was a nationalist rather than a purely Islamic movement.[60] This process required accommodating the country's large Christian population[61] and the liberal components of Lebanese society, and at the same time maintaining a degree of ideological flexibility that presents Hizbullah as a moderate, national party while simultaneously retaining its Islamic appeal and wide base of pious supporters.[62] The shift in strategy, however, required reinterpreting the doctrine of *wilayat al-faqih* to allow the party to maintain a foothold in the Lebanese multi-confessional system without compromising Hizbullah's doctrinal foundations. Hizbullah was able to promote its Islamic identity by following a pragmatic political programme, largely to attract Christians and other Muslims opposed to an Islamic state, while remaining faithful to its Shiite constituency using a 'bottom-up Islamisation process through working within the Lebanese state'.[63] Hizbullah maintained its populist approach while making clear that it continued to support the creation of an Islamic state in Lebanon; however, the group's leadership was now keen to stress that this objective was not a practical option in the immediate future given Lebanon's confessional and sectarian make-up.

Hizbullah's new *intifah* policy was outlined in its 1992 political programme, in which the group presented itself as a national Lebanese party willing to accommodate and represent the interests of all Lebanese groups, particularly the Christians. As Alagha writes: 'Hizbullah made compromises on some doctrinal issues by allying itself, in the legislative and municipal elections, on the same election slate, with ideological enemies, like any political parties that accommodated its protest by negotiations and bargaining with a wide spectrum of groups across the Lebanese myriad.'[64] In order to market itself in nationalist terms, Hizbullah partly relied on a public relations campaign[65] to show it was no longer solely a Shiite group but was a national Lebanese party that was able to represent all of society. On 18 February 1992, Hizbullah appointed Sheikh Hassan Nasrallah[66] as Secretary General, two days after Israel's assassination of Nasrallah's mentor and predecessor Abbas al-Mussawi, and his wife and son in a helicopter attack. Sheikh Naim Qassem was appointed as his deputy. Both remain in their positions at the time of writing. With Nasrallah's ascension to the party leadership, Hizbullah began a new and more public phase in its political communication strategy. This was reflected in Nasrallah's numerous public appearances, speeches and sermons, all of which were published in Hizbullah's media, as well as the increased use of posters, symbols and banners in public spaces[67] and a structural evolution in Hizbullah's media outputs and performance.[68]

In an intensive marketing campaign that reflected Hizbullah's intentions to join the political field in Lebanon, *al-'Ahd* published statements by Nasrallah and other Shiite clerical leaders, including Fadlallah, which supported its decision to enter Lebanon's first post-civil war elections, thus lending legitimacy to Hizbullah's gradualist-pragmatist approach. Nasrallah described the decision as an important move to bolster 'the option of resistance and to protect the rights of the people'[69] and to build a modern Lebanese state that would maintain the individual as its principal foundation.[70] *Al-'Ahd* also published detailed biographies of Hizbullah's candidates and their views on participation in political life. This was accompanied by Hizbullah's political programme, which began with the evocative call, 'O the honourable Lebanese, O the beloved deprived'[71] in order to summon the Lebanese people as a national collective and the Shiites, its main constituency, as the community whose struggle Hizbullah is obliged to support. The programme laid out the different aspects of Hizbullah's worldview, which remained rooted in the need for resistance as 'the natural gate towards the liberation … It has been proven that it is the only choice in the face of the enemy.'[72] It included references to education, society and development, as reflected in the following statement published in *al-'Ahd*: 'The reform of the infrastructure, the maintenance of the official education, and the development of the deprived areas, and halting of negligence … we are determined to protect the interests of the deprived in Lebanon.'[73] Hizbullah also called for 'technical development' (i.e. increased investment in media platforms and technology), which it described as 'an imitation of God's creations',[74] thereby setting the stage for a more intensive phase in the group's marketing of itself.

The visual turn in Hizbullah's communication machine

Once its participation in Lebanon's formal political sphere had been secured, Hizbullah began an intensive drive to build its own institutions, including its visual media outlets. In 1991 it established its own radio station, al-Nour, as well as a terrestrial television station, al-Manar. The primary audience for al-Nour was the Shiite constituency, which the station targeted through its religious programming and themes. Al-Manar, which Hizbullah described as *qanat al-muqawama* (the channel of resistance),[75] sought to consolidate the group's image as a defender of Lebanon against Israeli aggression and has played a central role in promoting Hizbullah's culture of resistance.

Al-Manar's local and low-budget broadcasts featured a mix of religious, political, sports and social programmes, as well as programmes designed for children. Initially, the channel was dominated by religious programmes such as 'My Trip to Light', which featured people who had converted to Islam, and programmes that focused on the resistance against Israel, such as 'The Resistance is Jihad and Victory', which chronicled the life of a Hizbullah martyr in each episode.[76] Al-Manar later began to produce historical drama series that made use of themes which would be evocative to a contemporary Lebanese audience. These included *The Four-Year War*, which was broadcast in the mid-1990s and dramatised the events of the First Barbary War (1801–5). During the first few years in which the channel began to broadcast, there were only a small number of political programmes addressing Lebanese and regional affairs, this type of programming only becoming a prominent feature on the channel in the 2000s. The largest share of al-Manar's programmes during Israel's occupation of the South, estimated at 40 per cent of its airtime, was its coverage of developments in the South, including Hizbullah operations that al-Manar's reporters often followed on site.[77] Al-Manar, however, eventually became nationally oriented. As a mass medium it allowed Hizbullah to communicate directly with the wider Lebanese audience, which was crucial for allowing Hizbullah to establish itself as a key political party. One way in which it achieved this aim was through its broadcasts of translations from Israeli news outlets—the only Lebanese channel to do this—which informed the audience what the 'enemy' was reporting, a tactic that helped to boost Hizbullah's credibility.

The creation of al-Manar marked a dramatic turn towards the use of images in Hizbullah's communication strategies, and this gradually became manifest in all its media platforms. *Al-'Ahd* began to use more images than text on its cover pages, with pictures of Israeli casualties, and Hizbullah fighters attacking Israeli posts, and images of Hizbullah and Iranian leaders, as well as pictures of events, rallies, Jerusalem Day celebrations and other ceremonies held to support the resistance. It was at this stage that Nasrallah began to become a more visible presence in Hizbullah media, speaking to his intended audiences in different spaces and diverse media.[78] The visual turn in the group's political communication practices was also evident in the production of space, particularly in the Hizbullah-dominated southern suburbs of Beirut, serving to accentuate and naturalise Hizbullah's presence in the everyday.

Throughout the 1990s Hizbullah created various forms of 'public presence' and commemoration in its territory, most notably through the use of rows of billboards depicting young men who had died in the resistance against Israel. At another level, al-Manar broadcast numerous programmes about the Palestinian refugee experiences in Lebanon,[79] reinforcing Hizbullah's image as a party concerned with the Palestinian–Israeli conflict and also as the party bearing the brunt of the confrontations with Israel. In the southern suburbs of Beirut, Hizbullah dominated the production of space by using symbols and images with bold references to the Islamic resistance, having largely supplanted its rival Amal following Hizbullah's military victory in the War of the Camps. Closer to the centre of Beirut, the rivalry between the two groups resulted in a fluid and overlapping symbolic 'competition between the two Shiite parties that directly reflected political and religious territorial competition and often seemed little more than a continuation of the intra-Shiite wars of the late 1980s'.[80] The city's squares were renamed Khomeini Square, Revolution Square and Nasrallah Square, while the streets were lined with martyr and orphan photos as well as adverts for the various social, cultural and educational services that Hizbullah provided. Although this practice of spatial demarcation is not unique to Hizbullah and, indeed, prevailed in other parts of Beirut, Hizbullah's production of space served to legitimise its presence in the everyday lives of the Shiites and helped it claim the place of their sole legitimate political representative.

A further way in which Hizbullah legitimised its everyday presence in the southern suburb of Beirut was through periodic parades of cars adorned with Hizbullah posters and affixed with loudspeakers broadcasting Islamic chants—mainly during the month of Ramadan and during 'Ashoura—political speeches and religious sermons, or songs adapting Lebanese folkloric rhythms with religious and political lyrics. Hizbullah also began producing merchandise, from cassette tapes of the car broadcasts to necklaces and stickers bearing the photographs of martyrs to calendars that its personnel would sell door to door, asking residents to 'contribute the price of a bullet' by buying one. As there was no clear pattern as to when a Hizbullah representative could show up at someone's door, or when a car might drive down a particular street broadcasting audio messages, or even when a parade might pass commemorating a martyr or an event, Hizbullah's domination of space also had a temporal dimension. These 'informal' practices increased Hizbullah's presence and visibility and supported its more 'formal' visual practices which peaked with the parades that Hizbullah regularly organised in public spaces in the South and the southern suburbs of Beirut. As the years went by, the parades became larger and more streamlined, and were not only covered in special issues of al-'Ahd with extensive photo spreads but also broadcast live on al-Manar, becoming spectacles of Hizbullah's power.

The most important parade in this vein is Jerusalem Day. Hizbullah began using this event to disseminate propaganda to Israel and political messages in the Lebanese context, as well as to rally the Shiite community around a 'strong' party that would defend its rights and elevate its status within Lebanon while liberating the country from foreign oppressors. Jerusalem Day parades, as discussed earlier, were an occasion to affirm Hizbullah's commitment to the liberation of Jerusalem through jihad. As a result, they always featured sculptures or images of the al-Aqsa mosque, which would be carried by a procession or displayed in the background. The image of Khomeini would often be placed above that of al-Aqsa, depicting him in such a way that he appeared to be looking down protectively on the mosque from the sky. Banners with slogans like 'Israel should disappear' would be hung behind a platform featuring Hizbullah leaders, who would give speeches about the Palestinian cause and Hizbullah's political position. But Jerusalem Day is also an occasion for Hizbullah to disseminate another key message, both to the West and to its own constituents and local Lebanese rivals: namely, power. Several units of Hizbullah fighters would march in precision, wearing military fatigues, black balaclavas, bandanas proclaiming 'we are coming', karate uniforms, gas masks and shrouds featuring the slogan 'lovers of martyrdom'. Women in black chadors would follow the men, carrying photos of martyrs. Children in military uniforms tagged with 'we heed your call, Khomeini' labels and carrying arms, or wearing the uniforms of al-Mahdi and Risalah scouts, would also march, affirming the continuation of Hizbullah's message over a number of generations. The processions would be accompanied by a parade of military vehicles and awe-inspiring performances, such as scaling walls on ropes or martial arts, as well as symbolic acts like the burning of the Israeli or American flag or of effigies representing Western leaders.

Hizbullah's media wars

As the discussion above shows, Hizbullah's communication strategy aims to reach multiple audiences both within and outside Lebanon—allies, competitors and foes. The turning point in Hizbullah's communication strategy came on 11 April 1996 when Israel launched its 'Grapes of Wrath' military operation. The operation culminated in the Qana massacre on 18 April when more than 100 Lebanese civilians were killed by Israeli shelling as they sought shelter in a UN complex in southern Lebanon. The events highlighted Hizbullah's need to compete with several other entities, including those of Israel, other Lebanese media outlets and the group's political rivals in Lebanon, in order to ensure that its own communication messages prevailed.

Following the first Israeli attack on 11 April, and despite the destruction of some of its facilities, Hizbullah intensified its short-range rocket attacks into northern Israel, thereby increasing its popular appeal as the only Arab entity able to stand up to Israel. As Hala Jaber writes:

For the first time since the group had come into being, Lebanese of all religions, sects and classes rallied around the Party of God's Islamic resistance in an unprecedented show of support and solidarity. Even Israel's old-time allies of 1982, the Christian Maronites, managed to put aside their political differences and supported the resistance.[81]

The attacks heralded the beginning of a media war between Hizbullah and Israel. Hizbullah used its radio station al-Nour to send a clear message to Israel in which it announced that its rockets would

continue to terrorise you. Death will continue to hover above your heads. Our terror will kill you, will destroy your economy, and your technical capacities will not be of any use. Rockets will rain on you today and everyday by the tenths, hundreds and thousands … You will not impose your will on us. You threaten us with two weeks and we are ready for two months; for two years, and we are ready for two decades. No matter how long the aggression lasts, our will would not be twisted or broken. Our spirits will not be sapped. Our blood will only lead to victory, and will shame and humiliate the Jews.[82]

The Qana massacre was covered extensively on Lebanese national television, Tele Liban, which sent reporters to the site who transmitted horrific live footage of mutilated body parts. The reporters remained in the South for days, where they chronicled in detail the search for casualties and the stories of the people who had died. The Tele Liban coverage upstaged that on al-Manar, sparking Hizbullah's launch of 'a more structured and re-organised media strategy … aimed at targeting new audiences in and beyond Lebanon'.[83] Zahera Harb, who covered the events for Tele Liban, wrote: 'What started with TL as an unstructured and unorganised media campaign aiming to defy the enemy by uniting the nation around its government and resistance fighters was translated by al-Manar into an organised, strategic plan to use the media systematically as one of the tools to achieve liberation.'[84]

The new media strategy saw the beginning of a 'restructuring phase' which, by the end of 1996, had led Hizbullah to place all of its audio-visual output—television, radio and a newly launched website—under the control of a new unit, called Qism al-di'ayah al-siyassiyah (the Political Propaganda Unit), with the aim of harmonising communication across all its media platforms. The unit began producing video-clips and short reports for al-Manar that praised the resistance fighters while sending threatening messages to Israel. Some of these clips were broadcast in Arabic and some in Hebrew, and some in both, thereby targeting Israel directly. This use of Hebrew went hand in hand with a tactic of placing billboards carrying warning messages on sites where they would face in the direction of Israel from the Lebanese border. One such billboard displayed black-and-white images of the body parts of dead Israeli soldiers and a message to Ariel Sharon in Arabic and Hebrew: 'Sharon, don't forget, your soldiers are still in Lebanon.' The billboard had been erected in the context of an ambush that Hizbullah had conducted on an Israeli naval commando unit in Ansarieh in September 1997, after which Hizbullah kept some of the body parts of the Israeli soldiers that it had killed. Hizbullah used its website to taunt Israel for its dishonesty regarding the number of soldiers whose intact bodies were returned to Israel in an exchange with Hizbullah after the ambush, sparking uproar in Israel and forcing the Israel Defence Forces to admit the cover-up.[85] While the creation of media content across all platforms was centralised, the delivery of media messages was decentralised, allowing regional party groups to take charge of the dissemination of content.

The propaganda unit remained in existence until the liberation of southern Lebanon in 2000 when it was integrated into the new Resistance Department. Throughout this period, al-Manar also operated under three other units. The first was the Military Media Unit responsible for sending cameramen with the Hizbullah fighters to record operations. The second was the Media Relations Unit, which was born out of the restructuring of the Central Media Unit that had been responsible for all Hizbullah-affiliated media outlets and for the dissemination of 'popular media', such as posters, regional parades, political festivals, sports and cultural activities. In 1996, al-Manar and the al-Nour radio station started to be run by an elected board of directors in accordance with the Lebanese Audi-Visual Law, while the Central Media Unit was in charge of dealing with Lebanese and international media personnel and institutions. The third was the Hebrew Monitoring Unit which tracked Israeli media and addressed Israeli soldiers and nationals in Hebrew.[86]

As the Qana massacre became an icon of national injury and joint Muslim and Christian sacrifice, Hizbullah integrated the event into its own narrative of resistance, with Qana being a persistent presence in Hizbullah's media long after the events took place.[87] This emphasis on the Qana massacre can be understood within the context of the group's rivalry with Amal, which had constructed a cemetery for the victims that became a popular visitor site frequented by busloads of Lebanese, including children on school trips. The site consists of white marble mass and individual graves on which the names of the victims are engraved, surrounded by a space that can be used for public events. Hizbullah, Amal and other political entities in the South, like the municipalities, held ceremonies at the Qana site. But Hizbullah became the most dominant in this context, arranging visits by its constituents to the site where they would be told stories about the heroism of the 'resistance'.[88] By claiming the memorial as a public site, Hizbullah can be seen as taking an active role in constructing and directing national memory, as the Qana massacre forms a key part of this memory for Lebanese citizens. Hizbullah's media reinforce this construction by commemorating the Qana massacre periodically through special programmes on al-Manar and articles in *al-'Ahd*. In one of its portrayals of Qana in 1999, *al-'Ahd* showed images of the Qana massacre on the one hand, with people carrying dead children and smoke rising from buildings, while showing acts of resistance as represented by Katyusha launchers on the other. The massacre is described in a commemorative piece entitled 'Lebanon with its Resistance Squeezes the Grapes of Wrath' as having totally failed to stem the tide of the resistance, thereby bringing the role of Hizbullah to the fore in the national narrative of Qana.[89]

A regime of truth

In the three years before the liberation of the South, Hizbullah increased its military operations (which peaked at 1,528 operations in 1999 alone), while al-Manar intensified its coverage in the area, using symbolically charged language to talk about Hizbullah fighters and the achievements of the group as well as inciting hatred towards Israel—key elements of conventional propaganda techniques. Al-Manar began providing round-the-clock coverage of operations in order to intimidate the enemy and show its weaknesses. It also exposed Lebanese collaborators working with the South Lebanon Army.[90] But propaganda was not the sole focus of Hizbullah's communication. A larger concern was maintaining the regime of truth that Hizbullah had constructed to present itself as credible in the eyes of its constituents.

An unexpected boost to this credibility came on 12 September 1997 when Hassan Nasrallah's eldest son Hadi was killed in a confrontation with Israeli soldiers in southern Lebanon. Nasrallah's dignified and largely unemotional reaction to his son's death—reported widely by Hizbullah's media outlets—rendered the martyrdom of Hadi Nasrallah, as well as the status of Hassan Nasrallah himself, even more heroic. Nasrallah gained a great deal of credibility from the fact that his eldest son had served as a Hizbullah fighter, which in turn gave a huge boost to the morale of the group's followers. Yet his public handling of the death also had a significant impact on how Hizbullah was perceived. In a speech televised on al-Manar the day after Hadi's death, Nasrallah declared:

I thank God and praise Him for His great bounty, that He generously blessed my family by choosing one of its members for martyrdom, and accepted me and my family as members in the holy assembly of martyrs' families. I used to feel ashamed when visiting the fathers, mothers, wives, and children of martyrs, and I will stay feeling humble in front of them.[91]

Al-Manar's broadcast intercut the speech with footage of Nasrallah visiting the families of martyrs, alongside images of the attending audience in the hall where he was giving the speech, during which the audience members twice responded to his statements by raising their fists in the air, chanting: 'God is great. Khomeini is the leader. Victory to Islam. Death to Israel. Definitely [reaching] victory. Advancing till [we reach] Jerusalem.' As this is the standard chant that Hizbullah has popularised in its public rallies, the audience's reaction suggested that his and their spirits had not been broken by this loss and that they remained firmly fixed on achieving their goals. Nasrallah's popularity subsequently soared and his reputation assumed mythic proportions, commanding a level of love and popular respect that translated into greater support for Hizbullah.[92] Less than two months after the death of his son, Nasrallah announced the formation of al-Saraya al-lubnaniya li-muqawamat al-ihtilal (the Lebanese brigade to resist the occupation), the name of which itself suggested a new phase, the 'Lebanonisation' of the resistance. In making the announcement, Nasrallah said the decision to found the brigade reflected a sensitivity to Lebanon's confessional dynamics and was meant to open the door for many Lebanese to work under this umbrella group 'which only reflects the commitment to the nation while the Islamic resistance will continue to operate independently drawing on the religious duty of *jihad*.[93]

However, the commemoration of Hadi Nasrallah's death remained modest when compared with that of Hizbullah's slain leaders, as Hizbullah was careful not to jeopardise its credibility by privileging the story of the young son of its Secretary General over those of martyrs with a publicly known legacy. Hizbullah maintained a constant presence of commemorative events and reports in order to keep the memory of those martyrs alive, thus strengthening its links with its community. Just before Martyrs' Day on 11 November 1999, *al-'Ahd* published a special issue on 26 October 1999 commemorating its two iconic leaders, Sheikhh Ragheb Harb (1952–84) and Sayyed Abbas al-Mussawi (1952–92). Children were invited to submit works of art to commemorate them and to celebrate their ideals of resistance and jihad:

The cultural section in the newspaper of *al-'Ahd* invites children, boys and girls to participate in the painting competition to express their relationship with the resistance and the feeling of love which they carry for it, and to express their vision regarding the meaning of resistance to the Zionist occupation and the defence of the homeland.[94]

This might suggest that Hizbullah was seeking to reach out to its constituents, encouraging them to share in the experience of creating communicative outputs. But a closer look at the group's history reveals that people have always been invited to create, but not to curate: ultimately, Hizbullah's communication tools and outputs are tightly controlled and centralised. Any output created outside of the realms of the organisation can only be embraced if it is selected by Hizbullah. In other words, throughout its history, Hizbullah has sought narrative agency over its own stories, as well as appropriating other stories as the need arose, which necessitates a top-down communication structure that does not allow for alternative interpretations or narrations, even from its own constituents.

Conclusion

Hizbullah, as this chapter has shown, was remarkable in making use of media spaces to assemble a 'repertoire of politics ' through which it represented itself, sought to call diverse publics to action and used frames relevant to its intended audiences to produce truth-claims about its role and identity. In this way, Hizbullah's discourse, comprising text, image and symbols, should not be seen as epiphenomenal but as critical to the image, production and sustenance of the group over time.[95] As it enhanced its standing, Hizbullah's various media platforms themselves gained new political dimensions, particularly through their capacity to record information about Hizbullah and construct a counter-narrative, or an archive, of Hizbullah's political repertoire. However, Hizbullah's archive cannot simply be read as a record of history written against the grain of other histories, or in opposition to them, as the literature on alternative history, oral history and post-colonial struggles shows.[96] Rather, it must be seen as a part of Hizbullah's efforts to construct and affirm a mediated regime of truth, the ultimate articulation of panoptical power.[97] As the following chapter will show, this articulation of its power intensified with the expansion of Hizbullah's institutional structures, media use and practices, allowing it to assert its presence in Lebanon and beyond.

3

HIZBULLAH IN THE TWENTY-FIRST CENTURY: THE STRUGGLE FOR POLITICAL SURVIVAL, 2000–12

*Lina Khatib**

Between 2000 and 2012 Hizbullah faced a range of opportunities and challenges both within Lebanon and the wider region which in turn led to a number of significant developments in the group's political communication strategy. The period began with a milestone in the group's history: the liberation of southern Lebanon from Israeli occupation in May 2000. The liberation launched Hizbullah as a regional force across the Arab world and consolidated its position as a credible resistance group. This growing influence was later strengthened further as a result of Hizbullah's media coverage of the second Palestinian intifada from September 2000 onwards, which brought the group closer to the hearts and minds of Arab audiences. But Hizbullah faced a challenge to its newfound credibility with the assassination of former Prime Minister Rafic Hariri in February 2005. In the period that followed Hizbullah came under severe pressure as it battled local Lebanese political opponents in elections and in popular protests on Lebanon's streets.

* Dina Matar and Atef Alshaer contributed sections to this chapter on *al-'Ahd* and Hizbullah's website and books.

THE HIZBULLAH PHENOMENON

The 2006 war with Israel provided an opportunity for Hizbullah to regain its 'resistance' tag, with its leaders and Media Department describing the eventual ceasefire as a 'divine victory'. This sense of 'victory' was embraced across the Arab world, consolidating Hizbullah's—and Hassan Nasrallah's—reputation as an Arab hero redeeming an Arab sense of dignity. The war also marked the start of a new era in which Hizbullah's image was framed in more 'modern' terms through visual saturation and innovation. But the local political tensions that followed the war presented Hizbullah with further challenges following the establishment of the UN Special Tribunal for Lebanon (STL), which was set up to investigate Hariri's assassination. Hizbullah viewed the STL as a Western conspiracy that posed a direct threat to its existence. In the years that followed Hizbullah oscillated between different narrative frameworks in response to the STL, particularly after its indictment of some of the group's members in 2010. Hizbullah veered between presenting an image of power and an image of victimisation, intimidating its local political opponents while simultaneously presenting itself as the victim of an international conspiracy. The Arab Spring further challenged Hizbullah's self-propagated image as the 'sole' representative of Arab dignity, despite the group's attempts to appropriate the Arab revolutions for its own benefit in a pattern it had developed over many previous years.

The twelve years between 2000 and 2012 were thus characterised by a number of important landmarks in Hizbullah's communication strategy as the group struggled for political survival. Examining these landmarks serves to reveal both the group's adaptability and its rigidity as to its modus operandi. While it successfully capitalised on 'achievements' like the 2000 liberation and the 2006 'victory', and was able to mould its communication tools to fit twenty-first-century trends, its tried-and-tested communication methods, such as the appropriation and use of familiar narrative frameworks, proved to be of limited efficacy in the face of unexpected political challenges. Hizbullah also remained restricted by an inability to transform its core political strategy, pragmatic though this strategy is. Ultimately, the group's continued reliance on weapons as a tool to sustain local political supremacy, its alliances with authoritarian regimes and its antagonism towards the West—all of which had previously served as assets in

Hizbullah's political strategy—began to undermine its credibility in the eyes of Arab audiences.

From a national to a regional force

The liberation of southern Lebanon on 25 May 2000 was a watershed in Hizbullah's history—it was the first time that Israeli troops had been forced to retreat from Arab lands at the hands of an Arab paramilitary group since 1948, when the modern State of Israel was created. This event, widely attributed to an increase in Hizbullah's resistance operations against Israeli forces, helped the group sustain its image as a national Lebanese party, a status which it had sought to achieve since the beginning of the 1990s in order to expand its support base in Lebanon.[1] The liberation also marked the beginning of an increase in measures that aimed to claim a space for Hizbullah in the pan-Arab imagination. Television provided the main communication tool in this process, with the liberation occurring in the same year as the launch of al-Manar's satellite television channel (al-Manar was previously a domestic, terrestrial channel). This allowed Hizbullah to communicate its messages directly to a regional audience in the Middle East, and to present Hassan Nasrallah as an Arab hero. The liberation of the South can thus be considered the moment that launched Hizbullah as a regional force to be reckoned with in the Middle East.

In his speech on the day of the liberation in 2000, Nasrallah addressed the Hizbullah flag-waving crowd in an open-air venue in the southern town of Bint Jbeil by standing in front of a large Lebanese flag and proclaiming: 'You have proven, and the resistance has proven—in harmony with the Lebanese government—that the people of Lebanon, and the Lebanese state, and the Lebanese resistance, and all the sects in Lebanon are worthy of victory.' This speech planted the seed of 'the people, the army, and the resistance' demarcation that Hizbullah would repeatedly return to in the years that followed, in order to justify its separation from state institutions like the Lebanese Armed Forces.[2] In the liberation speech, Nasrallah went on to dedicate the victory to the Arab people: 'We dedicate this victory to our oppressed people in occupied Palestine, and to the peoples of our Arab and Islamic nation.'[3] Nasrallah consequently sought to appeal to non-Shiite Lebanese and Arabs at large, presenting Hizbullah as being at the core of Lebanese and Arab identity.[4]

Hizbullah's media platforms began a concerted campaign to emphasise the group's transformation from a localised Islamist movement into an Islamist/national/Arab party, using the liberation as stark evidence while retaining Hizbullah's identity as a resistance movement distinct from the Lebanese state. The cover of *al-'Ahd* on 2 June 2000, for example, used an image of the Lebanese map populated in its entirety by a photograph of people carrying the Hizbullah flag, along with the headline 'Congratulations to Lebanon on the Victory of the Resistance', with a smaller circular photo in the bottom right-hand corner featuring Hassan Nasrallah.[5] Al-Manar continuously broadcast live images of Israeli troops leaving southern Lebanon to legitimise the image of Hizbullah as the Lebanese national resistance party. The image was further bolstered by pictures of thousands of hitherto dispossessed Lebanese returning to their homes and land in southern Lebanon, from which they had been driven by Israel during the years of occupation. Some of the most emotional coverage by al-Manar, as well as other Lebanese media, showed people trying to discover the fate of prisoners in the notorious Khiam detention centre in southern Lebanon after realising that Israeli soldiers had left without setting the detainees free. Zahera Harb, who covered the events for Tele Liban, writes of the scenes: 'People with camera crews crawled towards the centre and broke into the cells where the detainees did not know what was happening outside. Suddenly, those who had been behind prison doors were celebrating their freedom.'[6]

The prison where Israel detained and tortured Lebanese and other nationals for years had been an important visual and material symbol of the Israeli occupation. After the liberation Hizbullah quickly transformed the site, which was located in the heart of the village of Khiam, into a visitor centre. The prison was opened to the public and manned by Hizbullah personnel who marked the different sections of the prison with yellow signs with red (Arabic) and green (English) writing, mirroring the colours of the Hizbullah flag: 'torture rooms', 'solitary confinement rooms', 'women's rooms', 'room for interrogation with the help of the traitors [*sic*]' and so on. A matching yellow sign proclaiming 'Khiam Detention Centre' in English and Arabic was hung at the entrance to the prison, surrounded by two Lebanese flags. Inside the site, Israeli weapons seized by Hizbullah were displayed—signifiers of prowess over the enemy—and visitors could peer into the tiny, sparse rooms where detainees had been held, bringing the spectators closer to the experience of victimisation that Hizbullah strived to overcome. The crude presentation of the Khiam site soon evolved into a more polished experience for visitors—parking spaces for visiting cars and buses were subsequently added, along with a map of the grounds detailing the layout of the site and its different components, and, eventually, an official brown sign from the Ministry of Tourism in Arabic and French saying 'Prison de Khiam', affirming the prison as an official Lebanese tourist site. The early use of English and Arabic in Khiam's signage points to Hizbullah's awareness of the international media attention to the liberation of the South and the desire to disseminate Hizbullah's 'story' to a global audience, including Israel, while the decision to grant an official tourism sign highlights the Lebanese state's embrace of Hizbullah domestically. As the Lebanese army had proved incapable of liberating the South, this act provided a degree of state-sanctioned credibility to the triangle 'the people, the army, and the resistance' as separate yet complementary entities—a triangle that Hizbullah has repeatedly used to justify its possession of weapons in the name of national and regional defence.

Hizbullah's weekly newspaper *al-'Ahd* also reported the Israeli withdrawal in pan-Arab/pan-Islamic terms, showing jubilant crowds celebrating along with images of the departing Israeli soldiers as well as Hizbullah fighters under the inscription: 'The Arab and Islamic World: Congratulations to Lebanon on the Victory of the Resistance'.[7] At the bottom of the page a headline dedicated the victory to 'the martyrs', to al-Imam al-Mahdi, whose return from occultation many Shiites await, to Iran's spiritual leader Ayatollah Ali Khameini, and to Hassan Nasrallah. In order to enhance his credibility, Nasrallah's portraits were placed at either side of the page, merging the image of symbolic religious leaders from the past with the iconic hero of the present—a tactic Hizbullah had consistently used to endow itself with legitimacy and religious–historical continuity, as discussed in the previous chapter. For months after the withdrawal, *al-'Ahd* and al-Manar reported the stories of Lebanese prisoners, taking them to the site of their imprisonment to recall their memories about the places and tools of their torture, thereby providing a potent personal counter-narrative of memory that was individually and collectively empowering. All of these factors allowed Hizbullah to appropriate the label 'the resistance', so that 'the resistance' has become another name for Hizbullah; this labelling offers a way to cultivate legitimacy, which in turn means that resistance connotations come up every time Hizbullah is mentioned or even thought about, regardless of the context. In adopting this label, Hizbullah can also be seen as using an international framework to appeal to global audiences, as it has branded itself a resistance movement on a par with the anti-colonial movements of Africa and Latin America.

With the outbreak of the second Palestinian intifada (uprising) at the end of September 2000, Hizbullah's political communication strategy was adapted to project an image of the group as the main regional supporter of the Palestinians in their struggle against Israel, and as the most credible resistance force in the eyes of Arab citizens. Al-Manar covered the unfolding events non-stop during its hours of broadcasting, earning itself a position among the top most-watched regional and transnational broadcasters with the largest audience share in the region.[8] The liberation of southern Lebanon had sparked the launch of satellite broadcasting by al-Manar. While the station initially broadcast for just four hours a day, this was subsequently increased to eighteen hours with the onset of the Palestinian intifada.[9] Throughout the day, al-Manar would announce the timing of its programmes according to 'occupied al-Quds [Jerusalem] time',[10] and the station also commissioned fifty special music videos for the Palestinian intifada.[11] When Israel bombed the Palestinian Television building in Ramallah, al-Manar added the logo of the television station to its own as an expression of support for the intifada. The channel subsequently adopted a new slogan, 'the channel of Arabs and Muslims'.[12] Al-Manar's discourse also sought to show Hizbullah as the most significant actor in the ongoing regional existential 'war of position' (to use Gramsci's expression) with Israel and the United States, serving to enhance its image as a national Arab group. As Joseph al-Agha writes: 'in regional affairs, especially the issue of buttressing the *Intifada*, Hizbullah became more and more radical, using hard-line pre-Ta'if discourse that labels the US as "Great Satan" and the "Mother of all corruption" (*Um al-Fasad*)'.[13]

The terrorist attacks of 11 September 2001 and the ensuing US-led 'war on terror' saw a further radicalisation in Hizbullah's anti-US and anti-Israel rhetoric that spoke to pan-Arab sentiments and public opinion at the time. The group's stance was made clear in statements delivered by the party's Deputy Secretary General Naim Qassem. On various occasions, Qassem reiterated the impossibility of coexistence with the United States and its proxy, Israel, as well as the impossibility of compromise on the question of Hizbullah's arms.[14] Hizbullah consequently altered its image from the liberator of Lebanon to the protector of the country from potential Israeli and US aggression.[15] Al-Manar dedicated time and programmes for commentary and reports on US relations with the Arab world and with the Muslim *umma*, hosting a number of analysts, academics and religious scholars to talk about Israel's policies and its continued hostility to its neighbours and the Palestinians. Among its most popular talk shows was the programme *The Spider's Web*—a term Nasrallah uses to refer to Israel—which detailed Israel's weaknesses and provided scenarios on how it could be defeated. Another programme, *The Terrorists*, broadcast images of Israeli attacks and dead children as well as homes that had been burned to the ground to emphasise that it was Israel, rather than Hizbullah, which was the terrorist in the region—a clear attempt to distance the group from the label it had acquired following the bombing of Western interests in Lebanon in the 1980s.

The liberation, the second intifada, September 11 and the war on terror worked as political opportunity structures for Hizbullah, providing the group with ready-made 'proof' of the justice of its cause and its criticism of the United States and Israel. Hizbullah capitalised on these opportunities to spread its message across the Arab world, with television continuing to serve as the main tool in its efforts to reach a wider audience. The five years following the liberation of the South marked a qualitative and quantitative shift in the programming of al-Manar as it sought to engage Arab audiences through programmes other than its well-established current affairs, news and documentary programmes. Entertainment shows and children's programmes—which had featured only marginally on the channel before—joined existing political, social and religious programmes to appeal to Arab and Lebanese audiences in their leisure time. A key characteristic of all of al-Manar's output was—and remains—the fact that it presents a coherent message across the different genres that the station broadcasts. An example of this is *The Mission*, a game show in which contestants earn points by answering questions about US–Israeli relations. The more points the contestants earn, the closer they are moved to the location of Jerusalem, which is displayed on a giant map in the studio.

When a winner is declared, the refrain 'Jerusalem is ours and we are coming to it' is played.[16] The programme signifies two important tropes for Hizbullah: its declared commitment to the liberation of Palestine, especially after the liberation of southern Lebanon, with Jerusalem presented as the next target; and the display of knowledge as power. Demonstrating detailed knowledge about the 'enemy' is a sign of mastery over a weak object. The show joins a variety of other programmes dedicated to Palestine as a theme, such as the current affairs programme *The Palestinian Scene* and a number of documentaries. The most prominent programme in this vein is *Here is Palestine*, which attempts to reunite members of Palestinian families in the diaspora and the Occupied Territories while underlining their right of return to their homeland. The programme has different sections, starting with 'Not Forgotten', which consists of an oral history narrated by a Palestinian elder, often juxtaposed with 'before' and 'after' images of Palestinian villages in relation to the Israeli occupation. The programme then moves on to broadcasts of recorded messages from Palestinians to their families in the section 'I Send My Regards', followed by 'Till We Meet', a long section in which family members are reunited, and finally 'O Bird', in which on-screen guests ask viewers for assistance in tracing lost family members.

Hizbullah also appealed to the sense of pride among Arab audiences through its focus on the heroism of its martyrs. A show on al-Manar, *Sincere Men*, profiles Hizbullah's suicide bombers, whose images float across the screen while narratives of their lives and achievements are aired. Children were also targets for this message of heroism. Collectible martyr cards were created in the style of the Pokemon cards that were popular in the early 2000s, encouraging children to collect a complete set featuring the photographs, names and profiles of Hizbullah's martyrs. The cards were sold not only in Lebanon but also in the Occupied Territories.

The range of Hizbullah's merchandise for children has grown over the years to include stationery, such as ink stamps bearing the image of Nasrallah, puzzles again bearing the photograph of Nasrallah, and computer games that invite the player to assume the position of a Hizbullah fighter. These joined a growing repertoire of children's programmes on al-Manar, including cartoons. One example of the latter is *The Courageous Knight*, a weekly cartoon that tells the story of al-Abbas bin Ali as he fights 'infidels' in defence of Islam in the Battle of Karbala. This historical narrative can be read as an indirect representation of Hizbullah's fight against the West, especially the United States and Israel. The cartoon speaks directly to the Shiite community by representing one of its most eminent historical figures, the son of Imam Ali who is considered one of the greatest warriors in Arabia. Its representation of al-Abbas as a fourteen-year-old child riding a horse and slaying opponents with his sword can be seen as normalising the use of weapons in defending a cause regardless of one's age.

The challenge of the Cedar Revolution

Hizbullah's image as a Lebanese national party with the sovereignty and defence of Lebanon as its primary concerns was challenged by the Cedar Revolution following the assassination of the former prime minister Rafic Hariri on 14 February 2005. Hariri's death, which was widely regarded as an assassination orchestrated by Hizbullah's ally Syria, presented a significant challenge for Hizbullah, as mass public mourning for the former prime minister became a daily ritual in downtown Beirut. Attention to the Cedar Revolution went beyond Lebanon. Arab citizens as well as international observers praised the street protests and their calls for 'freedom, sovereignty and independence' (from Syrian control), with this slogan becoming one of the most memorable in Lebanon's popular history.[17]

Hizbullah was quick to condemn Hariri's assassination, calling him 'Lebanon's martyr',[18] and to warn against Western intervention or pressure in the wake of his death. For example, while condemning Hariri's assassination, *al-Intiqad* (formerly *al-'Ahd*) wrote: 'The assassination of Hariri opened their [Western] desire for exaggeration and the exertion of pressure ... Washington and Paris push the Lebanese situation towards further internationalization.'[19] The party also described its political opponents, particularly those who would later become known as the March 14 coalition, and the protestors calling for the withdrawal of Syrian troops from Lebanon as Western-oriented forces supported by the Americans and French. Hence, demands for the withdrawal of Syrian troops from Lebanon were portrayed as representing a minority position in Lebanon that was designed to advance US and Western interests in the country, a discourse Hizbullah would later use when describing groups that opposed its agenda. Syria and Iran were described by the newspaper as the 'protectors of the resistance' whose support should be appreciated, in contrast to the United States, which was seen as creating problems for Lebanon and siding with Israel.[20]

The March 14 coalition responded politically, symbolically and on the popular level to Hizbullah. Daily protests by people carrying the Lebanese flag and demanding the 'truth' behind Hariri's assassination took place in downtown Beirut, an area of symbolic significance not only because it houses the parliament, but also because it formed the heart of the post-war regeneration project led by Hariri both as a politician and as a founder of Solidere, the company charged with implementing the project. Hariri had also built a mosque inspired by the Ottoman Sultan Ahmed mosque in Beirut's Martyrs' Square. Following his assassination, the area adjacent to the mosque became the site of his grave as well as the tombs of his aides who were killed in the same incident. Public action in Martyrs' Square led Hizbullah to organise a mass rally on 8 March 2005 in support of its Syrian ally. During the rally, people carried the Lebanese flag to emphasise Hizbullah's nationalist stance, as well as placards directed at the West declaring 'No to foreign intervention.' The March 14 coalition responded by calling for a popular rally on 14 March 2005, which visually resembled the 8 March rally in its extensive use of the Lebanese flag as a patriotic marker.[21] Both rallies were about cultivating legitimacy through the invocation of popularity.

Lisa Wedeen argues that 'ideologues use spectacles to revise resonant symbols so as to convey current political messages',[22] and this is certainly the case in Hizbullah's use of the spectacle of the rally as a communication tool. Wedeen also argues that 'spectacles are taken simultaneously to represent dominance and to operate as a means of dominating'.[23] The 8 March rally, then, was a means for Hizbullah to display its power and exercise it over 'others'. In so doing, the group was able to assert its dominance over its political opponents, and by extension, to imbue its supporters with this sense of dominance. As a spectacle, the rally served as a visual anchor for the political ideas that framed the ways in which Hizbullah's supporters defined themselves.[24]

But as Wedeen also argues, spectacles are a way of disciplining the bodies of people by enacting political obedience.[25] The rally can therefore be additionally seen as a way to maintain the loyalty of Hizbullah's supporters by inviting them to participate in this public performance. The 8 March rally began a phase in which Hizbullah employed a number of public and private measures to ensure that it retained the undivided loyalty of its followers and to intimidate its rivals. This loyalty was important as Hizbullah once more found itself in a position in which further engagement in local Lebanese politics was a necessity, as parliamentary elections were scheduled for May 2005. Hizbullah competed with the March 14 coalition in the May elections, allying itself with a Christian political party, the Free Patriotic Movement, in a bid to sustain its Lebanese nationalist tag and to hold on to its political power. Hizbullah was keen to use the Lebanese flag alongside its own flag in its rallies and television broadcasts as a visual indicator of its nationalist sentiment.[26] However, March 14 representatives won the most seats in the election, leading Hizbullah to engage in further measures designed to discredit the coalition.[27]

Following Syria's withdrawal from Lebanon in April 2005 under populist pressure, Hizbullah began a political communication campaign against the March 14 coalition, highlighting what it called the coalition's subservience to France and the United States. Such campaigns are not unusual when different factions are jostling for power and for the hearts and minds of the public, and it should be noted that March 14 also launched counter-campaigns to discredit Hizbullah and brand it as an Iranian stooge. However, Hizbullah's campaigns differed from those of March 14 in that senior members of Lebanese society and political figures, who were not affiliated to Hizbullah and were not members of the Shiite community, were invited to speak on air or write in its newspaper to demonstrate that the group had nationwide support and that its ideology was not sectarian. In addition, several books began to appear supporting Hizbullah's viewpoint. In a book titled *Hizbullah: The Most Difficult Choice*, Ja'far Atrisi reiterates Hizbullah's position on the United States and France:

The Lebanese [political] weakness turned into a stage for the authority of the [foreign] embassies ... a harsh and blatant type of protectorate. In turn, the new mandate for [Western] embassies became a provocative and detailed intervention into every little matter: from the date of the elections, to the law of the elections, in administration, in the number of sectarian votes, in the exertion of pressure to make this or that person run for the elections ... it reached the extent of American Ambassador Feltman wandering around voting stations on election day in Beirut, 29 May 2005 … Indeed, Paris and Washington have become much closer [to Lebanon] than ash-Shaam (Syria) …![28]

Iran, Hizbullah's long-time ally, was portrayed as a paragon of resistance and independence, a discourse which implies that Lebanon should follow in Iran's footsteps.[29] When the former Iranian President Mahmoud Ahmadinejad won a landslide victory against his rival Hashemi Rafsanjani in the presidential elections of 2005, *al-Intiqad* used a headline that echoed the slogan of the Cedar Revolution: 'Independence, Freedom and the Islamic Republic'.[30] The cover of the newspaper showed an image of Israeli soldiers carrying the coffins of their dead colleagues juxtaposed with an image of Ahmadinejad in prayer after winning the elections along with the headline, 'Iranian Democracy: Transparency that Humiliated Enemies'.[31] In this way, the paper linked Hizbullah's triumph in its battles against Israel with the success of Ahmadinejad in the elections,[32] not only underlining Hizbullah's organic links to Iran but also showing that victory in the battle against Israel is ultimately an Islamist one. March 14 responded symbolically, raising a banner at the site of Rafic Hariri's grave that carried his photograph and the words: 'With you: He taught, he built, he liberated.' The banner referenced Hariri's education foundation and his effort to rebuild Lebanon's infrastructure after the civil war, and credited him with posthumously liberating the country from Syria. The slogan was a message directed at Hizbullah, which had established a monopoly over the label 'liberation' by applying it solely to its own effort to liberate Lebanon from Israel.

The 2006 war: visual and discursive spectacle

The visual saturation of the Cedar Revolution was embraced by Hizbullah, with the group increasingly using multiplatform media as part of its communication strategy in the period after 2005. But it was the July 2006 war that marked a key transformation in Hizbullah's image. As argued in the previous chapter, when Hizbullah first emerged as a paramilitary group its primary target audiences were Israel and Lebanese Shiites. As the group's political aims widened, so did its target audience. Although Hizbullah had been addressing Arab audiences through its al-

Manar satellite television channel since 2000, in the period prior to the 2006 war the station was perceived as representing the interests of a local Lebanese Shiite paramilitary group, albeit one that was nevertheless a key participant in Lebanese politics. The group's main appeal to Arab audiences was its consistent support for the Palestinian cause.[33] Israel's reaction to Hizbullah's kidnapping of two IDF (Israel Defence Force) soldiers on 12 July 2006 changed this image. Israel launched a military campaign targeting not just Hizbullah strongholds in southern Lebanon and southern Beirut but also vital Lebanese infrastructural sites, from bridges to power plants to Beirut's only lighthouse. Israel's attacks resulted in the death of more than 1,200 people in Lebanon, most of them civilians, and the displacement of 1 million others, a quarter of the Lebanese population.[34] The 2006 war saw Hizbullah once again market itself as Lebanon's saviour from Israeli aggression, but it also went beyond that: the 24-hour coverage of the war on pan-Arab satellite television widened Hizbullah's network of audiences, and helped transform its image into that of a primarily Arab paramilitary group.[35] The fact that Hizbullah emerged defiant after the war allowed the group to present itself as a heroic brand across the Arab world. Nasrallah's image as the new Gamal Abdel Nasser, a pan-Arab leader, was reconfirmed on a larger scale than before, and Hizbullah came to be widely viewed as the only Arab actor that had succeeded in resisting Israel and 'defeating' it in war.[36]

Hizbullah as a brand

Hizbullah's double 'victory', according to its own rhetoric, made the group a household name in the Arab world. It strove to cultivate a sense of legitimacy based on this reputation, with the ensuing combination of power and legitimacy paving the way for Hizbullah's rising authority in Lebanon and its broader popularity in the Middle East.[37] The group worked hard to reach Arab audiences by utilising all of its communication tools at the same time. Mass rallies were organised and televised live to celebrate the 2006 victory, in which Nasrallah gave speeches that often merged classical Arabic (to appeal to Arab audiences) with the Lebanese dialect (to appeal to the local audience).[38] Flyers, banners and billboards were created to commemorate the war. Al-Manar broadcast music videos dedicated to the war[39] and the *al-Intiqad* newspaper carried images from the twice-liberated South on its front pages. Merchandise commemorating the war was even created. A key characteristic of these communication tools is that they were marked by a high degree of inter-textuality and uniformity of message.[40] As such, they have helped con-struct Hizbullah as an identifiable brand.

Stuart Agres defines a brand as 'an asset of differentiating promises that links a product to its consumers'.[41] The associative aspect of brands is particularly important: strong brands have strong bonds with their target audiences. As Peter van Ham argues, brands serve as emotional appeals to people, granting them a sense of belonging and security.[42] Logos, in particular, serve as visual reminders to followers of their affinity with the brand, cultivating their sense of loyalty. The Hizbullah flag, with a distinct canary yellow background and the image of a rifle held high by an arm extending from the words 'Hizb Allah' in Arabic, acts as one such marker of identity and pride for Hizbullah's followers.

Hizbullah was aware of the importance of engaging with its wider audience after the war on a more personal, everyday basis in order to sustain brand loyalty.[43] It consequently created war memorabilia like t-shirts, key rings and baseball caps—for children and adults alike—bearing its logo and the colour of its flag, as well as the picture of Nasrallah, in addition to several DVDs of 'documentaries' about its achievements with titles such as *The Surprises*, *The Banner of Lebanon* and *The Days of the Truthful Pledge*. It also issued merchandise including a dart board featuring Israeli government officials and Israeli towns that the player was invited to throw darts at, and a new computer game ('Special Force 2: Tale of the Truthful Pledge') that allowed players to battle Israeli soldiers in the southern Lebanese villages affected by the 2006 war. According to its designer, the game aimed to make players 'feel the victory as if they were taking part in attacks they were cheering for from far'.[44] All of these products can be seen as material efforts to associate Hizbullah's image with specific, definite values (defiance, heroism) in the eyes of its audience, no matter how much the values are actually related to Hizbullah's 'real characteristics'[45]—as Andrzej Falkowski and Wojciech Cwalina argue, 'it is sufficient [for a brand] that [the values associated with it] have a definite meaning for the recipient'.[46]

David Aaker writes that the strength of brands lies in brand awareness, perceived quality, brand loyalty and brand association.[47] After the 2006 war Hizbullah's brand scored high on all four levels. Brand awareness is not just about recognition of a brand name, but also about its dominance in someone's mind over other brands. Hizbullah worked to achieve this through the repetition of its victory messages across all media, which turned slogans like 'the most honourable of people' (in reference to Nasrallah's characterisation of the people of the South, which was in turn popularly appropriated as a description of him) and 'The Divine Victory' (in reference to the 2006 war) into everyday expressions. The perception of quality was easy to achieve following the 'victorious' outcome of the 2006 war, but Hizbullah was keen to emphasise added value. In his address at the victory rally in September 2006, Nasrallah promised that those houses destroyed in the war would be rebuilt to an even higher standard than before.[48] This promise can be connected with ensuring continued loyalty, as those who suffered great losses during the war could be seen as those most likely to have lukewarm feelings toward Hizbullah. The group was eager to showcase people's loyalty by rallying thousands to participate in its victory celebrations. Loyalty was also communicated by cultivating the expression '*fida al-sayyed*' (meaning a sacrifice to Sayyed Hassan Nasrallah), which was mouthed in the media by those whose homes had been destroyed or who had lost loved ones, to indicate that all of the losses were worthwhile as long as Nasrallah prevailed—an expression of utmost loyalty to the brand no matter how dire the circumstances. This bond with Nasrallah strengthens Hizbullah's brand association, which refers to the emotional bonds that link a person to a brand. The latter are important for Hizbullah because it is through emotional bonds that people internalise Hizbullah's principles. As Claus Mueller argues, '[l]egitimating rationales, necessary to any system of domination, are effective only if their underlying principles have been internalized by the public, that is, collectively accepted as normative and thus as binding'.[49]

The brand that Hizbullah intends people to form a bond with invokes certain positive connotations like justice, liberty, honour, defiance and heroism. These connotations came to the fore during the 2006 war. The war was a media spectacle. While television coverage of the war in the Arab world highlighted the plight of civilians, Al-Jazeera's coverage in particular was marked by its clear stance in favour of Hizbullah:[50] Hizbullah was branded 'the resistance', with its fight against Israel being presented in heroic, David-versus-Goliath terms. The channel's normal schedule was suspended as attention was focused on the small villages in southern Lebanon where the fiercest battles were taking place. While there was little footage of actual Hizbullah fighters, the rhetoric used in the newscasts painted a picture of larger-than-life, almost mythical action heroes. The news reports coupled graphic footage of Lebanese casualties with stories about Hizbullah's defence operations in the South. A similar, if more pronounced, image of Hizbullah could be seen on its own television channel, al-Manar. By merging footage of war-torn villages and civilians with those of Hizbullah fighters in the field, al-Manar disseminated a message of defiance that was bolstered when Israel destroyed the station's headquarters in southern Beirut on 16 July 2011, only for the channel to continue broadcasting from a secret location after a mere two-minute interruption to its live transmission. Al-Manar's feat came just two days after Hassan Nasrallah appeared on television promising victory against Israel:

> The surprises that I have promised you will start now … Now in the middle of the sea, facing Beirut, the Israeli warship that has attacked the infrastructure, people's homes and civilians. Look at it burning.[51]

As Nasrallah spoke, Hizbullah attacked an Israeli warship off the Lebanese coast, with the camera cutting live to the action—of all Hizbullah's actions during the war, this was unquestionably the most potent symbol of its defiance. The Hizbullah brand was sealed. Defiance became even more firmly associated with this brand, emerging as it does from Hizbullah's name in the first place, which is taken from a verse in the Quran, 'the followers of God will conquer'.

Hizbullah capitalised on this defiant brand in 2011 when it produced and aired a drama series on al-Manar called *Al-Ghaliboun* (The Conquerors). The series tells the story of the resistance to the Israeli occupation in southern Lebanon between 1982 and 1985 and the rise of Hizbullah through operations against the Israeli army. The series, which is presented as historically accurate, features key characters in the history of Hizbullah, such as Sheikh Ragheb Harb, chronicling his rise as a resistance symbol even after his assassination by Israel. *Al-Ghaliboun* presents Hizbullah as an indigenous product of the socio-political milieu in the South, with all the families in the programme shown as providing support, protection and food for the '*shabab*' (men) of Hizbullah. It also invokes Hizbullah as a grassroots movement with a strong sense of unity, solidarity and heroism among its members. The group is presented as more courageous and shrewd than the hapless yet menacing Israelis, monitoring the Israeli army closely and studying carefully its on-the-ground movements and fighting techniques. A significant amount of time in the series is dedicated to representing the planning and execution of resistance operations against the Israeli Defence Force: how intelligence is gathered; how operations are planned; how roles are divided; how operations are executed; and what weapons and transport techniques are used in those operations. Time is also devoted to the commemoration of the martyrs of those operations, showing how the 'resistance' supports and looks after their family members. As such, *Al-Ghaliboun* presents 'resistance' and defiance as a way of life for the group's supporters, and legitimates the internalisation of the Hizbullah brand by people in the South and elsewhere.

The personified image

It is not just Hizbullah that has been internalised by its supporters—the same also applies to its leader, Hassan Nasrallah. Knut Bergmann and Wolfram Wickert write: 'In difficult times, a charismatic leader helps to give a sense of direction both at the objective and emotional levels';[52] he is both 'a director and a leading actor'.[53] Nasrallah plays this dual role as Hizbullah's leader and public face, as this book details in Chapter 5. But the 2006 war gave Nasrallah an additional role: he himself became 'the platform' of Hizbullah.[54] Nasrallah's image as a charismatic pan-Arab leader was strengthened by the end of the war. His 'extraordinary' deed meant that he became victory personified. Al-Manar broadcast music videos in his praise, one example of which is 'Message of the Rebels', a musical video clip that represents Hizbullah fighters as the 'men of God' who renew their allegiance to Nasrallah. Nasrallah, in turn, is presented as the leader holding together and motivating the fighters. He is shown among the fighters, as well as with their mothers who throw rose petals at him. The clip juxtaposes segments from his speeches with matching images, demonstrating the coherence of his words and actions against the enemy. This kind of representation serves to sustain his charismatic position. As Arthur Schweitzer argues, the ability to sustain charismatic leadership is dependent on extraordinary deeds, and this is mainly dem-onstrated in times of war when the leader gains possession of heroic charisma.[55] Hackman and Johnson add that through such deeds charismatic leaders can in turn help their followers overcome feelings of inadequacy: 'In validating a charismatic leader's extraordinary ability, followers may experience feelings of empowerment by submerging their own identities in that of a seemingly superior leader.'[56]

Through this two-step process, Nasrallah became a pan-Arab icon. Arab citizens demonstrated against the Israeli aggression towards Lebanon in 2006 in several countries in the region, with the image of Nasrallah often being used in public space as an identity marker. But it was the end of the war—and the 'victory'—that marked a new visibility for Nasrallah. As David Belt puts it, Nasrallah became 'Islam's most noble [doer]' (echoing Nasrallah's statement 'the most honourable of people').[57] Posters of Nasrallah were carried by people in Bahrain, songs praising him were sung in public gatherings in Egypt and Hizbullah souvenirs bearing his image could be bought alongside those of President Bashar al-Assad in Syria. Nasrallah represented a new hope for Arabs in the long battle against Israel, and he seemed the perfect candidate to fill the gap for a pan-Arab leader which had existed since the death of Egypt's President Gamal Abdel Nasser in 1970. In the summer of 2006, Nasrallah's picture was carried alongside that of Nasser in Egypt and in Lebanon;[58] the comparison with Nasser was pronounced not only because of Nasrallah's great deed in the 2006 war (which some saw as comparable to Nasser's nationalisation of the Suez Canal in 1956, and which Hizbullah constantly framed as defeating the largest Israeli military operation against an Arab country[59]), but also because of Nasrallah's rhetorical style and his ability to achieve parasocial intimacy with his followers, as will be discussed in detail in Chapter 5.[60]

Pels argues that parasocial intimacy between leaders and their followers disturbs the traditional political divide between elitism and populism. This disturbance is based on the linking of difference and familiarity. On one hand, Pels says, 'only through distance is the representer able to represent'.[61] This can be seen in Nasrallah's status as a larger-than-life person. On the second anniversary of the war, Hizbullah put up new billboards in southern Beirut and the roads to the South as well as to the airport. Unlike the 'national' colours of the billboards of the previous two years, the billboards in 2008 were in Hizbullah's canary yellow and displayed unfinished quotes, mainly of 'promises',[62] from Nasrallah's speeches. As the second anniversary of the war followed shortly after the release of the Lebanese detainees from

Israeli prisons that Nasrallah had 'promised' two years earlier, the two events were commemorated together, with the prisoner release used to emphasise Nasrallah's credibility. One billboard, for example, featured the words 'Even if the whole universe comes …' in reference to a speech Nasrallah had delivered regarding the kidnapping of the two Israeli soldiers in 2006: 'Even if the whole universe comes, the soldiers will not return except through indirect negotiations.' A second billboard stated 'We are a people …' in another reference to one of Nasrallah's statements: 'We are a people who do not leave our detainees in prisons.' The deliberate quoting of parts of these statements implies the complete internalisation of the leader's messages by the 'masses'—people are invoked as literally finishing Nasrallah's sentences, affirming his larger-than-life status. On the other hand, Pels argues, as the representer speaks in the name of the represented, his representation implies a sense of proximity. Nasrallah is thus at once 'one of us' and an untouchable star, displaying an 'extraordinary ordinariness'.[63]

Hizbullah capitalised on this ambivalence after the 2006 war through a 'documentary' produced by al-Manar and distributed on DVD called *Al-'Abaya* (meaning 'the cloak'). *Al-'Abaya* focuses on a Lebanese Shiite woman called Reem Haidar in order to construct 'a film about the importance of mutual affinity and commitment between the leader and his people', as she states at the end of the documentary. Reem Haidar was an 'ordinary' Lebanese woman who was interviewed on television as she walked to a café in Beirut two days into the 2006 war. One of the comments she made in the interview turned her into a new 'face' for Hizbullah:

I want from Sayyed Hassan—when this mess is over—his cloak, that he sweated in while he was defending me and my children, my siblings, and my land. I want it so I can roll around in its sweat, and roll my children around in its sweat. Maybe its pieces can be distributed to people so they can acquire some of its generosity, honour, and dignity.

When the war had come to an end, Hassan Nasrallah responded to this plea by sending Reem Haidar one of his cloaks, which she proudly displays in her house 'so that people can visit it and be blessed by it'. *Al-'Abaya* follows Reem as she talks to people from the areas destroyed in the war, intercutting her exchanges with monologues. The words she uses in the documentary echo those of Nasrallah. Talking to a woman whose home was destroyed in southern Beirut, Reem says, 'those of us whose homes were not destroyed have been humbled by you'. She then addresses the camera as she walks in the midst of the rubble: 'I wish my home were here. Why is it only them who have received this honour?' The film ends with a scene in which Reem carefully takes Nasrallah's cloak out of its clear plastic trunk, spreads it as she gazes at it, with the camera zooming in on sections of the cloak, inviting us to share this intimate gaze. She then holds it in her arms twice, before carefully placing it back in its trunk.

One curious feature of the film is the fact that it is only the women in it who specifically speak about their relationship with Nasrallah, whereas the men in the film focus on other subjects related to the war and to Reem herself. It shows the women praising Nasrallah: an elderly woman recites a poem comparing him to the sun; a young woman declares that 'what Sayyed Hassan has done could not have been done by any other human being or Arab leader'. Another says, 'We have been blessed by God for existing in an era when Sayyed Hassan exists'. This divine quality, according to Weber's theory of charisma, is an essential attribute for the existence of genuine charisma: the leader must believe that he possesses a divine grace and his followers must share this belief.[64] Through media images like those invoked in the film, Nasrallah himself becomes a message defined by a heroic act. As Groys puts it, '[t]he heroic act transforms the hero's body from a medium into a message. Making the body the message requires above all an arena, a stage—or … a public created by the media.'[65] The film, then, is an example of how Hizbullah uses the media to take its leader beyond familiarity and into the realm of intimacy, where he becomes internalised by the group's followers.[66]

The Divine Victory

Al-'Abaya was part of a larger multimedia political marketing campaign that Hizbullah launched at the end of the war in August 2006, which included several audio-visual and other products, ranging from documentaries to merchandise. The campaign labelled the end of the war 'The Divine Victory'. Bruce Newman lists three main components of political marketing: 'Social Imagery', personality politics and 'Situational Contingency'.[67] Hizbullah used all three in the Divine Victory campaign. Social imagery associated Hizbullah with issues relevant to its constituents; personality politics operated through Nasrallah's performances as discussed in detail in Chapter 5; and situational contingency was used by presenting hypothetical scenarios which created the illusion that Hizbullah would be better able to deal with them than any other political or paramilitary entity. In his analysis of Bill Clinton's 1996 presidential election campaign, Newman argues that Clinton's subsequent victory can partly be attributed to the campaign's 'positioning strategy'. He writes that this strategy constituted 'his ability to convince voters that the American Dream was getting easier to achieve, that he was the person who would give them a sense of control over their own destinies, and that the "age of opportunity" would make that happen for them'.[68] Hizbullah followed a similar model in using situational contingency, as it aimed to convince its people that defeating Israel was becoming easier to achieve, that Nasrallah was the person who would give them a sense of control over their own destinies and that, in Nasrallah's words, 'the age of defeats has gone, and the age of victories has come'.

But Hizbullah was also keen to market the 2006 war as a victory against Israel to an international audience. In order to achieve this, Hizbullah's communication strategies became more sophisticated and streamlined, relying on professionally designed visual products. As soon as the war ended, Hizbullah planted 600 billboards in Lebanon that commemorated the group's achievements, the most prominent of which were placed on the road from Beirut's international airport into the capital.[69] The billboards had several distinctive characteristics that marked a departure from Hizbullah's usual communication style.

First, as the billboards were meant for the cameras of the international media, they featured images and text in Arabic, English and French. While Hizbullah had previously used different languages in its communication messages (namely by installing billboards in Hebrew on the Israeli border to intimidate the 'enemy', and on al-Manar's multilingual website), this was the first time that the group had used foreign languages in this streamlined and self-knowing way.

Second, a clear distinction between Hizbullah's Divine Victory campaign and those which it had launched previously was that the Divine Victory campaign was less dense, both visually and verbally.[70] *Newsweek* interviewed the creative director of the public relations company Idea Creation which designed the campaign in 2006. In the interview, Mohammad Kawtharani revealed the intention behind this:

The international public 'expects a clear and single message,' he says. 'That's the language of the media these days.' So Hizbullah settled on the simple and catchy 'Divine Victory' slogan, and repeated it over and over.[71]

Third, when using images of casualties, Hizbullah chose not to display graphic violent images, as it had in previous campaigns:

Now that the war is over, says Kawtharani, publicizing what he calls the 'more aggressive' visuals can be counterproductive … The West already considers Hizbullah a 'bloody party,' Kawtharani acknowledges. Continuing to publicize carnage would reinforce this image, especially among foreign audiences.[72]

A fourth distinction is the use of humour, something that Hassan Nasrallah had started employing in his speeches, and which was now translated into a visual form coupled with ironic text:

Some of Hizbullah's most common ads use a tactic that Kawtharani calls sending 'double messages.' One example: a red banner featuring the slogan *extremely accurate targets!* juxtaposed against the rubble of Beirut's southern suburbs. 'In advertising, irony is part of the modern style,' says Kawtharani. 'The audience will receive the double message.'[73]

The campaign is also noteworthy for its appropriation of the religious and patriotic frameworks that Hizbullah had used in previous communication products. All of the billboards had a red background with the words 'The Divine Victory' written in white and green—a reference to the colours of the Lebanese flag. They also featured a logo in the same colours written in a modern Arabic font that spelt the slogan 'Victory from God' at the bottom. The same slogan, logo and colours appeared on al-Manar, on Hizbullah's websites and on a variety of merchandise. The choice of words was deliberate: in April 2006 the Hizbullah leader Hassan Nasrallah had promised victory against Israel, as well as the release of Lebanese prisoners from Israeli jails (hence the naming of Hizbullah's operation on 12 July 2006 as 'Operation Truthful Pledge'). Nasrallah's surname literally means 'victory from God'. Consequently, while the media campaign that followed the 2006 war sought to define the 'victory' as one of Nasrallah's personal achievements, it also elevated Nasrallah to quasi-divine status, as Lebanon's only saviour. Indeed, some of the audio-visual merchandise commemorating the war even bore the slogan 'God's promise was true' (*sadaqa wa'du allah*).

The use of a religious framework for its activities, as stated in Chapter 2, is a constant for Hizbullah. For example, Hizbullah's first anti-Israeli suicide bombing mission was called 'Operation Khaibar' to connect it with the historic Battle of Khaibar when the Prophet Muhammad and his army took over a Jewish area. But the 'Divine Victory' took this to another level, allowing Hizbullah to claim a position for itself above all other political parties in Lebanon. This use of religion makes Hizbullah's actions dogmatic and unchallengeable—to contest them would be equivalent to blasphemy. Indeed, in a speech Hassan Nasrallah delivered in 2008, he exclaimed that 'This is the party of God! It is not a regular party. It is the party of God!' One can understand the need for this dogma as Hizbullah faced a degree of criticism in 2006 and after, both within and outside Lebanon, for recklessly dragging the country to war.

This criticism was one of the reasons behind Hizbullah's efforts to gain narrative agency over the story of the war. This could be seen in the range of audio-visual products that Hizbullah's Media Department issued in the wake of the war, from documentaries in English, Arabic and French (such as the self-explanatory *The New Middle East: A Film Depicting the Massacres of the Israeli American Enemy*) to CD collections of photographs from the war (such as 'Eye on the Sun', featuring photos of material and human damage as a result of the war as well as images of humanitarian aid efforts), all branded with the 'Victory from God' logo created for the occasion, and the colours of the Lebanese flag appropriated for the campaign. These products were handed out to foreign journalists who were prohibited from reporting from Hizbullah strongholds like southern Beirut without explicit permission from the party's Media Department, and who often had to be accompanied by a Hizbullah minder while in the area. Although security was a key driver behind such control, constructing history from the perspective of Hizbullah was another motivation: Hizbullah wanted to ensure that its own version of the story of the war prevailed in order to counter those of its rivals and to write history in its own way.

Written material, in the form of website content and books, formed a vital part of this strategy. Hizbullah's website, which was launched in the mid-1990s, took several forms and names over the years, evolving from a propaganda tool targeting Israel into an online archive of Hizbullah's activities. The website covers all the activities and convictions of Hizbullah historically and in the present, yet it also engages with current affairs, which it analyses from a perspective that is consistent with the group's worldview and ideology. The website evokes the images of Hizbullah martyrs, asserting their presence and sayings. It also contains information about Hizbullah's allies, namely Iran and Syria, and exhibits their news and statements regularly, with both states often being described as guardians of the resistance. The 2006 war catalysed the creation of new sections on the website documenting the war and its atrocities, Nasrallah's speeches, the stories of the war's martyrs, collected media articles about the war and photographic albums depicting the war's physical and human impact.[74] Hizbullah later added an infographic section to the website which chronicled the major milestones in the group's history over the thirty-year period from 1982 to 2012.[75]

In the wake of the 2006 'victory', a crop of books was also published to 'archive' the war and compiled different statements from a range of actors, including some that had been made by Israeli politicians, as well as interviews and media coverage of the war. Examples include the two-part volume *Yawmiyyat al-wa'd al-sadeq: sumoud sha'b wa-muqawama* (The Diaries of Truthful Pledge: The Steadfastness of a People and a Resistance), published by Hizbullah in September 2006, the seven-volume *Hizbullah: al-muqawama wa al-tahrir* (Hizbullah: Resistance and Liberation), based on material produced by *As-Safir's* Arab Documentation Centre and also published in 2006, and *Yawmiyyat al-harb al-israeliyya 'ala lubnan 2006*, an encylopaedia published by al-Markaz al-'Arabi lil-ma'lumaat. The encyclopaedia offers a detailed description of the war. It lists the sites of Israeli bombardments, the incidents of the war and the stories of people killed and destruction in Lebanon. The book goes into extensive detail regarding Hizbullah's operations during the war, including the rocketing of Haifa and other cities inside the 1948 borders, as well as the appearances of Hassan Nasrallah and the performance of the fighters. It also contains essays by writers supportive of Hizbullah and the ideology of resistance in general.

In addition to these works, Hizbullah has chronicled the war in a series of short stories titled *Qalam Rassas*, with the subtitle 'The Encyclopaedia of Resistance'. The series was published in Lebanon by one of the party's publishing houses, al-Risalaat. Each volume is qualified by a caveat on the cover that reads, 'The short stories in this collection are inspired by real events which happened with the resistance in Lebanon'. Most of the stories contain narratives of resistance that revolve around depicting the martyr as a winner. In the first volume, the publisher elaborates on the main subjects of the encyclopaedia, saying that 'it discusses several topics, including martyrdom and martyrs, the wounded, the prisoners, jihadi operations, and a resistant society. There is no doubt that it expresses the feeling and the culture of resistance ...' The majority of the stories reflect heroism in the battlefield against Israel, with the theme of death for the sake of the cause of liberation being palpable. In a short story by Maryam Ali Jum'a, entitled *The Messengers of the Beloved*, for example, the narrator, who reports the martyrdom of someone who was engaged in the 2006 war between Hizbullah and Israel, writes about how the news was relayed to the martyr's anxious wife/widow:

she received the news of his martyrdom from one of the young men who accompanied him in the journey of his jihad until the moment of arrival (meaning, death) ... a moment in which he shouted amidst his wounds, 'I swear by the God of the Ka'ba that I have won' ... the Mujahid [jihadist] told her about the two bullets which penetrated his chest ... about the blood which exploded and watered the flowers of gardens, the chrysanthemums ... about his determination when he endured his pains and continued his jihad until he received the third bullet which was the key of his departure to the almighty God ...[76]

Arab authors began to write about the party too, underlining the shift in the pan-Arab imagination about the group. One book, authored by Egyptian Arwah Mahmoud and introduced by Hizbullah's Deputy Secretary General Naim Qassem, is particularly worthy of mention in this context. The book's cover is suffused with titles, a characteristic of Hizbullah's books and publications, which tend to saturate the reader with images and words that substantiate and limit their interpretations. One of these titles is *The Fighting of Hizbullah* (*qitaal Hizbullah*), another *Religion in the Confrontation against Israel* and the third *How did Hizbullah Win in the July 2006 War?*

In Mahmoud's book, which grew out of a thesis presented to the American University in Cairo, the writer explains why such a victory was able to happen, focusing on the individual valour of Hizbullah's fighters on the basis of their religious ethos. She writes:

What I realised from a close observation is that the religious motive is the first instigator, and it is the only evidence through which people saw their leadership and the Israeli aggression against them. And religion is not only as presented in different media channels affiliated to Hizbullah, but it is also inbuilt in the words of an old woman who comes out of her camp, in the dream of a ten year old child, and even on the walls of the streets in the south … it was a revolutionary soul that vows allegiance to God every day and to Hussein every hour; and it forewarns the usurper aggressor of defeat.[77]

Hizbullah's website and books can be seen as illustrations of the group's desire to control how its history is narrated. Hayden White argues that it is the presence of contest that produces narrativisation of history.[78] Possessing narrative agency is important because being the narrator allows one control over how a story is presented, which elements of it to emphasise and which details to overlook. Narrativisation is thus relevant not only in the context of competing with political opponents, but also in that of history. As Hegel wrote:

In our language the term *History* unites the objective with the subjective side … it comprehends not less what has *happened*, than the *narration* of what has happened. This union of the two meanings we must regard as of a higher order than mere outward accident; we must suppose historical narrations to have appeared contemporaneously with historical deeds and events. It is an internal vital principle common to both that produces them synchronously.[79]

White elaborates by highlighting narration's relationship to historical reality, or 'events that are offered as the proper content of historical discourse':[80]

The reality of these events does not consist in the fact they occurred but that, first of all, they were remembered, and second, that they are capable of finding a place in a chronologically ordered sequence … The authority of the historical narrative is the authority of reality itself; the historical account endows this reality with form and thereby makes it desirable, imposing on its processes the formal coherency that only stories possess.[81]

In seeking to gain authority over the writing of history Hizbullah established itself as the sole legitimate narrator both of its own story and of the story of the war. This latter story centred on Hizbullah as the hero of the people, protecting them against aggression from a foreign villain (Israel) and its sidekick (the United States).

The multi-actor story of the war featured on the billboards celebrating the Divine Victory, with individual billboards focusing on Hizbullah, the Lebanese people, Israel and the United States. In this story Hizbullah is the protector of the nation and the people, the protagonist and hero, as seen in one billboard that carried the image of a rocket launcher and two Hizbullah fighters as well as the Hizbullah flag, with the caption 'The arms of the mujahideen'. The Lebanese people are the defiant victims. While some billboards depicted casualties, the majority acknowledged the steadfastness of the people of the South (of Lebanon and Beirut). A billboard under this theme had the image of an old man with his fist raised in the air, standing in front of a burning home that had recently been bombed, along with the caption, 'With the patience of the steadfast people'. The Israeli army is not just the villain in the story—it is also the stooge. Several billboards belittled the Israeli army, such as one showing a picture of Israeli soldiers crying in a huddle, with the caption, 'It's Lebanon, you fools!' in Arabic and English. The United States is painted as a menacing Israeli accomplice in the war. A billboard showing a destroyed home had the caption 'Made in USA' in English, while a red banner erected at the site of a destroyed building stated in English, 'The New Middle Beast', in reference to Condoleezza Rice's speech on 21 July 2006 in which the war was described as representing the 'birth pangs of a new Middle East'. A notable feature in the representation of Hizbullah as a 'character' in the story is that the faces of its fighters are not shown on the billboards. Instead they are anonymous, almost mythical figures. This visual representation contrasts sharply with the images of the faces of Hizbullah martyrs displayed on posters commemorating their deaths, which have been a regular feature of Hizbullah's visual products in public space ever since the group's inception. By choosing to de-individualise its fighters, Hizbullah is appealing to the audience to identify with the group as a unified, larger-than-life entity, but also to imagine themselves as those heroic figures.[82]

A new era of challenges: Hizbullah and the Lebanese state

The period following the 2006 war and its celebration was politically challenging for Hizbullah. The United Nations endorsed the establishment of a Special Tribunal for Lebanon (STL) to investigate the death of Rafic Hariri, according to a UN Resolution originally issued in March 2006. Hizbullah had lost the parliamentary elections of 2005, with the group and its allies securing around 45 per cent of the seats. Hizbullah's ministers and their allies, empowered by the Divine Victory, resigned from the Cabinet in November 2006 in an attempt to halt the government's expected approval of the UN Resolution. A joint Hizbullah–Amal press release framed the resignation as a response to the 'politicisation' of the STL.[83] When this failed to produce the desired outcome, Hizbullah and its allies, the March 8 coalition, started a series of anti-government sit-ins in downtown Beirut on 1 December 2006 which paralysed life in the area as well as the normal functioning of the government. The sit-ins called on the government to resign.

The sit-ins quickly evolved into a protest camp in which political posters were used to discredit the government. One large poster depicted the US Secretary of State Condoleezza Rice as a primary schoolteacher instructing the Lebanese Prime Minister Fouad Siniora at the 'School of the New Middle East' in courses on 'corruption', 'sectarianism', 'the removal of sovereignty', 'meddling with security' and 'rigging elections'. It also saw the erection of posters displaying the image of Nasrallah. The 'Lebanese National Opposition' became the new title for the political coalition led by Hizbullah, which used an image of a rainbow as its logo, a reference to its claimed anti-sectarian agenda with each stripe in the rainbow representing the distinct colour of a political party in the coalition (yellow for Hizbullah, green for Amal and orange for the Free Patriotic Movement). Hizbullah tried to place the camp in a patriotic framework similar to the one used during the Cedar Revolution. The Lebanese flag was hung across the sit-in area and was carried by the protesters. Tents were erected in Martyrs' Square, populated by young people, creating a quasi-carnivalesque atmosphere, and the Free Patriotic Movement ensured that its supporters were photographed alongside those of Hizbullah, an image of sectarian unity against a divisive government. A Christmas tree was even erected in the protest camp as a sign of Muslim–Christian harmony. The rallies featured a significant presence of (often scantily clad) young Christian and Muslim women carrying the Hizbullah flag, wearing Hizbullah t-shirts or carrying the photo of Hassan Nasrallah. By appropriating what had become one of the dominant images of the March 14 rallies (as glamorous women featured prominently in those rallies), March 8 was sending a message that it too was cosmopolitan and 'modern'. In doing so, Hizbullah attempted to control the narrative of the protests as being about the spontaneous, bottom-up action of the diverse population of Lebanon.[84] Through this visual competition, March 8 tried to cultivate a sense of legitimacy and credibility for itself as the 'true' representative of the will of the people and as a symbol of a unified Lebanon.

March 14 responded in early 2007 through a billboard campaign titled 'I Love Life', a message implying that Hizbullah loves death and martyrdom, in reference to one of Nasrallah's famous sayings: 'The Jews love life, so that is what we shall take away from them. We are going to win because they love life and we love death.'[85] The campaign's website listed its mission as follows: '*We understand the **Culture of Life**, as opposed to the **Culture of Death**, as a deep, well-developed sense capable of discerning true values and interpreting authentic needs in our communities and society.*[86] The phrases 'discerning true values' and 'interpreting authentic needs' were a direct response to March 8's self-styling as the 'true' representative of the will of the people. The campaign was composed of a series of billboards with a plain red background, a white heart with green olive leaves at the top and the words 'I Love Life' written in white, thereby using the colours of the Lebanese flag. The billboards carried life-affirming messages like 'I have a class' and 'I am going to work'. March 8 was quick to launch a rival campaign, which appropriated the visuals of the 'I Love Life' billboards but added to them the March 8 rainbow flag, the signature 'The Lebanese Opposition' and rejectionist slogans like 'undictated' and 'in all its colours'. Hizbullah additionally responded with the publication of a book by Naim Qassem in 2008 in which he reframed the embrace of martyrdom in life-affirming terms:

We arrive at the virtues of martyrdom, for it is the real and beloved culture of life in contrast with the culture of death, the noble virtues of martyrdom, for martyrdom is life, and capitulation and humiliation are death. Sovereignty is life, and a hegemonic mandate is death. The liberation of land is life, surrender to occupation is death.[87]

The downtown Beirut protest camp soon became a ghost town as most protesters left the area, although the tent city itself and the protest movement remained for almost eighteen months, after which the tension escalated into a violent confrontation as Hizbullah took over the western area of Beirut, the stronghold of the March 14 leader Saad Hariri, in May 2008. The May 2008 events not only featured street fighting, but also involved attacks on Hariri's media companies, Future Television and the *Al-Mustaqbal* newspaper, whose buildings were set on fire. Future Television and al-Manar subsequently engaged in a media war, with each channel quoting the broadcasts of the other and branding them lies. Hizbullah needed to assert its political power. Although violence paid off with the signing of the Doha Accord that gave March 8 veto power in the Cabinet, Hizbullah also sought to communicate its political power through more peaceful means by affirming Nasrallah's 'pledge' of April 2006, when he promised the release of Lebanese detainees from Israeli prisons: the prisoners were released in July 2008. Nasrallah's matching of words and deeds further established an image of grandeur and dominance for Hizbullah.

From a challenge to an opportunity

One element of Hizbullah's image of grandeur is the almost mythical persona of Imad Mughniyeh. In contrast to the organic materiality of Nasrallah, Imad Mughniyeh, Hizbullah's head of external operations who was otherwise known as Haj Radwan, is an enigmatic figure whose existence Hizbullah originally denied. He was rumoured to be responsible for several terrorist attacks in foreign countries that have been attributed to Hizbullah, such as the attack on a synagogue in Buenos Aires in July 1994. His assassination in Damascus in February 2008 was the subject of much speculation, with some attributing it to the Mossad while others argued that the location of the assassination, in the heart of Baathist Damascus, meant that the killing was an 'inside job' that had been designed to stall STL investigations. The assassination took place at a time when Hizbullah was presenting a defiant, anti-American and anti-Israeli image following the 2006 war, and his death became a useful tool which enabled Hizbullah to disseminate stories about him that benefited this defiant image. It was only after his death that Hizbullah claimed him as one of its own and confirmed his responsibility for masterminding various attacks, including some which the group had never associated itself with before, like that on the American marines in Beirut in 1983. Mughniyeh's death was both operationally and symbolically useful for Hizbullah.

Very little was known about Mughniyeh in the public domain at the time of his death, not even the way he looked. But after his assassination, Hizbullah swiftly moved to add Mughniyeh to its public historical repertoire. To commemorate the Day of the Martyr on 11 November

2008, the photo of Mughniyeh was added to those of Ahmad Qassir (Hizbullah's first martyr) and the assassinated former leaders Ragheb Harb and Abbas al-Mussawi in a banner appearing on Hizbullah's website moqawama.org. He was given the title 'Prince of the Caravan of Martyrs'. Thus began a process of commemoration that continues to the present day. An avenue was named after him in the southern suburb of Beirut in 2010. Selected photos of him were uploaded on a special section of the website. Writings in English and Arabic were posted on the website praising his legacy and using it to address Hizbullah's opponents, such as one piece of prose titled 'Moghniyeh Haunts "Israel": Every Day, Every Year', stating: 'With every rising sun he asks revenge. With every passing month he asks revenge … If you ever bombed his towns, beware Moghniyeh … If you support those who killed him, beware Moghniyeh.'[88]

Banners and billboards commemorating his death appeared on the road to Beirut's airport and elsewhere. The banners carried another title for Mughniyeh: 'Leader of the Two Victories' (in reference to 2000 and 2006). Almost out of nowhere, the liberation of the South and the 'defeat' of Israel in 2006 now had one mastermind. Slogans were used to emphasise this. One banner of Mughniyeh in Beirut had his photo, in which he is wearing military fatigues and a baseball cap, in front of the Hizbullah logo along with the phrase: 'The grace of conclusive victory.' Another stated, 'Our wound is the pulse of weapons.' A further series of banners in the South had his photo with the phrases: 'Karbala is my weapon'; 'My blood is for Jerusalem'; 'Our enemy is one: Israel'; 'The key will is my will'; 'Jerusalem is ours'; '[Our] position is a weapon—my position'; 'My country is my spirit and blood'; 'Palestine is my cause'; 'Israel will be annihilated'; and 'My blood is victorious'. In another set of yellow banners celebrating the release of the detainees and displaying the 'Victory from God' logo used in the 2006 Divine Victory campaign, the impression of Mughniyeh surrounded by the halo of the sun was depicted along with the words 'The liberation of detainees is the achievement of God with our hands.'

One intriguing aspect of the phrases and slogans used in these banners is that none of them have been attributed to Imad Mughniyeh himself. Instead, they are a collection of pronouncements by other Hizbullah martyrs and leaders. 'The key will', for example, is a phrase from a statement made by Abbas al-Mussawi: 'the key will is the preservation of the resistance'. And '[Our] position is a weapon' was a statement made by Sheikh Ragheb Harb. By associating the image of Mughniyeh with the words of Hizbullah's martyred leaders, the story of Mughniyeh as another figure in the Hizbullah leadership was being woven. This was cemented visually through banners showing the image of Nasrallah above that of Mughniyeh, as if looking out for him, a visual layout normally used by Hizbullah in representing the relationship between the Shiite supreme leader and the Hizbullah leader (in the hierarchy, the supreme leader—first Ruhollah Khomeini and now Ali Khamenei—is always highest and depicted visually as such).[89]

But unlike other Hizbullah leaders who had known public personas, Mughniyeh as a man was unknown. Hizbullah consequently sought to create an individual persona for him by making his death the theme for celebrating the second anniversary of the Divine Victory in 2008. The group created an exhibition for the occasion titled 'Leader of the Two Victories' in a square in Nabatiyeh in southern Lebanon. The exhibition was set against the backdrop of a huge banner displaying Mughniyeh's photo on the right and a coffin covered with an Israeli flag on the left with images of injured Israeli soldiers in the middle, under the phrase: 'The martyr will remove them from existence.' The exhibition featured items presented as having belonged to Mughniyeh: his rifle; clothes; shoes; prayer rug, cap and beads; hair brush; eyeglasses case; bag; torch; and office chair and desk, upon which his now-trademark baseball cap was laid. As Laleh Khalili argues, such a display of quotidian 'non-heroic' objects serves to lend the martyr familiarity in the eyes of the viewer.[90] In Mughniyeh's case, the display also serves to ground the myth in material reality.

Yet Mughniyeh's absence is a useful component in the myth, creating a hyper-image. As Patrick Fuery and Kelli Fuery argue, '[t]he hyper-image ... can become the defining image for that which it comes to represent because it is such an extreme version ... What we do not see [in hyper-images], however, are the people themselves.'[91] In this way, the hyper-image of Mughniyeh has come to stand in for resistance as it is based on the absence of the man himself. Absence serves to keep the myth alive: 'The hyper-image relies on absences to construct and retain part of its power. Through these absences it seduces the spectator into a contributory role. In other words, the hyper-image self-perpetuates by convincing the spectator of its status.'[92] 'Imad Mughniyeh' thus becomes a postmodern tool for Hizbullah's image. It is a simulacrum, a sign without a referent, whose existence is derived through referencing other signs.[93] The sign's usefulness is due to the fluidity of meaning that can be ascribed to it. As Baudrillard says, 'simulation threatens the difference between "true" and "false", between "real" and "imaginary"'.[94] This simulacrum can be used by Hizbullah to project whatever messages it wishes to disseminate. As Ajemian argues:

the mystery surrounding Mughniyeh's life and activities provided a blank slate for Hezbollah's media apparatus to mold the myth of Mughniyeh through ceremony, discourse and imagery that frames his death, not as a defeat, but as an omen of victory that is part of a greater history of defiance.[95]

As such, 'Imad Mughniyeh' is a sign that serves 'cultic purposes'; it continues to be invoked by Hizbullah in its public messages as a rallying, intimidating and legitimating tool, even though Hizbullah no longer relies on the physical/visual display of Mughniyeh's image in abundance. As Walter Benjamin argues, the presence of such signs 'is more important than the fact that they are seen'.[96]

Mleeta: Defiant self-presentation

Mughniyeh's persona is part of a wider strategy to construct a larger-than-life image for Hizbullah in the post-2006 era. This image is manifested in a series of public visual displays. Three key displays form part of this strategy. The first is the organising of public rallies and protests to commemorate the Divine Victory and the ensuing release of Lebanese prisoners from Israeli jails in July 2008. The second is the series of billboards that Hizbullah installs in southern Lebanon and on the road from Beirut's international airport, which has now become an area for the exclusive display of the group's messages. And the third is the establishment of a permanent visitor site in southern Lebanon called Mleeta, which opened in 2010 having evolved out of a temporary exhibition in the southern suburb of Beirut called Spider's Web that took place in 2007.

Public rallies have served as a tool for Hizbullah ever since its inception. But after 2006, the rallies became larger in scale and more streamlined. Because of the threat to Nasrallah's life, most of his live addresses to the crowds have since had to be delivered through video on giant screens placed in football fields and other large community spaces.

Yet there have been exceptions. The most notable is the rally that took place in July 2008 to celebrate the release of Lebanese prisoners from Israeli jails. Standing next to Samir Quntar, Lebanon's longest-serving prisoner in an Israeli jail, who had been released after twenty-nine years (and who wore a Hizbullah scarf at the rally), Nasrallah appeared in person for the first time in almost two years, and addressed the crowd using the same phrase he had coined in 2000, which had become one of his trademark slogans: 'The age of defeats has gone, and the age of victories has come.' Behind them stood a huge yellow banner displaying the words 'Operation Radwan'. 'Operation Radwan for the Release of Prisoners and the Return of Martyrs' Remains' was a shrewd choice of name for the event as it referenced Imad Mughniyeh as the original planner of the operation, thereby immediately lending the event a larger-than-life status. Spectacular rallies, which are used to comment on specific political developments, have now become an established component of Hizbullah's communication strategies.

The billboards that have been used to line the sides of the road to Beirut's international airport have varied over the years. In 2007 they retained the red, white and green colours of the Lebanese flag, but in later years they reverted to the canary yellow of Hizbullah's flag, asserting the group's contribution to a 'free' Lebanon, which serves as a message to Hizbullah's Lebanese political rivals. But the most striking visual display of power was the opening of the Mleeta visitor centre in the spring of 2010. The centre, titled 'Mleeta: The Story of the Earth to the Sky', is perched on a hill close to the Israeli border that overlooks several villages in southern Lebanon and features a highly modern exhibition of Hizbullah's military operations and capabilities and its adherence to the tropes of sacrifice and land. Its message is a simple one: power—and as such, it is both an example of strategic warfare communication and internal propaganda.[97]

The site is divided into two parts, with the contents and layout of each serving to project power through the tropes of knowledge superiority over and objectification of the other. An indoor space is split into a screening venue where the visitor is invited to watch a film about Hizbullah's military history, and an exhibition space dedicated to military information about Israel. A banner of Nasrallah raising his finger with the slogan 'If you hit, we hit' faces the entrance. Another banner shows the map of Israel, on which key areas that could form military targets for Hizbullah are highlighted. Another map shows the location of Israel's military bases. Other banners display Israel's anti-aircraft missile capabilities, and information about Israeli drones and tanks. A flowchart illustrates the structure of the Israeli army. This part of the exhibition is a pure example of power in the Foucauldian sense, as a producer of knowledge.[98] It also places Hizbullah on an exalted level in relation to Israel, as it boasts of the party's epistemological superiority over its enemy. This superiority is coupled with representing the 'enemy' as weak (thus echoing the media representation of Israel in the series *Al-Ghaliboun*). The indoor space contains Israeli military equipment displayed in glass cases. Stripped of its power, the equipment is rendered an exotic object to be gazed at. The space also harbours a banner dedicated to Israeli 'Special Forces' which is illustrated with the photo of a distressed, wounded Israeli soldier supported by another. A further banner, titled 'The Israeli enemy army's battle ideology', is illustrated with a photo of seven Israeli soldiers crying. The display of such images is an example of modern political force that can be understood in the sense of 'the political sublime'[99] as presented by Edmund Burke in 1756. Burke used the term 'sublime' to refer to horrifying images, such as those of beheadings and torture in the pre-Enlightenment period, which invoke in the viewer a sense of intense emotion that is experienced as delight and awe.[100] The visitor to the Mleeta site is similarly invited to engage in delight and awe at the supposedly powerful Israeli soldiers whom Hizbullah has reduced to a bunch of crying, injured men.

The second part of the site is a vast outdoor space. A round, sunken area displays several Israeli military vehicles that Hizbullah captured during its many confrontations with the IDF. The vehicles are displayed in a way that signals impotence: one tank has its cannon twisted, and military vehicles are placed upside down, tilted or embedded in rocks, their bombs scattered for viewers to stare at, becoming paralysed, wounded, broken objects of the gaze. Tens of Israeli soldier helmets are arranged on the ground in a neat display, subjected to the ordering power of Hizbullah. Nearby, a path through the woods leading to an underground tunnel, where Hizbullah fighters engaged in live battles with Israeli soldiers, invites the visitor to walk in the fighters' footsteps, imagining their deeds and internalising them. The path is lined with displays of Hizbullah's missile power, with signs showing photos of different missiles and descriptions of their capabilities, along with specimens of the actual missiles. The outdoor space is immaculate and minimalist in its style, showing the aesthetic of war to full effect. It is a reminder of Marinetti's Futurist Manifesto of 1909:

War is beautiful because it ushers in the dreamt-of metallization of the human body. War is beautiful because it enriches a meadow in bloom by adding the fiery orchids of machine-guns. War is beautiful because it combines rifle-fire, barrages of bullets, lulls in the firing, and the scents and smells of putrescence into a symphony. War is beautiful because it creates fresh architectures such as those of the large tank, geometrical flying formations, spirals of smoke rising from burning villages, and much else besides.[101]

Mleeta can be read as a propaganda site. Hamid Mowlana argues that the socio-political effect of propaganda is that it becomes autonomous, leaving no space outside the ideology it disseminates.[102] The presence of Mleeta in Lebanon is an attempt to express this totality of the commitment to militarisation in Hizbullah's ideology. It is also a 'permanent' record of symbolic victory which serves as a political and military deterrent. As Robert Jervis argues in relation to states, a 'symbolic victory can lead others to see high resolve and risk-taking in a state's behavior. This image is apt to make other states retreat or act cautiously in conflicts with the first state.'[103] If Hizbullah is imagined as a state, then Mleeta can be seen as a message of caution aimed at Hizbullah's political opponents within and outside Lebanon. But it is also a sign of pride for Hizbullah's supporters, mainly within the Shiite community.

Courting the Shiites

Hizbullah's outreach to Lebanese Shiites affirms both a sense of Shiite loyalty as well as the group's care for its core constituents. This duality has its origins in the days of Musa al-Sadr's Movement of the Deprived which sparked the creation of institutions catering for the impoverished Shiite population, and evolved into the myriad of services provided by Hizbullah to this community.[104] As a significant proportion of this community was affected by the 2006 war, Hizbullah sought to compensate those whose houses were destroyed or whose relatives had been killed or injured. The flagship programme in this regard is 'Waad' (Promise), Hizbullah's Iranian-funded reconstruction programme. In much the same way as Nasrallah had promised to release Lebanese prisoners from Israeli jails, he also promised to rebuild the destroyed buildings in southern Beirut 'even more beautiful than before', as he stated in the 2006 victory speech. The Waad office in the area displayed a large model of the new buildings to be reconstructed, over which the large photograph of a smiling Nasrallah was hung on a wall—larger than life and benevolent, symbolically looking down on to the area to be reconstructed, in a visual manner reminiscent of representations of Khomeini. Hizbullah's media were rife with stories about Waad and its positive contribution to people's lives, with interviews on al-Manar featuring people praising Nasrallah's promise and dismissing their material loss as being a worthy 'sacrifice' in his name. In this way, Waad symbolises the co-optation of the Shiite community by Hizbullah, and the placing of this community as clients in the traditional socio-political sense found in Lebanon and the Middle East.

While Waad was similar to previous Hizbullah reconstruction projects, such as Jihad al-Bina', in focusing on provision of basic needs, it went beyond those projects by funding the creation of other edifices in southern Beirut and the South: places of leisure. Cafes, fast food shops and amusement parks were constructed as spaces of outreach to the Shiite community that had come to expect more than the mere provision of basic needs following the huge losses it incurred as a result of the 2006 war.[105] In the southern border town of Maroun al-Ras—one of the worst affected areas in the 2006 war—a public park funded by Iran was constructed, named 'Iran Garden', which overlooks Israeli settlements. The garden includes billboards with information about Iran, a picnic area and a paintballing section where people are invited to play the role of Hizbullah fighters (or Israeli soldiers). A tightrope (without a safety net) has been set up for people to walk, while a watchtower provides a bird's-eye view of Israeli settlements. The garden thus summarises familiar tropes in Hizbullah's communication, from permeating people's daily life to cultivating a sense of empowerment over the enemy to affirming the benevolence of Iran. Through all this, Hizbullah aims to maintain Shiite loyalty and a sense of legitimacy within the community that would allow it to continue pursuing its political goals.

Religious narratives also infused Hizbullah's appeal to the Shiites following the 2006 war. While religion had always been a cornerstone of Hizbullah's messages, after 2006 it took on a further mobilisational role through affirming the legitimacy of Hizbullah's actions in the war. This was achieved through the propagation of supernatural myths—

both orally and through the production of posters and books—which provided an otherworldly quality to the stories of Hizbullah's heroism during the war. One poster in the southern suburb of Beirut after the war showed the image of a robed figure, with white light for a face, launching rockets. The poster references a popular story told at the time (and narrated to the author by a man in southern Beirut), according to which Hizbullah fighters had been joined by Imam Ali (or Hussein, depending on the version of the story) as they were launching rockets at the Israeli army, with the Imam personally engaging in warfare in their support. Such supernatural stories were collected in a book by Hizbullah titled *Karamaat al-wa'd al-sadeq* (Honours of the Truthful Pledge). The book contains supposed 'eyewitness' narratives from Hizbullah mujahideen about undead martyrs continuing to fight, Hizbullah weapons operating against Israel on their own, the voice of Imam al-Mahdi encouraging the fighters, the apparition of Mary and Jesus to the mujahideen and the interception by Imam Ali of two Israeli rockets before they could land on a Hizbullah fighter, thereby 'proving' that the 2006 victory was indeed 'divine'.[106]

The return to victimisation

The communication strategy used by Hizbullah in reference to the points above served to cultivate a high-level of political, religious and military legitimacy for the group. Mark Suchman defines legitimacy as 'a generalized perception or assumption that the actions of an entity are desirable, proper, or appropriate within some socially constructed system of norms, values, beliefs, and definitions'.[107] Hizbullah cultivated this perception among the Shiites, the Lebanese at large and the Arabs by linking its behaviour to shared beliefs among those different audiences, centred on ideas of freedom, dignity and justice. Hizbullah's supporters believe the group to be trustworthy, and the group in turn views this growing support as a sign that it can persevere in its chosen courses of action.

This sense of legitimacy was to prove important for Hizbullah in the aftermath of the events of May 2008, when it used its weapons against other Lebanese. Hizbullah responded to criticism of its actions by framing the events as necessary to prevent an American-backed conspiracy against the group. This discourse was first set out by Hassan Nasrallah in a speech on 8 May 2008. Taking his cue from this speech, on 15 May, Hizbullah's political bureau chief Ibrahim al-Amin used this discourse in a strategic way to defend Hizbullah's actions on the ground, declaring that they were necessary to prevent more serious events from occurring later, in reference to the potential devastation that would be caused by another civil war. Al-Amin created parallels between the May events and the 2006 war, expanding on Nasrallah's speech by implying that both events prevented further planned attacks on Hizbullah from being carried out.[108] This association between the two events also aimed to transfer the meaning of an event with positive connotations (the July 2006 war) on to a controversial one. This adaptation of discourse aimed to re-brand the May 2008 events as an act of self-defence (something stated by Nasrallah himself in his speech). Instead of being the aggressor that took over West Beirut, Hizbullah became the victim of an international conspiracy.

The events of May 2008 show how the group, in addition to the larger-than-life image that Hizbullah has created to cultivate legitimacy, also has a tendency to resort to victimisation as an image-management strategy in order to justify a departure from norms. The return to the discourse of victimisation that began with the May 2008 events marked the start of a new phase in which victimisation—as a catalyst for 'self-defence'—became a vital tool for the group over the next three years as the STL's investigations gathered pace, and leaked reports indicated that the tribunal would indict members of Hizbullah. Hizbullah engaged in a dedicated multiplatform media campaign to discredit the STL as an American and Israeli conspiracy against 'the resistance'. Al-Manar's and *al-Intiqad*'s news coverage of STL developments consistently presented the court as lacking in credibility, while they also criticised the Hariri government which had supported the tribunal. In a speech on 22 July 2010, Nasrallah addressed his opponents with remarks that carried an implicit warning that the events of May 2008 could be repeated: 'I give you a chance to back down, as I have my facts ... I will not let you rest while calmly waiting for the [STL] decision, while you let me stress. I am capable of returning the fire.'[109] This was followed by a speech delivered by Naim Qassem on 30 July 2010 in which he framed the STL as an Israeli–American conspiracy.[110] On 9 August 2010, Nasrallah built on this argument in a televised speech in which he attempted to show that Israel was actually responsible for the murder of Rafic Hariri. What is notable about this speech is that, first, it came after a series of other speeches in preceding months in which Nasrallah stated that Hizbullah was preparing a 'file' that proved Israel's complicity in the murder, which would be released at a future date, and hence it can be seen as the crescendo in a carefully planned 'product launch' building up audience anticipation; and second, it utilised a number of visual pieces of 'evidence'. Nasrallah screened video footage intercepted from Israeli drones to show that Israel had closely followed the path taken by Rafic Hariri in his daily commute. The speech also included recorded reports using PowerPoint slides referencing Israeli statements about the STL as well as presenting key points about Lebanese collaborators with Israel. The reports and videos were intercut with Nasrallah's live commentary on them as he assumed the air of a professor or a legal investigator. In a reply to a journalist from the Iranian Arabic-language al-Alam television channel in the question-and-answer session that followed the two-hour speech, Nasrallah spoke directly about the necessity of image management:

The main aim of the indictment is to tarnish the image of Hizbullah and to show Israel as being innocent. So there is a battle of public opinion. Some spent 500 million dollars—only in Lebanon, what they had spent in other countries or on other satellite stations they didn't say ... for the sake of tarnishing the image of Hizbullah. So there is a war of image, of public image and public opinion. We are very cautious and we very much want to uncover the truth and we are also very much concerned, in waging this war of public opinion, to say that the resistance is subject to injustice.[111]

A significant trend in Hizbullah's campaign against the STL is the dissemination of the group's statements during public events, which are then covered by the mainstream media. These public events were part of the repertoire of Hizbullah's special occasions—religious and otherwise—including established ones like Jerusalem Day as well as resurrected or spontaneously created events, launched when the need arises, providing an almost daily pretext for Hizbullah personnel and leaders to use the occasions to give speeches presenting Hizbullah's position regarding political developments. Martyrs' Day, Ashoura, the opening of community facilities, funerals, cultural festivals and a myriad other, often obscure, occasions serve this purpose. This trend started early in Hizbullah's life before intensifying over the years, and had become an established mechanism of public dissemination by the 2010s. The speeches given on special occasions both reach out to constituents directly and address opponents through their coverage in the mainstream Lebanese media. During the Hizbullah-led campaign against the STL in the summer of 2010, a range of events were used as occasions for Hizbullah members of different ranks to speak out against the tribunal, including: the 'Day of the Wounded', on 15 July;[112] a commemoration event for the party's 'municipal work' bureau (al-amal al-baladi), held on 24 July;[113] an event marking the fifteenth day of the Islamic month of Shaaban (marking fifteen days before the start of Ramadan) on 30 July;[114] a tourism festival in the north-eastern town of Hermel, as well as a festival by al-Mahdi scouts in the southern town of Hosh and a funeral in Baalbek—all on 2 August 2010;[115] and an iftar in the southern town of Mashghara on August 16,[116] to name but a few.

Newspaper and television coverage from Hizbullah media and other outlets as well as the special occasion speeches were joined by 'popular public action' to affirm Hizbullah's 'victimisation' at the hands of the STL. In October 2010, when two STL investigators visited a gynaecological clinic in southern Beirut to obtain documents for their investigation, they were attacked by an angry mob of women; the incident was framed by Nasrallah as a response to an insult to women's honour. Hizbullah also sought to present the attack as a 'spontaneous' reaction by wronged 'ordinary people', similar to an earlier 'reaction' by people in the South against a United Nations Interim Force in Lebanon unit that was pelted with rocks in July 2010 after trying to investigate an explosion at a weapons depot in the area.[117] In doing so, Hizbullah thus extended the sense of victimisation from itself to the Shiite community as a whole.

As the STL crisis intensified, Hizbullah reframed its objections to the tribunal by referring to the need to protect national sovereignty. In December 2010, al-Intiqad invited the high-profile (and, notably, Christian) Lebanese judge Saleem Jraisati to support Hizbullah's opposition to the STL. He wrote: 'There is a fundamental mistake regarding the concept of national sovereignty, regarding the relationship between a sovereign state and the international community.'[118] In this way, Hizbullah was once again attempting to place itself as the legitimate guardian of the Lebanese state, and an alternative to the existing 'weak' government. This paved the way for Hizbullah's takeover of the Lebanese Cabinet by way of an orchestrated political 'coup' in January 2011. Yet this 'coup' did not eliminate the victimisation framework, which continued to be used by Hizbullah whenever the issue of its weapons or the STL was raised. When WikiLeaks began to release US State Department diplomatic cables in 2011, Hizbullah used them to present 'evidence' of the existence of an American–Israeli conspiracy supported by March 14 and their Saudi allies. Al-Manar's news bulletin on 6 April 2011, for example, claimed the cables revealed that a meeting had been held between the United States and Saudi Arabia during which 'they agreed to use US–Israeli money to support March 14'. The 'coup' also failed to eliminate Hizbullah's efforts to frame the (by then fallen, but remaining as caretaker) March 14 government as weak. In the al-Manar comedy show *Tarabeesh*, two comedians poked fun at the government's collapse by saying that they 'cannot bring it down because it was not there to bring down [in the first place]'.

Al-Manar's news continuously focused on stories that highlighted the impotence of the government. These ranged from reports on the government's inability to contain prison riots to a report claiming that the government was choosing to ignore the plight of Lebanese nationals who had become trapped in the conflict-ridden Ivory Coast. On 3 November 2011, al-Manar also broadcast a story about students who had been attacked near the home of Saad Hariri in Beirut despite the security belt around it; rather ironically, considering Hizbullah's large 'security quarter' in southern Beirut and its general insistence on assuming responsibility for the security of Shiite-dominated areas as opposed to trusting the state with this task, the belt was described as 'the largest security parameter in the history of Lebanon' and as a challenge 'to the sovereignty and authority of the Lebanese state'. Hizbullah, then, continued to present itself as the only viable alternative to the Lebanese state, a position it maintained even after claiming—with its allies—virtually all the seats in the Lebanese Cabinet in late 2011, thereby indirectly affirming its political ambitions.

While it was in government, the approach that Hizbullah had used in its communication strategy remained constant, with the group seeking to emphasise its role as a defender of the Lebanese in the face of an incompetent state. Following clashes sparked by the Syrian crisis between Sunnis and Alawites in northern Lebanon in May 2012, for example, Nasrallah gave a speech on 22 May calling on 'everyone to show restraint'. Both Sunnis and Shiites had engaged in public protests that included the blocking of roads with burnt tyres: the Sunnis protested against the arrest of a pro-Syrian opposition man in Tripoli on terrorism charges, and the killing of a Sunni sheikh at an army checkpoint, while the Shiites protested against the kidnapping of eleven Shiite Lebanese pilgrims in Syria who were on their way back from Iraq. Nasrallah was quick to address the Lebanese following the blocking of the road to Beirut's international airport by Shiite protesters. 'The Lebanese state and government have a responsibility to work toward the release of those kidnapped,' he said, placing the burden of responsibility on the state, but adding, 'We will work day and night until those beloved are back with us,' thereby reaffirming the state's weakness and Hizbullah's role as its rescuer.[119]

The challenge of the Arab Spring

Hizbullah's return to the victimisation framework was to prove useful with the onset of the Arab uprisings in December 2010. Hizbullah initially praised Arabs who had finally risen to claim their rights, with the Tunisian, Egyptian, Libyan and Bahraini uprisings viewed as useful occasions to advance Hizbullah's political position at a regional level. The first provided an opportunity to affirm Hizbullah's mistrust of the West. On 16 January 2011, for instance, Nasrallah delivered a television speech reflecting on the refusal of European countries to host the recently ousted Tunisian President Zine El-Abidine Ben Ali, in which the Hizbullah leader stated that he wanted to 'congratulate the Tunisian people for their historic revolution as well as praise their bravery. But we must draw a lesson from that revolution. The lesson, above all, is this: the Ben Ali regime and its entourage have always served the interests of France, the United States, and the West in general, but now no Western power takes them in.'[120] The Egyptian Revolution, on the other hand, was an occasion to delight in the fall of a political nemesis. After Hosni Mubarak was forced to step down from the Egyptian presidency in February 2011, Hizbullah issued a statement in which it said it 'congratulates the great people of Egypt on this historic and honourable victory, which is a direct result of their pioneering revolution'.[121] This quick embrace was in no small part due to Mubarak's previous accusation that Hizbullah had masterminded a number of attacks that were planned to take place in Egypt to destabilise his regime, leading to the arrest of a Hizbullah member in Egypt in 2009.[122] The third uprising, in Libya, was seen as a form of 'revenge' against the regime that had kidnapped the prominent Shiite leader Imam Musa al-Sadr in the 1970s. It took less than a week from the start of anti-Muammar Qaddafi protests in Libya for the Hizbullah MP Hussein Moussawi to speak out, calling on the international community to rid Libya of Qaddafi and condemning the Libyan regime for slaughtering its own people.[123] In the al-Manar comedy show *Tarabeesh*, two comedians made fun of those Arab leaders whose pictures had been pelted by shoes during the uprisings, while another mimicked Qaddafi's rambling speech on 22 February 2011, in which he had threatened the protesters and described them as rats in an effort to quell the uprising.

The Egyptian Revolution in particular was used by Hizbullah as an occasion to send different political messages. One message was an explicit criticism of its Lebanese and Arab opponents. An article in the 4 February 2011 issue of *al-Intiqad* with the headline 'The Arab Spring brings Down March 14 and Mubarak', for example, claimed that March 14 supported Mubarak because they were all American allies. A second message sought to paint the revolution as an extension of Hizbullah's own legacy of resistance. The 11 February 2011 issue of *al-Intiqad*, for instance, carried a story about Egyptian activists praising Nasrallah's speeches as having 'encouraged' them and 'taught us how to resist our enemy'.[124] In the same issue, Nasrallah is quoted as saying that the importance of the revolution is the same as that of the 'historic steadfastness of the Lebanese resistance in the July 2006 war', while the cover of the issue featured the headline 'The Era of Victories' in a direct reference to Nasrallah's speech of 2006.[125] Hizbullah also organised huge rallies in support of the revolutions in Tunisia, Egypt, Libya, Bahrain and Yemen, and used its 'trademark' verse from the Quran to bestow an Islamic/Hizbullah inflection on the Egyptian Revolution: 'a victory from God', *nasrun min Allah*. In the rally marking the 'Week of Martyred Leaders'—a special occasion that Hizbullah began celebrating in mid-February following the assassination of Imad Mughniyeh on 12 February 2008, which commemorates Mughniyeh's death as well as that of Abbas al-Mussawi and Ragheb Harb—Nasrallah addressed the masses gathered in the Sayyed al-Shouhada' complex in southern Beirut through a live video message. Next to the screen showing Nasrallah was another one with images of Egyptians celebrating in Tahrir Square, topped with the slogan 'The leaders ... of a victorious *umma*.' The slogan clearly frames the Egyptian Revolution as a victory for an Islamic world led by Hizbullah.

Hizbullah sought to portray the Arab Spring as a natural continuation of the 1979 Islamic Revolution in Iran. The 11 February 2011 issue of *al-Intiqad* opened with the full text of the Arabic-language speech given by Supreme Leader Ali Khamenei one week earlier that had praised the Egyptian Revolution.[126] Nasrallah also gave several speeches in which he lauded the Iranian model of revolution as a paradigm for Arabs to emulate in seeking to overthrow autocratic regimes. In a speech on 1 June 2011, for example, Nasrallah claimed that the main achievement of the Iranian Revolution was 'the establishment of a state, an alternative system to that of the [deposed] Shah ... which blocked what is called "counter-revolutions" which the [different] American administrations are used to support. With the Imam (Khomeini) the victory of the revolution was complete, the victory of the state was another, and it was more important ... the revolution did not stop being victorious until today [sic].'[127] Nasrallah's discourse has a clear implication in this context: the Arab peoples in Egypt, Libya and Tunisia should use the same strategy and eradicate all counter-revolutionary forces before political processes mired within the existing political institutions could start. On 11 September 2011, the daily television show *Al-Manar Morning* also described the Arab revolutions as movements of 'Islamic awakening' against Western influences and 'demonic' Arab dictators, inspired by the Islamic Revolution in Iran.

This discourse followed an earlier framing of Iran as a supporter of the Arab people, sparked by the uprising in Bahrain. Bahrain, a Shiite-majority country, witnessed anti-regime protests that began in Manama on 14 February 2011 which were met by a crackdown from the Sunni government. Al-Manar's news bulletin on 6 April 2011 featured an Iranian saying that 'the Muslim community, both Sunni and Shia, is being oppressed' and that 'they must stick together to defend themselves'. The news story then cut to images of large crowds gathered in the holy city of Qom in Iran to protest against the maltreatment of Bahrainis and to call for the withdrawal of foreign forces from Bahrain. Hizbullah's website meanwhile carried a banner declaring 'Save the people of Bahrain', and Nasrallah blamed the Bahraini regime for painting the protests in sectarian terms. *Al-Intiqad* ran constant reports on the human rights abuses of the monarchy in Bahrain and painted its victims as martyrs of a legitimate revolution. The last page of the 18 February 2011 issue of *al-Intiqad* is composed of graphic images of mutilated Bahraini bodies lying on the ground and bleeding with the words 'May God accept this offering from us' (*al-lahuma taqabbal minna hadha al-qurbaan*). Here, Hizbullah used the same language of resistance and sacrifice that it deploys in the context of its fighting against the Israeli occupation. In order to avoid provoking sectarianism, Hizbullah's discourse on Bahrain was cloaked in nationalist terms. In doing so, Hizbullah was attempting to capitalise on an opportunity to reach out to a wide audience all over the Arab world. But as the protests across the region gained momentum, Hizbullah's support also became driven by a sense of marginalisation: the Arab Spring had stolen the limelight from Hizbullah and shattered its status as the sole representative of Arab dignity.

Hizbullah's efforts faced a further challenge when anti-regime protests started in Syria. Hizbullah immediately adopted the Syrian government's line and blamed the protests on 'foreign forces' while trying to present the uprising as an American–Israeli conspiracy, using its familiar self-referential frameworks, a similar strategy to that used in 2009 to discredit the Green Movement in Iran. In an article on Hizbullah's main website on 28 June 2011, Naziha Saleh wrote:

The US went back to its planning room to work on its ever existing project of the 'New Middle East'—after the 'Israeli' failure in achieving it in the July war 2006, and after the US failure in hitting the stability in Iran, which is considered as the supporter of the resistance. To choose Syria because it is the protector of the resistance and the only Arab country that still stands in the face of 'Israel' for the Arab rights. In striking Syria, the US can achieve its goal and make the dream come true to isolate Iran geographically and politically after the UN economic sanctions resolution.[128]

Alongside this discourse regarding an American–Israeli plot, Hizbullah launched another audio-visual attack on the STL after indictments were issued in July 2011 that identified four Hizbullah members as being involved in Hariri's murder. Nasrallah gave another speech on 2 July during which he displayed images of documents which, he claimed, linked the tribunal with Israel. But the STL was to become an interlude for Hizbullah as it became more heavily involved in the Syrian conflict not only by providing strategic support for the Assad regime but also by sending troops to fight Syrian rebels. Hizbullah labelled its military involvement as pre-emptive action against Sunni jihadi '*takfiri*' groups who need to be stopped in their tracks before they threatened the sovereignty of Lebanon and the existence of the anti-Israeli 'resistance' triangle personified in the Assad regime, Hizbullah and Iran.[129]

Conclusion

Hizbullah's communication strategy experienced a number of highs and lows in the two decades following the liberation of southern Lebanon. The high enjoyed by Hizbullah after the liberation faced a serious challenge following the assassination of Hariri in 2005, but Hizbullah managed to reassert itself and its public image after the 'victory' of the 2006 war. Yet the sequence of events that followed, starting with those of May 2008, marked a downward shift in Hizbullah's credibility and ability to reach out to audiences beyond its constituents and allies in Lebanon. Hizbullah's political decisions cost it support in the Arab world at large and forced it to revert to relying on the framework of victimisation that had characterised its early days.

Reflecting on the use of victimisation as a strategy in the contexts of the May 2008 events, the STL and then the Syrian crisis illustrate the key components of this framework. First, it uses self-referential discourse that capitalises on Hizbullah's heroic legacy. Second, it uses adaptable discourse that reframes negative actions by Hizbullah positively. Third, it relies on 'support erosion':[130] this was used to destroy public support for the STL, a major driver behind the May 2008 violence, by equating Hizbullah's domestic opponents with Israel, and in the Syrian crisis by labelling all Syrian revolutionaries 'jihadi takfiris' threatening Sunnis, Shiites and Christians. Fourth, it makes use of Hizbullah's legacy and legitimacy to 'get away with' this departure from norms. As Suchman argues, 'legitimacy is resilient to particular events, yet it is dependent on a history of events. An organization may occasionally depart from societal norms yet retain legitimacy because the departures are dismissed as unique.'[131] Fifth, it relies on the strength of Hizbullah's brand to navigate its way through the criticism that surrounds controversial acts such as those of May 2008 or Hizbullah's military involvement in the Syrian crisis. Peter van Ham argues: 'Branding acquires its power because the right brand can surpass the actual product as a company's central asset.'[132] In this case, the positive connotations invoked by Hizbullah's brand supersede the actual 'product' it has become, a group involved in a violent attack on other Lebanese (and later, in a military conflict within Syria). Finally, it relies on Nasrallah's charisma, which had transformed the devotion of Hizbullah's followers into a sense of duty, leading those followers to obey his wishes regardless of the objective reality.[133] This is related to Nasrallah's success as a charismatic leader in building a relationship with his followers by presenting himself as a visionary, influencing his followers to the extent that they do not question his decisions or actions.[134]

The Arab Spring and the STL indictments consequently presented a set of complex challenges for Hizbullah's communication strategy. Audiences across the Arab world were too preoccupied with the Arab Spring to pay much attention to Hizbullah, while the STL indictments and Hizbullah's stance towards the Syrian uprising created a sense of doubt about Hizbullah's trustworthiness in the eyes of some of its Lebanese and non-Lebanese supporters. The fall of the regimes in Egypt and Tunisia also derailed the centrality of Hizbullah's image as an Arab hero. With dignity and heroism having come within the reach of the average Arab citizen as a result of the Arab Spring, the narrative of victimisation was the only way in which Hizbullah would now be able to stand out in a region that was witnessing a rise in individual agency beyond the umbrella of political organisations, a factor that Hizbullah's communication strategy had never had to address before. The Arab Spring, then, put Hizbullah at a crossroads, not only stealing its limelight but also testing its credibility in the Arab world, and consequently, its longevity . Thirty years after Hizbullah came into existence, the group's communication strategy appears to have come full circle.

4

THE POETRY OF HIZBULLAH

Atef Alshaer

While much attention has been given to Hizbullah's media, in all their forms, far less is known about its poetry, which is another important method through which the movement reaches out to its constituents in Lebanon and across the Arab world. Poetry has served as an essential communication tool for Hizbullah ever since the movement's early days, its role being consonant with the wider function that poems, both commissioned and popular, play in the socio-political context of the Arab world. Poetry is the primary form of artistic expression in the region. From pre-Islamic to Islamic history and to the contemporary world, poetry has always been acknowledged for its emotive value and for providing a repository of Arab lives, as the evocative and intimate phrase *'al-shi'ir diwan al-'arab*, 'poetry is the register of the Arabs', implies.[1] As Agha writes: 'Setting poetics aside, Arabic versified speech and the history of the Arabs are, in [the] Arabic sources, almost inseparable; so much so that one may even conjure up an outline (or a silhouette) of at least the major contours of early Arab history by solely tapping Arabic verse.'[2] Such an understanding remains relevant in the contemporary world as various politicians, political parties and state actors are often represented, and represent themselves, as much in verse as in normal speech. Thus it would be safe to say that Arab poetry, and particularly political poetry, might speak for one faction or state, one group or community, providing a rich insight into the language used by those entities—the communicative essence of existence that contributes to making up and representing social and political realities.

Poetry responds to the socio-political contexts within which it emerges. In this respect, two dates in recent Arab history are worth revisiting: 1948 and 1967.[3] The first represents the dismemberment of Palestine and the dispossession of the Palestinians, and the second the defeat of several Arab countries by Israel and the latter's occupation of more Arab land. These junctures saw the emergence of several important poetic figureheads who appealed and responded to local sensitivities and aspirations. Among these are the Palestinian poets Mahmoud Darwish (1941–2008) and Samih al-Qasim (b.1939), the Iraqi poet Abd al-Wahab al-Bayati (1926–99) and the Syrian poets Nizar Qabani (1923–98) and Adonis (b.1930).[4] But it is Palestinian poetry that has been notable for its entrenchment in the realities of the Palestinian predicament and for championing resistance against Israel.[5] Hizbullah has followed the Palestinian model in championing and popularising the trope of resistance in its poetry, in harmony with the focus on resistance seen in the group's other communication products and tools.[6] Yet in the context of Hizbullah, resistance is additionally a key Shiite paradigm, as the entire edifice of the Shiite faith is situated within narratives of resistance, sacrifice and endurance. Hence, the poetry of Hizbullah draws on multiple references including historical events and various tropes of colonialism and resistance.

The poetry of or about Hizbullah is diverse and can broadly be defined as that which is authored by Arab poets, writers, supporters and sympathisers as well as ordinary people who respond deeply to the events in which Hizbullah is a central player, and who are embraced by Hizbullah either formally or informally.[7] Though Hizbullah's poetry interacts with various historical events and serves to mark them, it is fluid and reiterative in its inclusion of several themes and reference points representative of Hizbullah's ideology and day-to-day political and social dynamics. In this respect, the themes of resistance, connectedness and continuity of past glories, heroism, certainty of victory, defiance and patience are notable as constant poetic preoccupations. These themes were substantiated by Arab poets who embraced Hizbullah and its ideology, suggesting that poetry, as a type of discourse, reflects a form of pan-Arab solidarity with Hizbullah, manifested in the repetition of discourses of connection and loyalty to the group through various poetic creations that represent one socio-political faction and reality rather than another.[8]

Poetry as political practice

The argument of this chapter is that poetry, particularly political poetry, is complementary to the other forms of political communication practices that Hizbullah uses. In the case of Hizbullah, poetry serves to solidify and constitute ideologies, hail Hizbullah leaders, fighters and affiliates, and enhance their appeal and authenticity.[9] Poetry is generally perceived as a residue of past authenticity, underlining the authority and legitimacy of those who use and embrace it, and this aspect comes across in the writings and speeches of Shiite pioneers whose ideas and activities gave rise to the organised political community epitomised in Hizbullah today, including Musa al-Sadr, whose conception of culture is worth noting here. For al-Sadr, culture is 'what connects heaven and earth, life and the afterlife, the individual alone and the society with God ... Thus culture acquires divinity, holiness and power, and in this, it satisfies all the feelings of human beings.'[10] Such an organic and holistic view of culture, according to Joseph al-Agha, has increasingly become symptomatic of Hizbullah as it operates and competes with other political players within Lebanon, and also in its 'treatment of Islam as a cultural and social force', underlining the fact that Hizbullah seeks, in effect, to be 'an existential necessity'.[11] It is in this sense that Hizbullah's poetry and the poetry associated with it are integral to the group's worldview of rootedness within its socio-political conditions. In other words, it serves as an integral part of its political communicative reservoir, partaking in all its political and existential aspects,[12] or as an extension of other communicative practices—another level of communication that bestows on its members and the wider Shiite community in Lebanon a sense of authenticity and rootedness.

THE HIZBULLAH PHENOMENON

Like other political actors in the Middle East, who fitted poets within their circles and within state structures to legitimise and authenticate their political programmes,[13] Hizbullah embraced poets within its ranks to project a comprehensive image of itself. To this end, throughout its history, and particularly after the 2006 war with Israel, Hizbullah staged poetry festivals, such as the 'Festival of the Poetry of Resistance', *mahrajan al-shi'r al-muqawim*, and published many poems aimed at enhancing its standing and appeal to its supporters.

Poetry is part of the socio-political fabric of the Arab world and Hizbullah is no exception in this respect. The creation and use of poetry are not subject to specific methods as such, as it is fused into gatherings, televised speeches, invitations, social meetings and exchanges and public readings. In the Islamic and Arabic traditions, which include the Sunni and the Shiite heritage, poetry has personal as well as communal values. In the case of Hizbullah, the public aspect of poetry resides in its affectative use in gatherings, where the audience hail their leader, heroes, community, values and way of life in general through poetry as a historical and authentic form of expression. Here the form corresponds to the value of the hailed object in the sense that the leaders, the heroes and the communal values are seen as authentic, and hence poetry corroborates their authentication as an exalted medium of expression. These primary functions of political poetry in the modern age are disseminated through films and video clips broadcast on al-Manar extolling the virtues of the resistance and hailing Hizbullah as its leading force. In this context, poetry is incorporated within a strategy of communication at whose heart lies the tendency for affectation, creating emotional solidarity and loyalty to Hizbullah and its methods.

Many poems are also turned into songs and repeated throughout the day on the television. The poems and songs are accompanied with imagined images of historic Shiite figures, Hizbullah fighters in the fields of fighting, retreating Israeli soldiers and jubilant scenes of victory in Lebanon and elsewhere in the Arab world. Poetry also extends to the social realms as in the *majalis al-'aza* (mourning congregations) for 'Ashoura, in funerals, weddings and other social functions. Almost all such occasions are announced with the aid of poetry, as reflected in *al-'Ahd*. These poems invited people to partake in the political and social activities of the party, while also seeking to reinforce the cohesion of the community through language that invokes its values, and which idolises those who take part in Hizbullah's activities. Furthermore, poems are either recited by their authors, or by affiliate members of Hizbullah or sympathisers with the party. And as often with disciplined political movements with ideological roots in history such as Hizbullah, the group also inspired several choral ensembles to emerge, as will be referred to in the course of this chapter. These choral groups amount to orchestral units and are invited to sing songs and recite poems at weddings, commemorations and rallies.

With its popularity increasing, Hizbullah began recording and archiving the poetry associated with it and its ideology on high-quality CDs and DVDs and distributing them through its media outlets. Thus, though poetry is often fluid and relates to emotive practices in the first place, it can also be used politically in intentional and calculated ways as part of communication practices and strategies, particularly when it is manipulated to lend legitimacy to political discourses and when the poets in question are fitted with or embrace a particular political ideology.

It is important to acknowledge the presence of Iran in Hizbullah's poetry which, like other forms of communication, projects the group as located both in the Arab and Iranian cultures. It is also worth noting that Hizbullah's loyalties and alliances are dynamic and varied, reflecting the hybrid nature of its identity. As such, it is a group enabled by an extensive apparatus of knowledge, which makes up its ideology as a structure and as a diverse content that merits interpretation in its own right.

Beginnings in oaths and sacrifice

Every member of Hizbullah is initiated in the party with a pledge, *qasam*, which is poetic in nature and congruent with nationalist and patriotic oaths of allegiance to the party and its ideology, thus forming what Michel Foucault implies to be acts of initiation in discourse.[14] There are two main oaths of allegiance, reflecting different periods of Hizbullah's history and referring to different leaders. The first oath relates to the period of resistance beginning in the 1980s and lasting until the 1990s, and the second represents the period from 2000 onwards when Hizbullah's cultural and political capital in the Arab world expanded. Broadly, in the first period, Hizbullah poetry is rooted in its Shiite milieu and Iranian connections; in the second, it is broadened to include wider Arab audiences. In the latter period, when Hizbullah's identity became more fluid, many well-known Arab poets also began to hail Hizbullah and celebrate its military achievements. In return, Hizbullah gave these poets a platform at poetry festivals, in publications and through media exposure, thus playing the role of the patron once preserved for the sultan and later by various Arab leaders, such as Saddam Hussein, who fitted poets within the hegemonic cultural apparatuses of the state. However, Arab poets who have embraced Hizbullah live in different Arab countries with their own cultures and authorities, and their relation to Hizbullah is therefore affinitive rather than one of binding to rulers by structures of power.

The first oath this chapter refers to goes as follows:

> In the name of Mecca and Galilee with the mount
> Martyrdom has eternally been our dream
> And our slogan is 'let us begin the noblest of work'
> For Glory, O Amal!

And the second reads:

> In the name of the blood of the stolen Jerusalem
> We have kept dignity, and we will not forget
> Khyber and the grand battle of Badr
> We will remain faithful to the oath, O Nasrallah!

The author of the first oath is unknown, but the oath is still in use as a relic from the past, while the second is more formalised and is used by Hizbullah members and supporters when they pledge allegiance and loyalty to the movement on formal occasions, in public rallies and in popular gatherings.[15] Both oaths represent continuity as well as the evolution of the party. The first oath refers to the revered leader Musa al-Sadr when evoking 'O Amal'.[16] The second is sealed with the evocation 'O Nasrallah', a reference to the longest-serving and current leader, Hassan Nasrallah, whose role and image are discussed in the following chapter. Both oaths register important points about Hizbullah's identity and its rootedness in a wider realm of convictions that transcend political calculations. As discussed in the previous two chapters, Hizbullah has always maintained its Islamist identity, while linking itself to important Arab causes and emotional sites, such as Mecca, the central site of Islam, and Palestine. Jerusalem also figures prominently in much of Hizbullah's discourses and actions. Both oaths emphasise Hizbullah's pan-Arab identity, thus dispelling suggestions that it is Shiite-centred in its worldview and concerns. It is noteworthy that the first oath underlines the commitments of Hizbullah members to fight the Israeli occupation of Lebanon. However, the statement 'that martyrdom has eternally been our dream' asserts the Shiite identity of Hizbullah in the importance of sacrifice/martyrdom and the rejection of humiliation, which is what the seminal figure in Shiite history, Imam Ali's son, Hussein, stood for in the Battle of Karbala (AD 680).[17] For Hizbullah, sacrifice and martyrdom are aspects of cardinal importance as means of liberation from the Israeli occupation.[18] In the second oath, it is the figure of Hassan Nasrallah that dominates. Again, the grand battles of Islam are evoked to reassure the fighters that the victories and glories of old battles will be repeated in the present. The first oath in particular is characteristic of the early period of Hizbullah's history, in which various discourses, including poetry, focused on reassuring and reaffirming old beliefs connected to the Shiite faith while reaffirming the centrality of resistance and sacrifice. It was during the 1980s and 1990s that several Lebanese Shiite poets and a few others interacted with the ideology of the movement and produced poems that were memorised and repeatedly recited by Hizbullah members and within Shiite circles. In this context, these recitals and interactions can be seen as active communication practices that helped reinforce Hizbullah's identity and appeal. Resistance as manifest in poetry highlights the collective endeavour and spirit of the community which are emphasised in the writings of Hizbullah's leaders, such as those of Naim Qassem.[19] The ideological resonance of the oaths and the cyclical view of history that they maintain highlight the importance of poetry as an essential form of communication that serves to authenticate Hizbullah's identity. Furthermore, it is the language of such poetry that constitutes, along with other language, the raw materials of ideology and faith, which this chapter aims to further explore.

The seeds of Hizbullah's poetry

Hizbullah's poetry initially appeared in the newspaper *al-'Ahd*. In the 1980s the paper began publishing a cultural supplement that contained poems and details of cultural activities, as well as cultural and historical reflections on the life of the Prophet Muhammad or the first community of the Shiites.[20] In that period, as well as later, political mobilisation went hand in hand with cultural activities that substantiated political objectives and helped give them historical legitimacy. *Al-'Ahd* regularly published poems and announcements for upcoming poetry evenings, thus reaching out to its intended audiences and calling for them to participate. These poems addressed resistance, and more often than not included references to particular figures or persons who fell in the course of fighting with the Israeli occupation. The bulk of the poetry published in the early editions of *al-'Ahd* refers to martyrs and martyrdom as essential ideals and practices, and is grounded in the Shiite faith and its emphasis on endurance and sacrifice as constituted in the first community of Shiites in Islam, and most significantly represented in the figures of 'Ali and Hussein.[21]

Two incidents in the 1980s that are represented in such poetry are the assassination of the Shiite leader Ragheb Harb on 61 February 1984 and the death of Iran's leader Ayatollah Ruhollah Khomeini on 3 June 1989. Their passing is extensively commemorated and portrayed as a turning point in history. Ragheb Harb is described as 'the son of Khomeini',[22] while a poem by Musa Mukhs, who is referred to in the newspaper as a friend of Harb's, commemorates his death as follows:

> At the forefront
> We are used to you, the pioneer of Shari'a, to be at the front
> Always in the path of righteousness as a guiding torch …
> That's how the heroes with firm positions undertake
> The strenuous journey of fear
> That's how it was with Moses … and this is what Jesus, the Messiah, said:
> The prophets of God are a permanent voice that returns …
> That's how the religion of Mohammad was firmly established
> As a nation that witnesses the renewal of each period
> That's how Hussein said it, heightening the determination of soldiers,
> That's how Khomeini shook the moving earth
> That's how Ragheb drew the horizons
> With the blood of the heart and verses full of good omens …[23]

The message is one of continuity on a path of sacrifice that was started by prophets and historical figures, such as Moses, Jesus, Muhammad, Hussein and Khomeini, and which continued with the martyrdom of Harb. The poet, Musa Mukhs, invites earlier historical characters whose sacrifices served as examples of courage and determination buttressed by a sense of righteousness. Sacrifice is a kernel theme in Hizbullah's poetry and is also to be found in the poetry commemorating the death of Khomeini, whose passing was widely lamented in al-'Ahd. Khomeini is portrayed as a milestone character whose death imbues the entire world with sadness and regret. In much of the paper devoted to him, prose is mixed with poetry in a way that invokes limitless lamentation over Khomeini's death. In one such poem, which is characteristic of Shiite commemoration practices called *latmiyaat'* (lamentations), with a rhapsodic undertone of descent into an overwhelming sorrow and grief, the anonymous poet says:

> Our salvation, where have you gone?
> Our protector, where have you gone?
> You left us early … quickly … and left us …
> You left us orphaned … perplexed … why …
> Why, O Imam?
> With whom have you left us?
>
> Who are we without you? Why us?
> And how … how could we be guided in this blackness which you left behind?
> Who will heal these endless wounds?
> My master …
> It was said that the strike that does not break the back strengthens it …
> But tell us: what can we do with our broken backs …?
>
> May an eye that did not weep over you go blind
> May an eye that did not weep over you go blind
> And may a chest that did not lament you get torn apart …[24]

Khomeini had exhorted and encouraged collective grief to mobilise publics and to consolidate the newly emerging Islamic nation state in Iran.[25] In the paper, he is given the status of a prophet with divine and worldly traits. 'Salvation' and 'protection', which his actual presence seems to have bestowed on people, have given way to loss, a loss which should be lamented not only by the Shiite community, but also by every human being. The lamentation shows a community enthralled by its leaders and doggedly loyal to them as Salvationists, guiding torches of light whose passing breaks a momentum endowed with great promises. However, though the spiritual and political leadership of Iran continue to be dominant figures in Hizbullah's poetry, culture and politics in general, they acquire more nuances with time, as will be seen further below, as pan-Arabism enters into the poetic veins of Hizbullah's world.

In addition to the poetry published in the paper, there were several Shiite Lebanese poets whose poems spread by word of mouth, and became known on that basis. These poets were part of the larger Shiite movement of revival, which Hizbullah championed, and hence interacted with their environments with poetry that echoed the broader concerns of the Shiite community as articulated by Hizbullah in particular. There is no serious conceptual difference between the work of such poets and the poetry published in Hizbullah's outlets as they both depict similar concerns, affiliations and themes. One such poet is Mohammad al-Qubaisi, who was born in the South of Lebanon in 1945. His words and poems are popularised through memorisation and recital by a large swathe of Lebanese Shiites who are loyal to Hizbullah, but he is unknown beyond Lebanon.[26] What follows are translated excerpts from his poetry:

> We are faithful to God
> For the sake of his love, we desire death
> We follow on the steps of the Prophet and his family until the appearance of al-Mahdi
> We are the valiant at heart
> We sacrifice ourselves for you, O the land of the south,
> We are on the path of martyrdom
>
> ***
>
> My homeland is strong and dignity is rooted in it
> The voice of the fighter is high
> O Jerusalem, we are coming,
> O fighter, do not fear the powerful, well-equipped,

And pursue dignity in life
Resist, for the souls of the fathers
Lived in your heart and eyes,
O Jerusalem, we are coming

* * *

In the south, a turbaned man had appeared
He has been taken notice of by lions
He (the turbaned man) yearns for heroes with burning desires
And people sleep with his memory peacefully
The mother had wiped away the tear with the handkerchief
Which had trickled down the cheeks of the orphaned
Why do I address a father who does not respond?
Why do I try to console a soul that cannot be consoled?
Why do I look at a south soaked in blood?
With the blood of the crime, spilt by the enslaver,
Melodies had come my way, beckoning children,
They sing, O orphaned, be patient, and recite:
Had Musa al-Sadr passed away with dignity
Or had the fire of oppression been extinguished,
You would have seen all creations killed with one stroke,
From your gigantic reaction when you threatened
But your face is a face of dignity,
It is to be worshipped after your God ...
I am seeing persecution as oppression
And by God, the right of people is being stolen ...

In al-Qubaisi's poetry, Jerusalem represents an ultimate point of reference whose liberation is called for as the key to Islamic salvation, but it is also the spiritual and political leadership of Musa al-Sadr that dominates, particularly in the third poem, conveying similar sentiments to Hizbullah's other poetry and songs. To this end, it can be argued that poetry grounded in a tradition is not like political discourses, which often can and do correspond to the political moment in a parallel way that can be relatively classified. Poetry with reiterative political and cultural messages tends to escape rigid classification, as at heart, it depicts, and in this case, it confirms, the epistemological identity of the movement in question with its emotional and spiritual package, as will be further revealed.

Another popular poem turned into a song through the choral singers of *husayiniun lan narka'* (Hussein's followers who would never bow down) which Hizbullah uses as it lays its victims to rest, and which belongs to the above-cited genre of poetry, is:

> With blood and Hussein, we follow on the steps of al-Khomeini
> We have pledged ourselves to you, Hizbullah,
> With soul and religion,
> We walk and death had returned
> For us, as lovers of martyrdom.[27]

Such poems and songs assert Hizbullah's early identity, its primal connection to the seminal figures of Shiite history, such as Ali, Hussein and others; martyrdom as a tool of liberation; its claim over a wider Islamic identity referenced by the Islamic Republic of Iran and with Jerusalem as its symbolic heart; bemoaning of injustice and oppression; and finally, fighting as the way forward out of injustice. These samples of poetry belong to an era when Hizbullah was relatively limited in its appeal and reach, and therefore they carry messages of suffering, defiance and reassurance through faith and a certainty rooted in Shiite tradition and history.

Political and poetic milestones

Hizbullah's popularity in the Arab world increased in 2000 following the Israeli withdrawal from southern Lebanon and during and after the 2006 war with Israel.[28] There were several other events which demonstrated Hizbullah's power, but these did not engender as much attention and adulation in the Arab world as the Israeli withdrawal. When Israel withdrew from Lebanon in 2000, Arab poets of outstanding calibre paid tribute to the liberation, praising the resistance and Hizbullah's role in it. Among these were the late Palestinian poet Mahmoud Darwish and the Syrian poet Adonis. While neither penned poems on the occasion, they delivered elegiac speeches impregnated with poetic authority. Adonis was particularly admiring of the resistance, approvingly articulating its perception about itself. To this effect, he wrote:

> When I see what Hizbullah did to 'Israel' and its soldiers in the South, on the borders with Palestine, I feel an inclination towards comparison. Poor people, armed with primitive weapons and in possession of tremendous faith, but they have held their lives in their hands to decide their own destiny. If we compare what Hizbullah did with the Israeli soldiers, we would find that it has affected Israel more than all the Arab armies combined for four decades. Why? Because if the people took charge of their own destiny, and all of them are involved in decision-making and responsibility, then they cannot be overcome.[29]

Adonis's statement elevates Hizbullah's position by asserting its disciplined and determined outlook, using it as an example of how victories can be made. Mahmoud Darwish, on the other hand, did not refer to Hizbullah specifically, but referred to Lebanon's 'culture of resistance':

> We love Lebanon more today, because it had triumphed over the pervasive culture of defeat inculcated within the Arab elites which have turned the concept of personal freedom and sacrifice to materials for daily sarcasm ... we applaud beautiful Lebanon, without exaggeration or interpretation, because it has triumphed over its legend, over its playful folkloric weakness; and it has won over the myth of the invincible Israeli army. The consequences of the withdrawal will not halt the infection of the grand hope which small Lebanon had awakened in a continent thirsty for freedom. And so long as the culture of resistance is part of the fabric of the society, then the withdrawal is possible ... and eloquence requires no eloquent.[30]

Both Adonis and Darwish highlighted the collective dimension of resistance that led to liberation in southern Lebanon. Both figures, being representative of the highest standards of poetry in the Arab world, in effect enlarged Hizbullah's grand sense of itself as a paragon of resistance.

The poetry connected with the Israeli withdrawal in 2000, however, specifically reiterates Hizbullah's rhetoric, symbols, themes and images, while drawing on the Shiite faith. Thus the Lebanese poet Mohammad Ali Shams ad-Din, in his poem entitled *The Blood of Hussein Coined the Dawn*, writes:

> Graves are moving
> I see heads raised at the arrows
> I see the roots resisting the winds

And I hear the graves grinding anger
I feel the sand traversed in the field
And the waves of the sea thrown over the fire
And I say with tears in my eyes
And I do not know, if I should laugh or weep,
Praise be to the one who gave the Umma of the Arabs its new Jesus
From the blood of Hussein
And coined its dawn.[31]

The aesthetics and power of this poem reside in its evocation of nature as having been animated with the liberation of the South, as if it had regained a lost order through acts of resistance and steadfastness. The other notable trope in the poem is the evocation of Jesus Christ in the figurative phrase 'blood of Hussein' (as in the blood of Christ). Both are considered figures of resistance and persistence in demands for justice and resurrection, all of which ultimately lead to the beginning of a new dawn, or a new beginning. In addition, other poems related to this period were used to commemorate particular martyr-figures, such as the poem written by the revered cleric Mohammad Hussein Fadlallah whose poem is headed with a dedication 'to the Sheikh of the resistance fighters, the revered martyr Sheikh, Ahmad Yahiya'. The poem celebrates the life of the martyr in light of the liberation, suggesting that it is through sacrifice that liberation was attained, as in the following excerpt:

Longing had attracted you, and fate had saved you
O descending happily …
Your turban, soaked with blood,
Is a compass for travelling.[32]

Martyrdom is a major cultural trope in Hizbullah's poetry and discourse. In this poem, it is associated with travelling in that it leads to another stage in people's lives, liberation. Thus, martyrdom is portrayed as an indispensable tool of liberation, which is celebrated through the invocation of the blood of the martyrs. In fact, many of the poems from this period are steeped in the celebration of resistance and the persons who perished on the road to its attainment. It is worth noting that al-'Ahd also published specific chants used after the liberation that engaged with several dimensions related to resistance. Most of these assert loyalty to Hizbullah and its leader, Hassan Nasrallah. Here are some examples:

> Look at you, Hizbullah, you have asserted your presence ...
> The Jews went ... and you left no collaborators behind

Another chant runs as follows:

> Bint Jbayl calls out
> We have liberated the land of our country
> May God preserve Abu Hadi
> Bint Jbayl, the glorious ...
> Bint Jbayl, the southern,
> Will remain Lebanese
> It has regained freedom
> Through the victorious soldiers of Hizbullah.[33]

These two chants glorify Hizbullah's resistance in southern Lebanon and register issues and places which were part of the struggle for the South. The word 'collaborators' refers to the Israeli-allied South Lebanese Army, as led by General Anton Lahd, which dissolved and whose members largely fled to Israel after the liberation of the South; 'Abu Hadi' is Nasrallah.

The expansion of Hizbullah's poetic repertoire

The major historical poetic juncture for Hizbullah was the 2006 war with Israel, when poets from outside the Shiite community in Lebanon and the Arab world celebrated Hizbullah's role in the war. It is worthwhile to start with Omar al-Farra, a popular Syrian poet born in 1949 in the city of Palmyra in central Syria. Al-Farra's poems deal with social phenomena in Syria and elsewhere in the Arab world, but he became particularly well known for a poem called *Hamida*, where he gives a voice to a Bedouin girl who prefers death to being forced to marry her cousin. The poem starts and ends with the defiant statements, *ma aridak, ma aridak, ma aridak*: 'I don't want you. I don't want you. I don't want you.' The poem is clearly one of protest against and apprehension about a longstanding social phenomenon which the poet is ardently opposed to. As such, al-Farra gained popularity invested with influence, and for Hizbullah to have his passionate endorsement is a testament to how far its appeal has reached.[34]

In his famous poem entitled *The Men of God*, a clear reference to the fighters of Hizbullah, we find al-Farra at a different front, a pronounced political one underlined with ideological overtones. The poem, which he wrote following the 2006 Israeli onslaught on Lebanon, is an elegy to the fighters of Hizbullah and to the South of Lebanon in general. Though it includes familiar Hizbullah themes, as seen in the above poems, it is richer in language and imagery. The fact that it was recited to large audiences in Lebanon and used in various media outlets adds to its political and emotional value in the wider Arab world in general:

> That's how the Arab blood became a knife that kills
>
> And poetry after silence became resounding
>
> That's how we became, and we will not be if we forgot the Jihad of righteousness and faith
>
> And that people despite humiliation and oppression wave the banner of rebellion
>
> They decide to take the land by force, and they take it
>
> That's what the men of God did in the day of conquest in Lebanon
>
> My heart inclines towards the south; and how beautiful that the love of my heart is southerner,
>
> Here our journeys have assembled, somebody said; take your shoes off,
>
> I could beg you to kneel
>
> We are walking on a holy land
>
> If I could, I would cross it on my eyelashes
>
> Here, they were robbed, here they were crucified, here they dwelled, here they prostrated,
>
> Here they were rocketed, here they stood, here they hoped, here they ascended the wings of God,
>
> Here they fell down, a stream of martyrs,
>
> Before they vanished, they wrote books without titles
>
> You will read in our school about the men of God, in the day of victory in Lebanon
>
> Because the people reject the idea of capitulation
>
> Because their wounds have bled, their pride of belonging had cried out an anthem of glory for the homelands

Because the land is their compass
The light of righteousness is their guide
Amongst them, believing men who read
That if they have promised, they will fulfil their promises,
As they have wished, their purity had united them,
Most of their speech is silence, and some of their silence is gestures
They erupted like a volcano that sends to perdition everything on its way
In death, they have a philosophy
They do not fear Him if they were ordered
For their country, they raised the banner of victory, and triumphed
Southerners: the sand of the earth knows them; the salt of it knows them,
A scent from the wellsprings of paradise
Southerners, known by the lightning of thunder,
The spells of rain, the magic of flowers,
The stars of the night know them; the sun of the morning knows them,
And the revelation of water to waterfalls
And they have known the birds of love, the sharpness of the sword,
The poetry of the Persians, the Greeks, the Phoenicians and the Romans
They have understanding and knowledge of those who governed and those who perished,
And they have knowledge of the rules and scales of poetry,
And how man gets liberated
Southerners, God used to know them, was their leader,
And their commander, so with all humility,
They were the men of conquest in Lebanon.[35]

It is instructive to highlight some of the images and linguistic constructs used in the poem in order to explore how ideology operates in poetry, how it elevates, delineates and creates an aura of authority of its own that imbues the organisation in question with an importance that amounts to sacredness. The poem capitalises on familiar tropes related to Hizbullah's ideology. It locates its point of departure in the humiliations (defeats) that Arabs faced, which consequently, and because of the responsibility placed on Hizbullah fighters, turned their blood into 'a knife that kills'. Hizbullah is the knife of the Arabs, an effective knife that emerges out of humiliation and oppression, and since it is a knife sharpened with a divine sense of righteousness, those who carry this knife 'decide to take the land by force, and they take it'; and as they take the land, liberate it, they become 'the men of God … in the day of conquest in Lebanon'. Hizbullah incorporates religion in its very name, the party of God; and the poem does the same, the men of God, creating a conceptual parallel between the name of the party and that of the poem, the men of God. In this sense, the poem grounds itself in the very beliefs of the party, drawing on the fact that such references to God have historical and contemporary political resonance.

The poem also evokes the South, and how dear it is to the poet. So many literary trends direct their compass towards the South, the southern part of the globe as historically or presently dominated by occupation, colonialism and struggles for liberation.[36] So the South is sung for, made an object of longing and promise, but here the South is specific, it is the South of Lebanon, so the international South is wedded to a local South where the struggle for liberation and freedom rings loud. The South is portrayed as holy; its holiness stems from the many events and travails it witnessed, 'Here they were robbed, here they were crucified … here they fell down, a stream of martyrs'. Even the image of the crucified Jesus, highlighting the severity of the suffering of the people of the South in Lebanon under the Israeli occupation, is evoked to highlight how courageous the fighters were in the face of the enemy, in overcoming this suffering. The poem is replete with images that evoke Hizbullah's ideology and feed into it. The use of the word philosophy, as in the phrase, 'In death, they have a philosophy', explains—to those who condemn Hizbullah and Islamist movements in general for their alleged pursuit of mindless violence that results in deaths—how death is accepted as a philosophy when it is rooted in a struggle for rights, a struggle over a land that is intimately connected with the fighters: 'Southerners: the sand of the earth knows them; the salt of it knows them …' Al-Farra widens the space of his portrayal for Hizbullah fighters, suggesting how they are knowledgeable, professional in fighting, sensitive and aware of various traditions. And because they are equipped with knowledge, poetry and history, God was alongside them and aided them to triumph in southern Lebanon, and they were humble in their victory. In addition, al-Farra adds to Hizbullah's prestige and popularity by including images from the Christian and Arab traditions, such as the Cross, which is a typical image in much of the secular Arabic poetry of the twentieth century.

Geertz reflects on how ideologies construct a world imbued with meanings and assurances that ground them and legitimise the endeavours and activities of their upholders. He writes: 'It is ... the attempt of ideologies to render otherwise incomprehensive social situations meaningfully, to so construe them as to make it possible to act purposefully within them, that accounts both for the ideologies' highly figurative nature and for the intensity with which, once accepted, they are held.'[37] However, while highlighting the significant role of ideology in moulding its subjects, it is equally important to give credence to history as a ground that gives rise to particular orientations that legitimise a diverse set of actions and authenticate them without an ideological guardianship attached to them as such. The poem of al-Farra can be read as a historical product of a particular era, in which Hizbullah is seen as a special liberating force in its resistance to Israel. Therefore, ideology in this context is more than an unchecked subscription to discourse and actions; it is also a historical product which individuals partake in and embody, thus becoming willing, active and obedient subjects at the same time.

The 'Lebanonisation' of Hizbullah in poetry

While it is characteristic of Hizbullah's songs and poems which are produced by members and direct affiliates, mainly from the Shiite community in Lebanon, to be profusely referenced with historical figures and allusions to the past and history, poets like al-Farra internationalised their struggle and added significant existential elements to it. The existing literature on Hizbullah attests to stages in the evolution of the movement from being Shiite-centred theologically and politically to becoming more inclusive, as is discussed in reference to its Lebanonisation and later Arabisation.[38] Hizbullah's poetry and songs reflect this evolution while remaining grounded in Shiite history and traditions. An example is the following poem, initially written by Rida Shu'ayb and later made into a song after 2006. Performed by the choral group al-Fajr, the poem was adapted by Tarik Sharifa and produced by Hizbullah's Dar al-Manar:

THE HIZBULLAH PHENOMENON

O, Lebanon, the garden of Eden,

My fascinating homeland

There is no place like you

This horizon belongs to you

O, Hussein, your soldiers have returned,

O, Hussein, we returned with the God's victory and the blood had won

You have come back, and Abbas, the faithful, leads us,

O, Imam, we and your companions, are in the same orbit

When we are afflicted,

The thirst of Hussein burst in Abbas's veins,

The earth shocked and the world thundered.[39]

Interestingly, the first part of the song echoes the thinking of one of the quintessential poets of Lebanon in the twentieth century, Saeed Aql (1913). This refers to the popular characterisation of the country before the 1975–90 civil war as 'the garden of Eden', a unique place of flourishing trade, high culture and civilisation. In the introduction to his play *Qadmus*, Saeed Aql refers to Lebanon as 'a powerful and genius message in the world, which qualifies us to the Lebanonization of the world, *labnanat al-'alam'*.[40] Hizbullah's celebration of Lebanese nationalism, even though it evokes religious references to the Garden of Eden, reflects Hizbullah's bid to project its identity as a Lebanese party with shared nationalist imaginaries about Lebanon. In this sense, Hizbullah sends a message to those who accuse it of being more loyal to other states (like Iran) than to Lebanon, asserting that it is a Lebanese party. At the same time, the song shows another aspect of Hizbullah's identity, the one rooted in the theological and historical convictions of the Islamic Shiite tradition. The poem refers to Hussein, one of the principal figures in Shiite history, a reference which, as we saw above, is evident in the early period of Hizbullah poetry as well. Hussein's journey to Karbala, having been invited by the people of Kufa in Iraq to rule over them after the death of the fifth Islamic ruler Mu'awiyah in AD 680, is portrayed as a return. Return here is embodied and continued through the men of Hizbullah who fight with the spirit of the Imam Hussein in them, providing a powerful symbol which invites Imam Hussein to bear witness to the Hizbullah fighters' sense of sincerity and righteousness as descendants and protectors of the faith, 'O, Imam, we and your companions, are in the same orbit.'

History remains a powerful connection insofar as the Shiite tradition is concerned, with past events, such as those in Karbala in Iraq to which Hussein travelled to rule its people, often connected to the Lebanon of today. Abbas, the brother of Hussein who showed strict loyalty to him when he went to Karbala, is continuously evoked, as well as his thirst in solidarity with Sakina—the daughter of Hassan, the other brother of Hussein, who endured extreme thirst during her arrest and was killed prior to Hussein's arrival in Karbala—endowing the song with emotional values and powerful historical and political echoes. The events and stories of Karbala offer lessons in sobriety, patience and steadfastness in the face of harsh adversities. And since the song evokes return, return often suggests preservation of an order that existed before. In this way, the continuity of history is contingent on ideologies, more so than it is on cultures, which are less reverential and accept criticism of the sacred. In addition, the song's use of such historical figures and allusions to battles without explaining their details suggests there exists a 'culture of communication'—one that, in this context, is particular to Hizbullah— which is shared by members of the Shiite community already familiar with this potent history and its meanings.[41]

Themes in Hizbullah's poetry

Apart from references to Iran and Shiite historical figures, Hizbullah's poetry includes other constant tropes: reverence to leaders, most notably Hassan Nasrallah; the commemoration of martyrs; the evocation of significant historical milestones pertaining to the party's history; and references to Palestine and Jerusalem. These themes will be elaborated on in what follows. Iran is a constant thread in the narrative of Hizbullah, and one of the major references whose force of presence does not lessen with time. Thus references to Iran in Hizbullah's poetry persisted even after its heightened 'Lebanonisation' in the post-2006 period. In this context, the Iranian influence on Hizbullah's poetry is connected to Hizbullah being inspired by Iran, and acting as an arm of its ideological representation and propagation in the Arab world. Iran, whether through its leaders, political stances or regional power, is seen as a source of inspiration and principles that are rooted in the Shiite tradition which the Iranian regime acts upon and which should be emulated by the Arab world. Thus in the following poem/song, released after 2006, the late Iranian leader Khomeini is constituted within the spiritual genealogy of the Shiite tradition. His authoritative evocation is particularly important as the poem references his revival and advancement of *wilayat al-faqih*, in which the ultimate power and authority are invested in religious jurisprudence and guardianship over a spectrum of social and political matters:[42]

> We trust the *wilayat*
> It's enough for you (Khomeini) that you had Mohammad in you
> You are the imam and in the *wilayat*, we trust
> Righteousness is his sword and fairness a witness to that
> The fires of Khomeini remain as a banner
> To the forthcoming Mahdi, witnessed by tomorrow
> The reign of Mohammad was entrusted to our Ali
> And to your trust, and the forthcoming Khomeini,
> Righteousness is his sword
> And fairness is a witness to that …[43]

Although the song above does not necessarily project a structural integrity, being composed more of statements rather than a tightly interwoven poetic composition, it holds an ideological cohesion which conveys meanings and themes constitutive of Hizbullah within its Shiite milieu. The lines of the song underpin the Shiite faith, while ascertaining its continuity and embodiment in present figures and events. Khomeini is embodied in the Prophet Muhammad, who, according to the Shiite tradition, handed the reins of power to Ali on his deathbed in AD 632. Thus Ali's descendants are the rightful upholders of power, including Mahdi, the Twelfth Imam who went into occultation (*ghayba*) in the tenth century AD. In this poem/song, Khomeini is also depicted as a guiding torch to Hizbullah, as reflected in the verse 'The fires of Khomeini remain as a banner'. Iran, in this respect, is an important backbone to Hizbullah, and the strength of this backbone stems from the theological convictions in the first place. Hence, as opposed to political alliances alone, religious ones are perceived and communicated as often being stronger and more enduring. The song also sheds light on how integral revolutionary Iran is to Hizbullah in terms of its founding principles as enshrined in the *wilayat al-faqih*, as well as the figures that spearheaded the Iranian Revolution and later the Iranian state and moulded its intellectual and spiritual guidance.[44]

However, while it is important to focus on the Iranian dimension to Hizbullah which is present in all of its outlets, Hizbullah's Arab identity and image are equally significant. This identity manifests itself in clear terms in poetry. In the following song, also released after the 2006 confrontations between Hizbullah and Israel, from which Hizbullah emerged as a pan-Arab hero thanks to its resistance and steadfastness against the Israeli onslaught, Hizbullah's Arab identity is celebrated through the use of familiar Arab nationalist tropes:[45]

> I am the Arab, I am the Arab
> I who do not fear the tyrant
> To die proudly is the highest of wishes
> I am the Arab
> I am the Arab, I am the faith
> The son of the Bible, the son of the Quran
> I am the Arab
> I am human being
> I am the countries
> I descend from 'Adnan
> I am the Arab who refused to be afflicted with tribulations
> I am the Arab
> I am the Arab, I was born free
> I am the determination, the revolution,
> Fire follows my anger
> I am the Arab who refused to be afflicted with tribulations.[46]

The repeatedly assertive declaration 'I am the Arab' leaves no room for doubt as to the ground on which Hizbullah raises its banner, recalling the evocations and constituents of pan-Arab nationalism which classic figures such as Sati' al-Husri (1882–1968), Michel Aflaq (1910–89) and others called for at the end of the nineteenth century and well into the twentieth century, such as language and shared history.[47] The shared history of the Arabs is interestingly captured in the song by the line, 'I descend from "'Adnan".' In the classical historiography of the Arabs, 'Adnan and Qahtan are the two major (figures) tribes from which all

Arabs hail.[48] 'Adnan is the father of the northern tribes of Arabia, extending from the Hijāz of modern-day Saudi Arabia all the way to Syria, Lebanon, Palestine and other adjacent areas; he is essentially the father from whom it is believed the Prophet Muhammad descended. To go as far as 'Adnan is to confirm roots, demonstrate allegiance and authenticity endowed with pan-Arab resonance and values. As characteristic of nationalist discourses, Hizbullah celebrates pan-Arabism in this song, conjuring Arab ancestry and alleged Arabic traits, but also hinting at being a particular Arab, one who does not accept humiliation and tribulations, but fights against odds to regain and assert rights.

In this, Hizbullah hits back at those who went down the path of peace agreements with Israel and capitulations to Western powers, chiefly the United States, which it views as hostile to Arab values and aspirations: 'I am the Arab who refused to be afflicted with tribulations.' Refusal requires an active agent, one who initiates and makes history, rather than being overwhelmed by it. Thus Hizbullah projects a principled image, in which only those who accept its underpinnings, its narrative, are included. Moreover, Hizbullah paints itself not as partisan or of one religious conviction rather than another, but more as an inclusive body, 'I am the Arab ... the son of the Bible, the son of the Quran.' The reference to the Bible and the Quran embraces the three major monotheistic faiths, Judaism, Christianity and Islam, within its fold and claims them as an integral part of its worldview. However, it is important to recall the context of the song here, which coincided with the outburst of popular support and embrace of Hizbullah in the Arab world during and after the 2006 Israeli attack on Lebanon. The party which used to adorn itself and rely on its allies, Iran and Syria, found itself at the centre of attention and admiration by a large section of Arab citizens, including secularists, nationalists, Marxists and Islamists. Since heroism, admiration and defiance are familiar tropes in what is known as the literature of resistance in Arabic literature,[49] Hizbullah was embraced and adulated by many Arab poets who applauded its steadfastness and paid flowery tributes to its leadership, particularly Hizbullah's Secretary General Hassan Nasrallah.

As was mentioned at the start of this chapter, Arab poetry is rife with examples of elegiac poetry to rulers and figures in positions of power in general. Hizbullah and its leaders are no exception in this respect.

Hassan Nasrallah has been the subject of many poems and songs, particularly after 2000 and 2006, the two events that cemented his reputation as a leader with a significant popular power base in the Arab world.[50] In the following song, released after 2006 by Firqat al-fajr, the legitimising force of history is bestowed on Hassan Nasrallah, with several images which bind and constitute him as a leader in his faith, Shiism, and of Hizbullah. The poem is full of images of heroism which are characteristic of Islamist poetry in general.[51] It opens with:

> The sun is colder than the heat of our pride …
> We have given our allegiance to Nasrallah, your grandson,
> The Hassan of Hussein found Haidar[52] steadfast
> The laments of Zeinab are still in our limbs
> Until we drew our sharp swords
> The Mahdi here has come with the wound of our Hussein
> We will follow him, and will heal the wounds
> O, Hussein, we have come back with Nasrallah
> And the blood has won.

History is presented as a linear narrative in which key figures in Shiite history, Hussein through to Zeinab, Mahdi and Nasrallah, have the main roles. It is particularly noteworthy in this narrative that Nasrallah, to whom the fighters vow allegiance, is referred to as the grandson of Hussein, a common mode of reference in the Arabic tradition as emotional bonds of affiliation overcome spatial boundaries.[53] In addition, the poem/song includes an image of return, a theme that dominates Hizbullah's poetry. This is a return to the eternal presence of mystical Shiite models, and their rebirth in figures such as Hassan Nasrallah. The historical links are made through images of intense passion: 'The sun is colder than the heat of our pride …' and strong historical affiliation and remembrance, 'The laments of Zeinab are still in our limbs …' The historical journey which remembers and evokes the principal Shiite figures, including Zeinab, the daughter of Ali who was captured in the Battle of Karbala and humiliated by the army of Yazid, the son of Mu'awiyah, highlights the literal and uninterrupted historical narrative of sacrifice and steadfastness in the face of persecution as exemplified in Karbala.

After the 2006 war, Arab poets joined in the praise of Nasrallah, following a historical trend in which poetry served as the highest form of expression and virtue in terms of its interaction with and absorption of political and social events. In the following poem, the young Palestinian–Egyptian poet Tamim al-Barghouti (b.1977), who acquired fame through his presence on the pan-Arab television programme *Sha'ir al-malyun* (The Poet of the Million), pays homage to Hassan Nasrallah:

> The doves of the towers pray for you
> You teach them generosity, you, the son of the prophet,
> You hand them ripe grains with your right hand
> They carry them and fly south
> They do not eat the grains, but scatter them on the mountains,
> For some women and men
> They ask them about the direction of fighting
> And carry your greetings to them
> If a journalist asked the doves
> They would say that the sky is there, shading you,
> And that you have spread out the sky before them
> The air of the country prays for you
> The flowers of the meadows pray for you.[54]

Nasrallah is evoked in a way that suggests heroism and hope. Tamim al-Barghouti's use of such references as 'doves', 'generosity', 'ripe grains', 'shade', 'flowers' and 'meadows' speaks of fertility and openness to a bright future, which according to him is what Hizbullah represents. Unlike other poems and songs by close affiliates and members of Hizbullah, which are carefully crafted along ideological lines, this poem is from an outsider, at least to a certain extent. But al-Barghouti's poem is not detached from Hizbullah's foundational ideology as he refers to Nasrallah as 'the son of the Prophet'. He thus affiliates himself with Hizbullah in his evocation of nostalgic and nationalist directions, where battles were fought and notable events involving Hizbullah took place, as when he says: 'You hand them ripe grains with your right hand; they carry them and fly south.' The poem is clearly grounded in celebrating heroism and paying homage to its representative for having 'spread out the sky' before the Arabs after their horizons had narrowed, given the many defeats and setbacks Arabs faced at the hands of Israel. Thus even phrases such as 'the air of the country', 'prays for you' and 'the flowers of the meadows pray for you' suggest that the poet should also join them—the forces of nature—in eulogy to Nasrallah, whom he credits with invigorating the Arabs with hope of ultimately overcoming Israel, the state responsible for so many of their woes, given its occupation of their land and repeated humiliation of them. Moreover, al-Barghouti embraces one of Nasrallah's famous statements which he expressed in one of his speeches in July 2008, following the release of prominent Lebanese prisoners from Israeli prisons, in which he stated that 'identity is resistance'.[55]

Broadly, committed poetry that interacts with reality and deals with socio-political issues and manifestations gives authority and opens further venues to those whom it hails. Tamim al-Barghouti's eulogy serves to enhance Nasrallah's visibility and authority on several levels. It hails him; it almost makes him a 'brand'.[56] The hailing and branding are not unique to Hizbullah, for that is how many politicians and political parties thrust themselves onto the public sphere, objectifying themselves and their convictions to the point of saturation. Here, Nasrallah becomes the embodiment of the very ideas and discourse he puts forward. This is reflected in a famous song by the renowned Lebanese singer Julia Butrus, released after 2006. The lyrics for the song are taken from Nasrallah's letter to Hizbullah's fighters during the 2006 Israeli onslaught on Lebanon. Nasrallah's letter is indicative of the complementary roles played by the various strata of Hizbullah's members, including the leaders, the fighters, the professionals, members of Lebanon's Shiite community and Arab supporters. The letter is itself a poetic engagement by a leader aware of the value of poetry in boosting the morale of fighters during hard times and as a medium of authenticity and truthfulness that speaks to people's humanity.[57] Since the song, titled *Ahibba'i* (My Beloved), has been referred to elsewhere,[58] and in this book, here are a few lines:[59]

> My beloved, my beloved, my beloved
> I have heard your letter
> In which there is pride and faith
> For you are, as you said, the men of God in the battlefield …
> You are the builders of a civilisation …
> You are our forthcoming victory …

The land will be liberated through you

With you, we change the world and build the best tomorrow

And with you, we march and triumph, we march and triumph …

The letter/song underlines the interactive nature of Hizbullah's communication practices. It starts with the evocative construction 'my beloved' and is followed with the active verb *istama'tu* (I have heard), echoing an emotional bond that resonates with paternal feelings, similar to what a father would say to his children, *istama'tu*. It acknowledges their description of themselves, 'the men of God in the battlefield'. On such a basis, where there are loyalty and religious convictions, the fighters become 'builders of a civilisation' as well as a means by which the world will be changed. It is an upbeat letter/song rooted in confidence and an unshakeable faith in the veracity of the path, the path of resistance that Nasrallah and Hizbullah champion in their discourse.

Poetry, songs and art in general accentuate the discourse of this path, impregnating it with an emotional resonance and virtuous authenticity. The following poem, read as an introduction to one of Nasrallah's speeches in 2010, makes use of Nasrallah's words in poetic constructions imbued with mysticism:

Four

And the impossible travel … our travel …

The glowing timbers … our bracelets

And the horizon is wider …

Four

And the water still inhabits the warmth of our swords

And the names surmount our longings

And the victory which had been accustomed to our heroisms

Has found a homeland for itself here …

And it will not be overcome …

O, our people, the most honourable of people …

The verses were recited prior to a speech Nasrallah delivered in the stadium of Ar-Rayah in the southern suburbs of Beirut on the anniversary of the 'Divine Victory' on 3 August 2010. They are close to surreal, symbolic poetry, poetry which, though anchored in the reality of Hizbullah, is not entirely Hizbullah. It has a cadence of its own which exceeds the object of which it speaks. There is ingenuity in the images, such as: 'And the impossible travel ... our travel ... The glowing timbers ... our bracelets.' However, it is only when the poem is read backwards that we see the elevated style of hailing Nasrallah as it evokes one of his most memorable lines as he emerged following the 2006 war, calling the people of the South of Lebanon 'the most honourable of people'. The poem is sealed with Nasrallah's phrase, conveying the sense of mysticism the poem embodies and revealing in the process the subject of its evocation by using the very language Nasrallah utilised to highlight the importance of an event and the people who were at the heart of it. It speaks of the difficult and painful moments for the Lebanese who bore the brunt of Israeli attacks, but endured the fighting and shielded the fighters of Hizbullah from this attack. Nasrallah's language is used to reassure, create further effects, encapsulate historical moments of significant values and draw a conclusion to a poem wrapped in mystic references.

Palestine is another constant element in the political discourse of Hizbullah, projected in various media outlets and highlighted in almost all of Nasrallah's speeches as a usurped land that should be liberated and redeemed from the Zionists (the term Hizbullah typically uses when referring to Israel). In the following anecdotal poem, the language amalgamates existential aspects and political messages, intertwined within an anecdote, told with panache and style by the poet Omar al-Farra. The poem was read in 2007 to a packed audience of Hizbullah supporters in an auditorium in Beirut, who looked mesmerised by the performance. The relationship between the audience and the poet in this case is one of intimacy and mutual recognition of the topic of which he speaks and the language of the poem, as it is written and recited in colloquial Levantine, rural Arabic, with folkloric dimensions to it. And it adds to the poem and makes it vivid that there is a love story at its heart. The poem's title is *Khuttar* (the uninvited guests, or the guests who come without prior notice):

> *Khuttar* (the uninvited guests) came to us in the evening and we were not prepared for their coming
>
> As I glimpsed the beloved of my heart with them, my mind went absent,
>
> We wanted time to melt, and the clock to stop,
>
> And forget the nights of sadness and the greedy eyes

THE HIZBULLAH PHENOMENON

With my eyelashes fluttering in order to see you
Looking with delight, when you say goodbye,
My fear is that our separation and your absence will be long,
Those daggers will strike at me for a long time,
One night, I came to you while in desperate need
With the heat of timbers as our witness, and the poetry of love at night,
It is possible that I could die at dawn, if you leave this night,
You who are going to Jerusalem, my love travels with you,
To attend the wedding nights, and grow apple trees,
We missed the sun, while the bosom is full of wounds,
O, my wound, murmur, murmur,
The sound of darkness is shameful
I have befriended estrangement and longing
And the singing bulbul
I did not see a day of companionship, nor is my heart comfortable even for a moment
O, you who are driving the stars,
My aim is the robe of the uninvited guest, just go
Stay with me after your absence, but now go,
'Alilah (I) awaits the arrival of the beloved,
Say to my people that the girl is in love
She is looking for the right time, cover her, she is cold,
She hopes for a peaceful sleep, and she hopes for a pomegranate,
O, time, time evolves with us, and I am wounded,
I saw hope with patience, a string in the wing of an eagle,
O, the exile, the abode of my people, they have forgotten me wounded,
Every time, I call out, O beloved, one wave after another,
My eyesight drifts and so does hope, and the wave goes away,
Time has betrayed me, O, time has betrayed me and I said, I have grown bored,
Through the eye of a needle, after your separation, I have grown bored,
If I could pour out tears, for I have grown bored of the sea, and no longer tolerate the drips of the clouds
Yesterday, in the day of farewell, I strayed, I saw tears as tears,
I no longer recognise the eclipse of the sun
I did not realise that the sweet had bid farewell, O my heart, the ashes of sadness,

I do not think that he will come back,

We heard the music of the wedding, and their bullets aflame,

Khuttar, unannounced guests, came to us in the morning; they cut the wing of a raven,

And narrated a story about him,

They brought a handful of sand with them, they said to me, your love has gone (died) yesterday,

While afflicted with the love of the land

Reciting a love poem

Under the shade of a grapevine

Every time, the wound bleeds and I hear a sound of absence (disappearance)

My tongue enchants with happiness

O, mother, the moon is by the door![60]

This is not a poem that is written by an affiliate of Hizbullah; nor does it have any of the prominent figures or even themes, in the strict sense of the term, of Hizbullah figures in it. But it situates its subject within the context of Hizbullah, southern Lebanon and the long drawn-out battles waged by Hizbullah fighters in the South to regain their land from the Israeli occupation. Besides that, it is a notable love poem with familiar emotional dimensions, such as longing, sadness at separation, affection, romanticism and deep hope, suffused with almost universal symbols of love emblems, such as 'the moon', 'apple', 'pomegranate' and so on. The marriage of these two contexts, love and battles, wounds and death, yields a vivid story, hence the mesmerising effect that al-Farra's recital brings. The audience reacts ecstatically to his story by applauding the poet and approving the sentiments and meanings that the poem embodies. The poem demonstrates Hizbullah's enhanced status in the Arab world, as witnessed by the moral support and solidarity Hizbullah received following that war, reminiscent of the support the Palestinian national movement garnered in 1968 as it seemed to rattle the power dynamics in the region with its stiff resistance to the Israeli occupation of Palestinian territories.

The poem *Khuttar* tells the story of fighters who went to southern Lebanon to carry out a military operation in the occupied Palestinian territories. This could be read as a veiled reference to Hizbullah fighters who abducted the two Israeli soldiers in 2006, an act that triggered the

Israeli onslaught on Lebanon. At one point in the poem, those Hizbullah fighters sought refuge in one of the houses in southern Lebanon to wait for the moon to disappear so that they could camouflage themselves aided by the darkness of the night and undertake their operation inside Palestine. The poem is narrated by a girl in the house who fell in love with one of the fighters. In his introduction to the poem, al-Farra refers to the girl as 'a symbol of the land'. That the poem anchors its subject in a group of fighters, heading south to launch a military operation and along the way, for tactical reasons, going uninvited to a house in the South, suggests the intimate interaction between the fighters and the people of the South. In this case, this interaction between the fighters and the people results in perhaps the highest form of human bonding, romantic love, one that the lover, the girl, evokes vividly and longingly: 'Those daggers will strike at me for a long time; one night, I came to you while in desperate need; with the heat of timbers as our witness; and the poetry of love at night; It is possible that I could die at dawn, if you leave this night.'

But since Hizbullah believes that the liberation of Palestine can only happen through resistance, and since it has appropriated resistance as its essential identity, and the girl in love knows that, she cannot stop her lover from continuing his journey with his group of fighters. Lovers usually long for their beloved to stay, but she puts the land, as she is the land herself, before herself: 'You who are going to Jerusalem, my love travels with you … O, you have who is driving the stars, I am after the robe of the uninvited guest, just go; remain to me after the absence, but now, go.' But as they embark on their journey, longing with all that it potentially gives rise to by way of tears, anguish and sleepiness, 'She hopes for a peaceful sleep, and she hopes for a pomegranate.' As her lover seems to disappear for a long time, she despairs and feels the worst: 'No longer the sweet and tender, O, my heart, the ashes of sadness, I do not think, he will return.' Her intuitions are confirmed when she is told that he died during the operation: 'They brought a handful of sand with them, they said to me, your love has gone (died) yesterday.' However, she does not wallow in despair at her lover's passing. Instead she sees hope and expresses pride in her lover. Hence the appearance of the moon, the reason for which the uninvited guests (the fighters) sought refuge in the house of the lover, becomes a sign of hope for her and happiness that this earth will always shine for her when she defends it while armed with hope and optimism: 'My tongue enchants with happiness; O, mother, the moon is by the door.'

Omar al-Farra's poem is filled with meanings and references situated within Hizbullah's space of ideology, practice and presence in Lebanon and the Arab world. He widens the appeal of Hizbullah in the Arab world by including Palestine and using it as a direction to which the fighters of Hizbullah head. To this end, it could be said that at so many points in its history, Hizbullah has succeeded in expanding its base and space, using political, cultural and literary agencies and activities to prove itself potent and invaluable to the Arab world and indispensable to the Lebanese state. However, with the Arab revolutions in mind, constituted within the Arab Spring, Hizbullah's position and identity in general, particularly in relation to the Syrian Baath regime which Hizbullah publicly endorses, are increasingly being questioned. Al-Farra himself is known to support the Syrian regime. That Hizbullah is a close ally of the Syrian regime translates in al-Farra's endorsement of Hizbullah. He sees Hizbullah as the embodiment of resistance and steadfastness which the official Syrian discourse advocates.

Whether other poets from the Arab world will flock to praise and sing for Hizbullah given its unpopular siding with the Syrian regime, which has committed serious crimes against its own people, is a trajectory to be followed. Ahmad Fouad Negm, one of the famous Egyptian poets who (along with his daughter) played a prominent role in the Egyptian January 25 Revolution in 2011 and who had penned a poem for Hizbullah and praised it after 2006, has asked for clarifications about its support for the Syrian regime, calling on Hassan Nasrallah during a live television programme from Tunisia to denounce the Assad regime and distance himself from it: 'Do you like what the Baath regime is doing to the Syrian people ... is it useful to support what is happening in any way?'[61]

Conclusion

Hizbullah, like all other political entities, was not founded in a cultural vacuum. From its inception, it tucked itself within an existing literary and cultural Arabic tradition that dates back centuries. Even its name 'Hizbullah' is derived from one of the major constituents of the Arabic tradition, the Quran: 'Surely the *party of God* (Hizbullah) are they that shall be triumphant'. Poetry in the Arabic tradition has often reflected the authenticity of culture and acted as a guardian of its language and an expression of its values and norms.

The poetry of Hizbullah revolves around its identity and taps into the cultural and political Arabic tradition. As this chapter has shown, this poetry serves as an effective form of communication, symbolising values of rootedness and virtues of resistance and steadfastness, and hailing supporters. It highlights the beliefs, references, battles, victories and views of Hizbullah, whether in relation to its own self or to the others with whom it interacts—from local agents within the complex sectarian make-up of Lebanon—to Iran, its intimate and co-religionist ally, to Palestine and to the Arab world, and to Israel and America which the party portrays in its discourse as the arch-enemy of the Islamic world. The poetry of Hizbullah becomes particularly important and visible after 2000 and 2006, two significant dates in the history of the party and its appeal. As Lila Abu-Lughod shows in her study of the Bedouin society in Egypt and the role of poetry in openly expressing hidden sentiments,[62] poetry serves as an invaluable ethnographic material that broadens the scope of analysis. This applies to Hizbullah insofar as the movement and its political and cultural base are concerned. Though Hizbullah's poetry is predictable and the tropes it covers sound familiar, it still sheds light on the language and sentiments that underpin its ideology and its relationship with ordinary people. It strengthens that relationship through language that has been familiar and earthly, and, in this way, it demonstrates the poetics of an ideology that is rooted in particular socio-political conditions and the emotional reservoirs it creates and inhabits.

HASSAN NASRALLAH: THE CENTRAL ACTOR IN HIZBULLAH'S POLITICAL COMMUNICATION STRATEGIES

Dina Matar

Populist movements, as well as formal and informal political groups, have often used charismatic leaders, symbols, imagery and language to mobilise supporters and enhance their appeal. Hizbullah is no exception to this—indeed, the group has proven to be remarkably persistent in terms of its efforts to cultivate and disseminate a symbolic and inspirational image of its secretary general, Hassan Nasrallah, as a uniquely charismatic leader whose own personal ethos, integrity and credibility have created a following even outside Hizbullah's main constituency. Nasrallah is depicted in numerous articles, books and media commentaries, as well as posters hung in public spaces, as a modest cleric-cum-political ideologue with 'genuine'[1] charisma, whose political path has emulated to a certain extent that of Iran's supreme and spiritual leader Imam Ayatollah Ruhullah Khomeini, as well as other figures within Lebanon's Shiite community, including the equally charismatic Imam Musa al-Sadr.

Since his appointment as secretary general in 1992, but particularly following the liberation of South Lebanon in 2000 and the 2006 war with Israel, Nasrallah has been a highly visible celebrity-like leader who is rarely absent from the public sphere, with a superstar status and a substantial following. His appearances—speeches, interviews, rallies and engagements—are publicised ahead of time and presented by Hizbullah's multimedia platforms as dramatic political performances that demand urgent attention and action. Political performances, or spectacles, are key constituents of political life as they play an important role in securing the consent of the public, reinforcing obedience and sustaining the conditions under which political elites rule, particularly in authoritarian states.[2] As Lisa Wedeen argues in her analysis of the state-constructed cult of the late Syrian President Hafez al-Assad, political performances and spectacles serve 'to anchor visually and audibly politically significant ideas' and to frame the ways people see themselves as citizens.[3] In the digital age, the mediation of political performances can create a false sense of intimacy, reducing the distance between the leader and the led, and disrupting the traditional divide between the elites and the masses.[4] Such aspects of the mediation processes are true of Nasrallah's political performances, which, along with his conversational mode of address and his use of potent religious–political language, have produced an effective, if not powerful, 'image of presence' that served as a tool for mobilisation and as a model of compulsion.[5]

Hassan Nasrallah is without doubt the key medium (actor) in Hizbullah's political communication strategies—the combination of his persona, demeanour and language has provided powerful imaginary significations that helped him and Hizbullah mobilise alternative collective identities over time and at particular historical junctures.[6] Hence, this chapter pays particular attention to how Nasrallah's 'image of presence' and charismatic authority were cultivated, institutionalised and validated in culture. Using a socio-historical analytical framework, the chapter begins by tracing Nasrallah's rise within Hizbullah's hierarchical power structures and his evolution from a devout humble cleric into a larger-than-life charismatic leader at the beginning of the twenty-first century. It then explores the methods and practices Hizbullah used to institutionalise and validate his religious–political persona, and the ways in which Nasrallah himself was involved in processes of self-mediation that served to centralise power in his public persona, to engage his target audiences' loyalty and to obscure faultlines in his and his party's rhetoric during particular historical junctures. As Roger Silverstone argues, mediation is dialectical, balancing potential opportunities with structures, but it is also uneven, with some actors more powerful than others.[7] The chapter concludes with an evaluation of the challenges posed to Nasrallah's mediated image of presence and charismatic authority by Lebanon's contentious internal politics and his support for the Syrian regime in its battle to suppress the popular uprising that began in March 2011.

Nasrallah: on the path to leadership

Hassan Nasrallah was born in a neighbourhood in East Beirut on 31 August 1960. His family was not particularly religious or political. His father Abdelkarim Nasrallah was a vegetable and fruit salesman, who moved to Beirut from Bazouriyeh, a small Shiite village 3 miles east of the coastal town of Tyr in South Lebanon. From an early age, Nasrallah was attracted to learning and theological studies because, as he put it, 'of the milieu I lived in',[8] in reference to his early association with the fledgling community of politically engaged Shiite Islamists that began to emerge in the 1960s and 1970s. Nasrallah's father recalls that his son, the eldest of nine children, developed an interest in Islamic teachings and politics by reading newspapers and books about Islam and politics.[9] His mother echoes these sentiments, noting that her son showed signs of responsibility and maturity from an early age in 'looking after his younger siblings when she would be out of the house helping her husband ... he would help me pick the olives even if he had much homework to do. Since his early childhood, he was brave ... and religious.'[10] In fact, while his brothers helped at the vegetable and fruit stall, Nasrallah, as the story goes, would walk to the city centre in search of second-hand books, and then spend the time reading and praying in various mosques in the mainly Christian part of Beirut. Speaking of his childhood, Nasrallah says:

My father Abdulkarim used to sell fruit and vegetables; my brothers would help him. When my father's financial status improved, he opened a small grocery store in the neighborhood, and I would go there to help him. We had a picture of Imam Musa al-Sadr hanging on the wall of the store. I would sit on a chair in front of the picture and stare at it. I wished that I would become like him one day. We did not have a mosque in our neighborhood (*Karantina*), so I would go to the *Sin El-Fil*, *Burj Hammoud*, or *Nab'ah* mosques for prayers. I would read anything I found, especially Islamic books. Any book that I could not understand, I would put aside to read it when I grew older.[11]

Nasrallah's family relocated to Bazouriyeh at the beginning of the Lebanese civil war in 1975. It was during this period that he began to be drawn to political organisations, joining *harakat al-mahroumeen* (the Movement of the Deprived), which had been established by Imam Musa al-Sadr a year earlier, and which later became known as Amal. Though most politically active young men preferred to join leftist secular groups at the time, Nasrallah decided to gather several friends who shared his religious leanings and helped organise meetings in the village's Islamic centre. Nasrallah says of this period: 'My choice to join Amal was a conscious and deliberate decision because I greatly admired Imam Musa al-Sadr. I was only 15 at the time. My interest in my village Bazouriyeh was decreasing because it became the magnet for secular and Marxist intellectual activists, particularly supporters of the Lebanese Communist Party. My brother Hussein and I joined Amal, and despite my young age, I soon became the representative of Amal in our village.'[12]

Nasrallah maintains that his main ambition was to travel to the city of Najaf in Iraq in order to pursue religious studies at the popular *hawzah* (religious seminary) run by Sayyed Mohammed Baqir al-Sadr, one of the foremost Shiite scholars and theoreticians of the time. Al-Sadr was reported to have discerned greatness in his new pupil even at this early stage, saying: 'I smell (in you) an aroma of leadership; you are one of the *Ansar* [followers] of the *Mahdi* ...'[13] In Iraq, Nasrallah was introduced to Abbas al-Mussawi, al-Sadr's 25-year-old disciple, who took him as his protégé. Nasrallah's memories of those days show him to be an ordinary young man interested in religious studies:

I went to Najaf when I was 16 years old. When I arrived, I had no money left in my pockets. But, there are more than a few strangers and lonely people there. More important, of course, is the fact that a scholar must learn how to live a respectable life with empty hands. My food was bread and water, and my bed was a rectangular piece of sponge mattress. As soon as I arrived, I asked the other Lebanese scholars living there how I could get my letter of recommendation to Ayatollah al-Sadr, who was considered as a pillar of the religious seminary. They told me that the martyr Abbas al-Mussawi could do that for me. When I first met him, I assumed he was Iraqi because of his darker skin, so I spoke to him in classical Arabic. He then arranged for me to have a room next to his *hawzah* and gave me some money to buy some books and clothes. This was how our acquaintance and close friendship began.[14]

Life in the seminary was simple. Nasrallah shared a room with other students, sleeping on a foam mattress on the floor—a habit he continued to be attached to even after he had become Hizbullah's leader—and living off a handful of dinars each month given to him by his tutor. His studies were demanding; he had little free time as Mussawi expected his pupils to work hard. In fact, he did not take any time off from his studies, completing all requirements in two years as opposed to the usual five. Mussawi introduced Nasrallah to Iran's revolutionary and spiritual leader Ayatollah Ruhullah Khomeini who had by then formulated the theory of *wilayat al-faqih*, which advocated the creation of an Islamic state ruled by sharia law and administered by an expert of Islamic jurisprudence—the *faqih*.[15]

During that period, little was known about Hassan Nasrallah or of his oratorical skills and charisma. However, an early sign of what was later to be publicised as his unusual personal qualities is revealed in an unverifiable testimony by a fellow cleric who knew him in Iran: 'I was mesmerised, he is more than charismatic if you listen to him—he is mythic. But as soon as you start asking him [theological] questions, you're surprised how little knowledge he has.'[16] Indeed, Nasrallah has yet to achieve the highest rank in the Shiite clerical hierarchy, that of an ayatollah, though he is already a Sayyed.[17]

Nasrallah did not complete his studies as he had wanted. In 1978, he was forced to escape to Lebanon when the Iraqi Baathist regime launched a major crackdown against Shiite Islamists, arresting and subsequently executing Baqir al-Sadr, and expelling dozens of Lebanese students on the grounds that they were working as spies for Syria. In Lebanon, he enrolled at a newly established religious school in Baalbek to continue his studies. His return to Lebanon coincided with the beginning of a critical phase in the history of the country. In March of that year, Israel invaded South Lebanon to drive out the Palestine Liberation Organisation from the area, beginning a 22-year occupation of the South. In August, Musa al-Sadr[18] disappeared while on a trip to Libya.

Nasrallah's political and activist profile took off when he re-joined Amal on his return to Lebanon.[19] In 1982, the year of the Israeli invasion of Lebanon—which is often cited as the catalyst in Hizbullah's crystallisation into an effective resistance movement in the South—Nasrallah was put in charge of the Beqaa' region in the east and appointed to serve with the movement's political bureau. However, he opted to leave Amal when the schism between the secular-oriented founders of the movement and other members who sought to Islamise the movement widened. In an interview about his decision, Nasrallah says: 'From the organisational point of view, we in the Bekaa' took issue with certain political positions taken by Amal ... [it] was no longer up to the task required at that particular juncture and we established the nucleus for a new movement, which became known as Hizbullah ... We enrolled in military camps until the arrival of the Iranian Revolutionary Guards who fired us with the spirit that prevailed in Iran and helped us on the organizational level.'[20] By 1985, the year when Hizbullah published its Open Letter, its quasi-political manifesto that outlined the party's aims and ideology,[21] Nasrallah was put in charge of Hizbullah's organisational activities in Beirut, where he had close contacts with the Iranian embassy, and affiliated militants like the late Imad Mughniyeh, Amal activists and Shiite fighters across Lebanon.[22] Within two years, he was appointed chief executive officer in Hizbullah's *shura* (consultative) council and began delivering rousing speeches to party supporters and new recruits. Attesting to Nasrallah's increasingly vital role within the party, a veteran Hizbullah official recalls that even when Sheikh Abbas al-Mussawi was elected secretary general in 1989, 'it was his protégé who drew the eyes of the party's files and ranks'.[23]

The political transformation of Nasrallah

Hassan Nasrallah was elected Hizbullah's secretary general on 18 February 1992, two days after the assassination of Abbas al-Mussawi. Sheikh Naim Qassem was elected as his deputy. Mussawi had replaced Sheikh Subhi al-Tufaili, the party's first secretary general, with whom both Nasrallah and Mussawi disagreed, particularly with regard to Hizbullah's public stance on the Taif Accord.[24] Such disagreements, it was reported, contributed to Nasrallah's decision to depart for the Iranian city of Qom in order to continue his interrupted religious studies.[25] Nasrallah was Hizbullah's *shura* council's unanimous choice, though he had been reluctant to take on the duty of head of the party, preferring to continue his religious studies:

As far as I was concerned, and from the very beginning, there were no obstacles to my assuming the position [of secretary-general]. Some of the brethren proposed that I fill that position, and then my name was proposed a second time; we always took into consideration extraordinary circumstances, and my name was always there, regardless of whether or not these extraordinary circumstances had taken place, or whether the legal period had simply elapsed.[26]

His appointment coincided with a radical transformation in Hizbullah's image from an Islamist resistance movement working outside the Lebanese system to a national Lebanese party playing by the political rules. Nasrallah supported Hizbullah's participation in Lebanon's first post-civil war elections in mid-1992, a stance reflecting his pragmatic political attitude when dealing with internal Lebanese issues. He initiated an expansionist campaign aimed at widening Hizbullah's reach— supervising the development and acceleration of his party's social, educational and communication services, and approving investments to expand Hizbullah's multimedia platforms.[27] At the same time, he oversaw a substantial rise in the number of military operations against Israel— attacks against Israeli forces in southern Lebanon rose from nineteen in 1990 to 187 in 1994, for example. In the few months before the liberation of the South, Hizbullah was launching as many as 300 attacks against Israeli forces per month.[28] While Nasrallah could not have claimed full credit for the number or the success of these military operations, he was largely responsible for the consolidation and institutionalisation of the group's political communication strategy and propaganda campaigns, which eventually won Hizbullah broad Shiite support in Lebanon[29] and helped transform his own image into the Arab world's foremost charismatic leader in the twentieth century.

The roots of the transformation of Hassan Nasrallah's image were laid in the second half of the 1990s when Hizbullah's resistance operations against Israel boosted its domestic credentials as well as Nasrallah's own negotiating powers in the country. 'Operation Grapes of Wrath' in 1996 served to draw attention to Hizbullah's role as a viable national resistance party. As different Lebanese media and nationals rallied behind the right to resist, Hizbullah intensified its media campaigns and strategies in order to appeal to the wider Lebanese public while warning Israel against further attacks.[30] The signing of the April Understanding provided political legitimacy to Hizbullah's military operations in the South and restricted Israeli attacks on civilian areas. It also saw the transformation of Nasrallah's image into the undisputed leader of the resistance and gave him increased negotiating powers in the Lebanese political sphere. Nasrallah constructed the agreement as a victory for Hizbullah,[31] a discourse he would enunciate on other occasions to legitimise his party's role as the protector of Lebanon's civilians: 'We can say this Understanding is a new attempt at ensuring the protection of Lebanese civilians … that we are bound by it, and agree to its terms. As for the movement of resistance, it remains intact … We believe that what happened was a great victory and that it was above all a victory for the Lebanese people—for Lebanon, Syria, the Arabs and Muslims. … we intend to preserve it. To this end we are prepared to tolerate, to a certain degree, those who take advantage of the situation, even at our expense …'[32]

On 12 September 1997, Nasrallah's image changed almost overnight. The date marked the martyrdom of his eighteen-year-old son Hadi in a military operation against Israel. Nasrallah's dignified reaction to his son's death and his *tadhiya* (sacrifice) of his son (according to Hizbullah and popular discourse) saw a cross-sectarian, impassioned outpouring of emotions and support for a man who had lost his eldest son, just like many ordinary people. Nasrallah's speech reacting to the news was broadcast live on al-Manar, blending it with footage showing him visiting the families of other martyrs. It then repeated the broadcast numerous times,[33] thus turning Nasrallah's performance into a pseudo-media event[34] that brought Lebanese nationals together as a collective. In an interview almost four years later, Nasrallah revealed that he had resisted weeping in public for his son because he did not want the Israelis to take this as a sign of weakness, but that he wept in private as any father would do:[35]

I had to give a speech and as normal in these moments, I felt the sweat coming down my face and into my eyes … I wanted to get a tissue paper to wipe my sweat … at least from my eyeglasses, but I thought these television stations … reporting the event might be selling their film to Israel … and people will assume I was wiping tears … and I preferred not to give the enemy an image of a grieving father breaking out in public over the death of his eldest son while asking others to become martyrs.[36]

From that date onwards, Hizbullah's media platforms as well as other Arab commentators constructed Nasrallah as a selfless leader with deep organic roots in culture, and as 'a man among equals', an example of ultimate dedication and sacrifice that should be emulated by Arab leaders and nationals. In Egypt, Magdi Hussein wrote in *Ash-Sha'b* newspaper:

'This aggressive action has turned into a new victory for the *mujahidden*. No one knew that Sheikh Hassan Nasrallah would send his son of 18 years old to the front lines … At a time when many (Arab) politicians in government and in opposition provide their children with different aspects of a life of luxury, we see here an ascending Islamist model [of selflessness]. This wonderful model shows us how Nasrallah refused negotiations with Israel to retrieve the body of his martyred son. … it is a model that will remain a source of inspiration for all in the Arab and Muslim worlds.'[37] When a deal was reached to exchange the remains of dead Israeli soldiers for Lebanese prisoners and bodies, Nasrallah did not put his son's name ahead of other resistance fighters' bodies, leading one commentator to opine: 'He [Nasrallah] is more than a symbol; he is charismatic, articulate, straightforward and a mastermind in politics … With Hassan Nasrallah, the political scenery seems to be different.'[38]

The liberation of the South enhanced Nasrallah's public image as a national and Arab hero. To mark the occasion, Nasrallah addressed a 100,000-strong crowd in an open-air venue in the southern town of Bint Jbeil, his language merging Hizbullah's Islamic identity with Lebanon's national one while also framing the withdrawal as a victory for all Lebanese people, irrespective of their political or religious affiliations:

On the day of resistance and liberation, on the day of the great historic victory … We meet here to celebrate the victory achieved by martyrdom and blood. … I would like to say to all the Lebanese people; you have to see this victory as a victory for all the Lebanese, not only for Hizbullah or for any other movement … this is Lebanon's victory.[39]

A few months later, the second Palestinian intifada (uprising) that erupted at the end of September further boosted Nasrallah's domestic and regional standing, particularly as he was quick to announce in public and on many occasions Hizbullah's support for the Palestinians, whose plight and right to self-determination every Arab leader had embraced to boost his national and Arab credentials. Speaking to the Kuwaiti *al-Rai al-'Aam* newspaper less than a week after the start of the uprising, Nasrallah claimed that the liberation had changed the rules of the regional conflict with Israel: 'I always thought than an *intifada* would break out after the victory in south Lebanon, as both a reaction to it and a consequence of it … We are committed, in principle, to supporting this *intifada* and standing side by side with the Palestinian people.'[40] Less than three years after the liberation, Nasrallah negotiated a prisoner exchange agreement with Israel under which Israel freed twenty Lebanese and 400 Palestinian prisoners in exchange for one Israeli businessman and the bodies of three Israeli soldiers. Nasrallah, along with a full state delegation, a guard of honour and thousands of Lebanese nationals, was at Beirut airport in person to meet the released prisoners, including eleven Hizbullah affiliates, the occasion lending him a statesman-like image and status in Lebanon's domestic space.

However, the assassination of Rafic Hariri on 14 February 2005 led to domestic political tensions and disquiet about Hizbullah's ascendancy and its insistence on keeping its arms, as well as its close alliance with the Syrian regime, which was viewed as being behind the assassination. Nasrallah called a rally of around 800,000 supporters who gathered close to Hariri's memorial in Martyrs' Square in Beirut on 8 March 2005, sparking a counter-protest on 14 March. Nasrallah condemned the assassination as an anti-nationalist act and called for parliamentary consultations to appoint a new prime minister. However, while calling for national dialogue and unity, Nasrallah issued a clear threat to Hizbullah's domestic foes, his language serving as a good example of what Judith Palmer Harik has labelled Hizbullah's 'ideological ambiguity',[41] a constant strategy Nasrallah has used in his speeches and addresses:

We gather to remind the world and to remember our partners in the nation that this is the square that pulls us together … it is the square that Israel had destroyed, that civil wars had destroyed … its unity has been supported and safeguarded by Syria and its soldiers … we condemn the heinous crime that led to the assassination of the leader and comrade Hariri … This assassination is a national cause and should be extracted from political affiliations and concerns. Lebanon … is not Somalia … If some people imagine that they can put the state of Lebanon, its regime, security, stability and strategic option in disarray, or thwart its relationships and positions through street demonstrations, banners, slogans or the media they are simply deluding themselves.[42]

The 2006 war between Lebanon and Israel completed the transformation of Nasrallah from a humble religious leader into Hizbullah's first charismatic leader in the media age. The war was the first in the region to be televised round the clock by diverse transnational broadcasters, including Al-Jazeera and al-Manar. All of Nasrallah's political performances, including his interviews, statements and speeches, were televised in full and repeated constantly to audiences in Lebanon, the Arab world and beyond, helping him transcend the prosaic role of party functionary to become the very embodiment of the group.[43]

Nasrallah gave a stream of interviews and delivered numerous speeches in which he detailed military operations, actions, strategies and plans while articulating a utilitarian and instrumentalist language evoking a powerful concept of resistance that was more nationalistic than religious and more inclusive than exclusive—the war was a war against all of Lebanon and all Lebanese. But it was his speech marking the end of the war that captured the Lebanese and pan-Arab imagination, cementing his evolution into a national and Arab charismatic leader. In the speech, Nasrallah fused religious and political language to emphasise his image as a religious and political leader, declaring the end of hostilities as both a 'Divine Victory' that only Hizbullah could have achieved, and a 'political victory' for all Lebanese:

Our victory is not the victory of the party … it is not the victory of a party or a community; rather it is a victory for Lebanon, for the real Lebanese people, and every free person in the world. … Your resistance, which offered in the 2000 victory a model for liberation, offered in the year 2006 a model for steadfastness; legendary steadfastness and miraculous steadfastness. It is strong proof for all Arabs and Muslims, and all rulers, armies and peoples … The *Lebanese resistance* provided strong proof to all Arab and Islamic armies. … This is the equation. Today, *your* resistance broke the image of Israel.[44]

By the end of the war, Nasrallah's 'image of presence' had reached unprecedented levels of mediated visibility, enhancing his mythical status in popular culture and validating his charismatic authority and power.

Constructing Nasrallah's image and charisma

The available literature on Hassan Nasrallah—mostly a collection of quasi-biographies, books, articles, images and archival material of his speeches, his achievements and his religious engagements—recounts his life story as a classical linear narrative of a 'genuine' or 'pure'[45] charismatic leader endowed (according to these accounts) with pre-authored, extraordinary skills. While there is as yet no book-length work on Nasrallah's life history in a Western language, a handful of books, pamphlets and other material detailing aspects of Nasrallah's life, his heroism and his charismatic appeal are available in Arabic. A majority of these publications have been produced and disseminated by Hizbullah's media institutions, including its mainstream website, al-muqawama, its satellite television station, al-Manar, and its various publishing houses. Most of these works were published after the 2006 war with Israel and all tell the same story—that of a humble, religious, visionary, authentic and credible leader who has charisma and who was destined to follow a revolutionary path.

One example is a book titled *Zaman Nasrallah* (The Time of Nasrallah: The Heavenly and Strategic Visions in the Leadership of Hassan Nasrallah) published in 2008 by Dar al-Amir, a Hizbullah-affiliated publishing house. The book discusses in some detail Nasrallah's political strategies and objectives over the years as well as his personal traits and religious credentials. Another example is a children's picture book titled *Al-fares al-arabi: sirat hayat assayed Hassan Nasrallah min al-wilada hatta al-qiyada* (The Arab Knight: The Life Story of Sayyed Hassan Nasrallah from Birth to Leadership) published by Dar al-Mahajja al-Baida', a Hizbullah publishing house which is mainly dedicated to religious issues. The date of publication is not given, but its contents indicate that it was published after 2006. The book uses cartoons, images of Nasrallah, posters and newspaper clippings to construct an image of the Hizbullah leader as an extraordinary religious, national, Islamic and Arab hero, while tapping into a reservoir of symbolic and sacred figures to appeal to children already familiar with this reservoir and its meanings:

Nasrallah became the leader of Hizbullah through his own efforts, hard work and the strength of his belief and love for the homeland and his fellow believers … he managed to unite the *mujahideen* and bring them together to struggle for freedom … it is through belief and reliance on God's will that the resistance managed to expand and improve its operations against the oppressive occupier.[46]

The book is thus part of Hizbullah's wider process of cultivating loyalty among constituents from an early age. Nasrallah, in this context, is presented as a hero in terms that appeal to children's imagination. This personalisation of heroism is sustained through the production of a variety of children's merchandise featuring the image of Nasrallah, from school stationery to toys, making engagement with the figure and symbolism of Nasrallah an everyday experience.

In his systemic, functional and broadly Eurocentric analysis of authority structures,[47] Max Weber argued that 'genuine' or pure charisma was a feature of ancient societies. He wrote: 'Where charisma is genuine ... its basis lies ... in the conception that it is the duty of those subject to charismatic authority to recognize its authenticity ... Psychologically, this recognition is a matter of complete personal devotion to the possessor of the quality.'[48] In Weber's categorisation of the different modes of authority, he suggested that charismatic authority was different from other forms of authority as it was distinctly personal and rested on the 'devotion to the specific sanctity, heroism, or exemplary character of the extraordinary charismatic order, but that genuine charisma becomes unstable as enthusiasm and fervour disappear through discipline and habituation'.[49]

Ruth Willner draws on Weber's articulation to propose four criteria that distinguish charismatic leadership from other types of leadership. These are: the leader's image, which suggests that followers believe the leader possesses superhuman and extraordinary characteristics; receptivity, which means followers believe the leader's statements because it is he or she who makes them; compliance, meaning followers obey the leader; and emotions, which mean a leader provokes intense emotional responses from his or her followers.[50] Willner also argues that a common misconception about charisma is the linking of the qualities of the charismatic leader directly to the personality of the individual who is credited with it: 'There is a popular notion that charisma is located in a quality or combination of qualities of a person and that some leaders naturally possess a charismatic personality while most do not.'[51] Hence, attempts to locate a set of qualities that would qualify calling political leaders charismatic—whether personality, character, temperament or style—are unlikely to yield results because 'charisma is defined in terms of people's perceptions of and responses to a leader. It is not what the leader is, but what people see the leader as that counts in generating the charismatic relationship.'[52] Thus the distinction between charismatic political leadership and charismatic authority rests on the extent of the radius of charismatic support. 'If and when a charismatic political leader converts the majority members of a system into his charismatic constituency, his charisma also becomes the basis for authority in that system ...'[53]

Statements by ordinary people, in fact, suggest they believe that Nasrallah is an extraordinary and charismatic leader—paradoxically, he is also described as a man of the street and a brother among equals. 'He is like us' is often heard on the streets or in private. Such comments, as well as references to his unusual characteristics and leadership skills, are reiterated by commentators writing in Hizbullah's multimedia platforms. For example, in one such commentary in the Lebanese *al-Diyar* newspaper,[54] Nasrallah is described as:

the politician, the fighter, the leader, but before anything else he is the decent human being, the loveable and truthful person, who you feel glad to meet. Anyone who meets him longs to speak with him directly and to sit with him, whether he is politically in agreement with him or not, a source of attraction in the political landscape towards whom everyone gravitates.[55]

Nasrallah's 'one of us' persona is enhanced by his austere and simple lifestyle (it is reported that he chooses to sleep on a hard mattress on the floor rather than a sumptuous bed), reinforcing an image of Nasrallah as an organic leader with close ties to the people. Statements about his austere lifestyle are common. For example, as Suha Sabbagh, a writer and artist from Beirut, comments:

Nasrallah comes across as a normal man who does not irritate people with his airs and graces like other Arab leaders. I like his way of talking, no high politics or subterfuge. During the 2006 war, I was looking for a hero, and I found him in Nasrallah. And this was not a movie. Nasrallah does not exaggerate or make things up. He is one of those rare leaders who is and remains youthful. He has the spirit of youth in him, unlike those other [Arab] leaders who look like fossils. He uses the language of the street, but it is not street language.[56]

Such rhetoric is suggestive of a deep emotional bond, or a 'dialectical relationship',[57] which exists between Nasrallah and his followers, forming what Simon Coleman has called a 'charismatic presence and landscape that constitutes the charisma of the exemplar'.[58]

The potential for a charismatic response may be conditioned and helped by a society's pre-existing symbolic system, or as Atef Alshaer has argued, the existence of a culture of communication. A feature of all societies, a culture of communication refers to the compendium of religious, historical, literary and mythological linguistic and symbolic references used, communicated and reiterated by any community, state or organisation as valid tropes for all times, and which are acted upon and treated as having authenticity.[59] However, as will be shown in the following sections, the maintenance of a charismatic presence, such as Nasrallah's, requires continuous amplification and appropriation, as well as visibility, in popular culture in order to transform personal charisma into an image of presence, legitimate organised support and forge what Antonio Gramsci has called an ideological hegemony within his own constituency and outside of it.[60] As Roy Wallis has argued in his discussion of the maintenance of charisma:

The putative charismatic leader, emboldened by this flattering recognition of the status and identity to which he aspires, then seeks to realize in his behaviour the powers and status with which he has been credited, to live up to the image with which he has been endowed. In the process, others are elevated with him as intimates or lieutenants. Their significance derives from his. Having been raised up, and recognised as special by him they add to the recognition of the leader, endowing him with still further significance as author of the movement and their own fortunate condition, leading him to take evermore seriously the conception of himself as someone out-of-the-ordinary. [61]

Institutionalisation of Nasrallah's persona

Hassan Nasrallah was in his early thirties when he was appointed Hizbullah's leader following the assassination of his predecessor. Within only a few years of his appointment, he had become the central actor in almost all of Hizbullah's political and military decision-making processes. His appointment, according to most accounts, was agreed upon by elites within Hizbullah's highly hierarchical organised power structure[62] and approved by the Iranian supreme leader Ayatollah Ali Khameini. On this Ahmad Nizar Hamzeh writes:[63]

Structurally, the party is headed by a collective leadership, rather than a charismatic personality, such as Amal was under (Imam) Musa al-Sadr ... However, despite this [structure], the post of secretary-general has lately become the party's centre of gravity, the 'imperial secretariat.' ... The longest-serving secretary-general in the party's history, Hassan Nasrallah may, and does, function within the bureaucratic culture of Hizbullah's collective leadership, but 'he [also] has demonstrated significant religious, political and military skills that made him a charismatic leader indispensable as secretary-general and propagator of the *wilayat al-faquih* (jurisprudence) ... There is no doubt that Nasrallah's combined leadership skills and his unquestionable loyalty to (Iran's spiritual leader) Ali Khameinei made him the central actor in almost all of Hizbullah's political and military decision-making.'[64]

Nasrallah himself alludes to the role of Hizbullah's institutions in key decision-making processes, including his appointment, and entrusting him with the task of appealing to would-be supporters.[65] As he puts it:

Hizbullah's structures place the secretary-general at the movement's summit … today, the party has no official spokesman, so the secretary-general assumes that role; this means that when he expresses an opinion he also commits the party to it. He, therefore, has to have cultural and scientific abilities, political acumen and administrative skills, and he must have the trust of the party's leaders, since they have entrusted him with an important responsibility … the command structure should be convinced [the party leader] has attributes and abilities that qualify him for this position … this does not mean that he is the only one who possesses these attributes, or that others in the leadership structure are any less capable.[66]

While Nasrallah was well known to party insiders, few outside of the close circle of early Hizbullah activists and fellow colleagues at the seminary in Najaf would have known much about his charisma or political talents. In fact, there is little evidence from his early life that he had unusual characteristics or was a charismatic persona. A recording of one of his speeches delivered sometime in 1982, and available via YouTube, shows him as an engaged, albeit dogmatic, religious figure preaching Hizbullah's foundational doctrine—that of allegiance to Iran's *wilayat al-faqih*. It is not possible to verify who recorded the speech or how it made its way into the public space—Hizbullah began recording key events as well as resistance operations in the late 1980s.[67] However, video recording of sound and image is a suitable format for sermons and speeches as it allows the full play of the emotional and dramatic power of culturally and religiously meaningful symbols and tropes as well as the recitative repetition of language aimed at community-building.[68] In this sense, as Annabelle Sreberny-Mohammadi and Ali Mohammadi note, 'religious knowledge does possess authority, not only as the received word of God but because it is community-building … and of necessity authoritarian'.[69]

In the video, a youthful Nasrallah is seen wearing his trademark black clerical garb and black turban (which signifies that the wearer is a descendant of the Prophet Muhammad), a style of dress he always wears in public apart from the few occasions where he is photographed wearing military fatigues in some unknown location. However, his mode of delivery is monotonous and stern, lacking the humour or jokes he began to introduce in his speeches as early as the 1990s and the conversational narrative style he adopted when he began addressing audiences via television screens. Furthermore, Nasrallah's message is unambiguous and his language heavily infused with a Shiite-specific religious aesthetic and political rhetoric reflecting Hizbullah's then uncompromising position about alliances with Iran. Unlike in later years, particularly when he began addressing a wider Lebanese constituency using the local dialect, Nasrallah speaks in *fus'ha* (classical or formal) Arabic, his sentences interspersed with citations from the Quran and references to revered Shiite leaders in order to court the Shiite constituency in Lebanon. What is evident, however, is that even at an early age—he must have been in his late twenties when the speech was recorded—Nasrallah comes across as a confident public speaker, a skill he would have likely developed through the delivery of attention-grabbing sermons and speeches in his early career as a religious persona.

However, in an interview with the *al-Khaleej* newspaper of the United Arab Emirates in March 1986, Nasrallah's rhetoric changed slightly, providing an early signal of his skills in adapting his discourse according to socio-historical juncture while maintaining ideological ambiguity—he opens the door to negotiations with other parties in Lebanon, for example, while at the same time leaving Hizbullah's rivals and enemies guessing as to what its next step would be. This combination of intrigue and revelation was to become a recurring feature in his later statements and speeches, a tactic he used to grab attention. In the interview, Nasrallah insisted that Hizbullah's strategy of resistance against Israel and its commitment to Iran were long-term, but that the party would accommodate a national consensus on the question of whether or not to impose Islamic rule, even though it remained committed to the idea as a matter of principle:[70]

From the point of view of ideology and *sharia*, we are required to establish God's rule over any part of this earth, regardless of particularities and details; this can only happen, however, if the nation adopts this ideology and safeguards it. We would like to allay the fears of those who think that Hizbullah intends to impose Islamic rule by force, and to tell them that we shall not impose Islam; for us, this is a matter of general principle.[71]

Following his appointment as secretary general, Nasrallah's rhetoric became more accommodating and flexible—in fact, he used every public opportunity to emphasise the idea that Hizbullah's transformation into a mainstream political party was authentic rather than opportunistic, and that Hizbullah was nationalist rather than purely Islamic.[72] To this end, Nasrallah adapted his image and language to appeal to the various publics he intended to reach and to ensure support for Hizbullah's discourse of resistance against Israel and its ally the United States.

His skilful manoeuvring was evident in several of his public pronouncements in mid-1992 when Hizbullah was preparing to take part in the first post-civil war elections in Lebanon. In these statements Nasrallah used a language aimed at convincing Hizbullah's main supporters of the need to enter a more inclusive phase in Hizbullah's history while projecting a self-image (to other Lebanese nationals) of a national Lebanese leader whose concern is all of Lebanon: 'We enter the elections in order to build a modern state and our programme is for a civilised and a non-sectarian human being … as we have announced previously and we reiterate this now that our alliances will be made according to political considerations and not according to sectarian allegiances.'[73] However, aware that the core party membership was committed to the Islamicisation of society, Nasrallah kept them loyal by maintaining strict internal disciplines and a strict Islamic culture within the party, endorsed and publicised by his deputy Sheikh Naim Qassem.

In public, Nasrallah put his weight behind Hizbullah's *infitah* or Lebanonisation phase, opening the party to the Lebanese political system and promising not to pursue an Islamic state in Lebanon, while issuing an invitation to the secular Shiites and the rest of Lebanon to support Hizbullah's stance against Israel. This position was evident in a speech he made in 1995:

We cannot enforce an Islamic state by force. An Islamic state is a just state and aimed at promoting justice and is based on people's support of it. There is no Islamic movement that can carry out a military coup to impose an Islamic state. There is no Islamic party that can work to found an Islamic state. In Iran's experience, a revolution took place and this led to an Islamic state without civil war. The Islamic republic was built on a popular referendum and some experts were elected and proposed a constitution … In Lebanon, we see many sects and groups and the situation is totally different. … If there were an Islamic movement in one country and this country is not ready because of its make-up and its diversity, then the alternative is not chaos, but order and this is where we start discussions about the nature of the order we would like.[74]

HASSAN NASRALLAH

Mediating Nasrallah's image of presence

The transformation of Hassan Nasrallah into Hizbullah's foremost charismatic leader at the beginning of the twenty-first century did not come about by accident. Rather, his charismatic authority and image of presence were an intended outcome of Hizbullah's political communication strategy which creatively appropriated his image and rhetoric in different media platforms and spaces in ways that, as Roland Barthes suggests, intervene 'without warning on the place of denotation … in order to pass off as merely a denoted message which is really heavily connoted'.[75]

The 'visual' appropriation of Nasrallah's image and its validation in mass popular culture was a vital component of Hizbullah's political communication strategy, as discussed in Chapter 3. While few details of the decision-making process surrounding his appointment were made public, *al-'Ahd* published two front-page black-and-white images of the new leader under the headline and inscription: 'The Best of Successors to the Best of Predecessors'.[76] The phrase is an example of the powerful, symbolic, religious and resonant discourse Hizbullah used to legitimise Nasrallah as a credible and authentic religious–political ideologue and broaden his appeal within the group's target constituency. Within a few days, the paper printed in full Nasrallah's first interview as secretary general conducted with the Lebanese daily *as-Safir*, in which Nasrallah sought to construct an image of himself, and his party, as more inclusive than other actors in Lebanese society:

When we were just a small *jihadi* group fighting the Israeli enemy, we were able to hide underground whenever we read in the papers that there was a reason for us to disappear … but soon we became a large movement and started viewing our project as non-partisan and non-factional, and one that operates at the level of the Lebanese people and the nation as a whole and not a sectarian or party project … The fact that we are engaged in an existential battle with Israel is an honour … we view the Israeli enemy with a different eye—namely, that its very existence in the region poses a constant threat to Lebanon as a whole.[77]

Along with the interview, *al-'Ahd* published a short, sentimental commentary by Ibrahim al-Amin, a vocal Hizbullah supporter, who detailed Nasrallah's personal traits and described them as the perfect qualifications to produce a great leader:

Hassan Nasrallah is distinguished for his calm demeanour so that anyone visiting him would feel becalmed in his presence … an imposing man, with a beautiful appearance. He is well-mannered and knows how to use language. He is a seasoned politician … who knows how to … use spectacular oratorical skills.[78]

John Corner has argued that the 'mediation' of political personas can project leaders in three broad modes: iconically—in the sense of displaying the demeanour, posture and associative contexts of the political self; vocally, reflected in the increasing blurring of 'what' is said with 'how' it is said[79] as well as between the personal and political; and kinetically, which is associated with the choreographing of political performances and actions.[80] All three revolve around style: the first referring to the image of the leader; the second to the manner in which the leader addresses the public (as well as what he says); and the third to the ways in which his performances are constructed and choreographed by diverse media outlets. From early on in his political career, Nasrallah's public performances suggested he was aware that image and language were central to politics, which, to paraphrase the French philosopher and critic Jacques Rancière, 'revolves around what is seen and what can be said about it, around who has the ability to see and the talent to speak'.[81]

For this reason, and in order to engage the loyalty of his target publics, Nasrallah used a religious–political language that not only responded to the longings or the aspirations of the masses, but also sustained an image of his virtues in a world of conspicuous consumption. But while maintaining a humble appearance and asceticism that contrast sharply with the public images of other Arab leaders, Nasrallah also projects an image of a powerful ideologue (as on the occasions when he would lead or address rallies and celebrations showcasing Hizbullah's military power and reflecting its massive popular support) tempered with a more personalised and intimate image of a traditional religious leader. Nasrallah's image is carried via mass media (particularly television) into thousands of households, creating a sense of false intimacy that is further accentuated by his mode of address (Nasrallah often goes off script), his use of vernacular rather than classical Arabic, and the jokes and humour (he often makes himself the first butt of his jokes) that have endeared him to his audiences and humanised his political persona. Nasrallah's skills as a public speaker are well known: as a master in adapting different linguistic, cultural and religious registers, Nasrallah is able to craft a powerful religious–political language that he renders accessible and comprehensible to all of his intended audiences. His statements are rich in imagery, symbolic references and culturally meaningful frames of reference that resonate with his intended publics, integrating Islamic frames of reference and heroic figures from the past with a potent discourse of resistance that suits, according to his rhetoric, present historical and political contexts.[82] His speeches often follow the same preordained sequence and structure, taking the form of a simple, yet resonant, storyline that is rich in detail and analysis and mixes frames of suffering and redemption with resistance and/or struggle for the land. All these narratives promise divine rewards for those who follow and respond, and therefore offer a model of compulsion rather than obedience.

Nasrallah is also adept at adapting his image and language to summon different audiences in diverse contexts. For example, he presents himself as a religious persona by constantly reminding Hizbullah's supporters of the need to follow the right path (the path of resistance and struggle) and of the significance of martyrdom as a religious duty; as an Arab leader by reiterating the significance of resistance against Israel and through leading (and addressing) Jerusalem Day celebrations; and as a Lebanese national by calling for cooperation and national dialogue among the country's various factions to preserve Lebanon's sovereignty.[83] While his language often changes to suit diverse audiences and contexts, his speeches have three main features which have remained constant: first, Nasrallah always peppers his talks with citations from the Quran and, references to the Prophet Muhammad and his descendants. Second, Nasrallah frequently addresses his audiences with the Arab personal pronoun 'antum' (you), provoking a sense of familiarity enhanced by his switching from intimate language (such as when he uses colloquial 'ammiyya Arabic) to formal Arabic (as when quoting from the Quran). Finally, Nasrallah employs different layers of speech, each designed to appeal to a particular audience:[84] to a mainly Lebanese Shiite audience, Nasrallah frames jihad (struggle) as a purely religious duty that transcends all other aims, and the conflict with Israel as the first part of a campaign aimed at liberating Jerusalem and other Muslim holy places; to a wider Lebanese audience, Nasrallah frames jihad in national terms, invoking the term muqawama (resistance); when addressing a larger Arab audience, Nasrallah presents armed struggle as part of a wider Arab nationalist cause against Israel and the United States as well as their allies; and to an international audience, Nasrallah frames Hizbullah's activities as aiming to fulfil the right of oppressed people to self-determination and as part of a liberation struggle against an illegal occupation force.[85]

The power of mediation

The cultivation, institutionalisation and mediation of Nasrallah's image and persona began when he was appointed secretary general. But his mediated visibility reached new levels during and after the 2006 war with Israel, serving to affirm his extraordinariness as a leader and turn his political performances into visual representations and mediated spectacles of power, which, as Lisa Wedeen has suggested, 'anchor visually and audibly politically significant ideas' and, frame the ways people see themselves as citizens.[86] It was after the war of 2006 that Nasrallah's role and standing gained unprecedented levels of popular support, not only in Lebanon but also elsewhere in the Arab world. Hence, it is worth paying attention to the different communicative methods Hizbullah used to enhance his persona and public standing.

Nasrallah's speeches, interviews, rallies and engagements—indeed, his every utterance—are constructed by Hizbullah's various media platforms as dramatic political performances that demand urgent attention and action. This urgency is mediated in a variety of ways. For example, before Nasrallah is due to make an address, which is always televised in full, al-Manar will begin the broadcast by showing him addressing audiences on other occasions, the clips often interspersed with images of Hizbullah fighters in battle and pictures of destroyed Israeli armoury. Another example is the use of songs, most of them with anti-Israeli rhetoric, accompanied by images of Nasrallah speaking to fighters or ordinary people, heightening expectations about what he is planning to say. Hizbullah's media outlets announce all of Nasrallah's appearances, whether on television or in public spaces, ahead of time—some of these announcements are in the form of printed informal invites detailing the time and place of Nasrallah's engagements and published in *al-Intiqad* and on Hizbullah's main website al-muqawama al-islamiya (Islamic Resistance), while others are open invites to the general public advertised by al-Manar at regular intervals. While these practices can be interpreted as attempts to reduce the formal distance between the leader and the led, they are also examples of 'dramatised media events'[87] that are mobilisational and agitational at the same time. The sense of drama is heightened by the fact that Nasrallah has rarely appeared at rallies or public events in person since 2006 owing to concerns regarding his safety, provoking affective associations with the occultation of the revered religious and symbolic leader, the Mahdi, whose return is still awaited by many Shiites. Hizbullah's media outlets rarely disclose whether Nasrallah will appear in person at rallies, but they always dramatise the occasion when he does appear so that his appearance creates associations in his intended audiences' mind with the return of the revered occluded leader. Nasrallah's televised image is always projected on a huge television screen set above a platform, providing a virtual iteration of pulpit addresses by politicians and religious leaders, a practice meant to reflect authority. While he speaks, the camera moves to audience members to register their appreciation and attention to his every word. At the same time, responses to Nasrallah's appearances and speeches, such as images of crowds carrying Nasrallah's pictures and the word *labbaika* ('we will act on your demands') are disseminated simultaneously in Hizbullah's diverse media outlets, which turns slogans like 'the most honourable of people' (in reference to Nasrallah's statement about the people of the South) and 'The Divine Victory' (in reference to the 2006 war with Israel) into everyday expressions. In the mid-2000s, Hizbullah provided Nasrallah with a live video stream of the audience as they listened to his speeches, enhancing the interactivity of his televised speeches.

Following the 2006 war, Hizbullah's media outlets began publishing sentimental songs and poems in praise of his persona and achievements.[88] Some of these are authored by Arab nationals, such as the Syrian Omar al-Farra.[89] In one poem, al-Farra goes as far as to refer to Nasrallah as a 'noble knight' from *ahl al-bayt*[90] who had come along with a 'flock of angels' to alleviate the suffering of the deprived, a language that resonates with popular Shiite aesthetics and collective memory. A popular song dedicated to highlighting his religious credentials ends with the phrase: 'Oh Hussein,[91] we had come back with Nasrallah,' thus making links to the lineage of the most revered leader in Shiite history. Another song that appeals to the larger Lebanese and Arab publics is *Ahibba'i* (My Beloved) whose words were adapted from Nasrallah's victory speech following the 2006 war. The climax of the song comes with the appearance of a group of able-bodied Hizbullah fighters running through Lebanese woods and the words: 'You are the glory of our nation, you are our leaders, you are the crown on our head; you are the masters.'[92] Al-Manar has also produced several videos about Nasrallah's life history and achievements.[93]

In the public space, Hizbullah planted images and religious iconography depicting Nasrallah with other revered Muslim Shiite leaders along roads, on the walls of buildings in the streets of Beirut and elsewhere.[94] Some of these are simply portraits of the Hizbullah leader, but many also have inscriptions referring to his religious and national credentials. For example, one poster has the image of the leader with the words 'Nasrallah, the sun of Palestine' inscribed under a photograph of the Dome of the Rock, the mosque that symbolises Jerusalem to many Muslims and Arabs. Others show Nasrallah holding children, laughing, addressing crowds or with Hizbullah fighters. Although such portraits were used before 2006, after the war the style and language of these portraits changed, reflecting the transformation of Nasrallah's image from a religious leader into an iconic national figure—there are some that reproduce the style popular in portraits and symbols of global cult revolutionary leaders, such as Che Guevara. These images complement and coexist with older images of Nasrallah, where he is sometimes shown in a reverential embrace with Iran's spiritual leader Ali Khameini, indicating his submission to the power of the Iranian Islamic republic. Hizbullah also produced and sold a varied assortment of merchandise— key rings, posters and other memorabilia—to reflect support and admiration for Nasrallah. There are stickers that show Nasrallah in different guises and places, and there are even some showing his well-known bodyguards who are a constant presence at all his public appearances. Nasrallah also appears in posters of Hizbullah martyrs, in which he is often seen smiling, suggesting that their death should be celebrated, not mourned. Combined, all these products maintain what Barthes calls a 'photographic syntax', or 'a discursive reading of object-signs within a single photograph'.[95]

The 2006 war was the ultimate historical moment in which Nasrallah's image of presence and charismatic authority helped his party impose an ideological hegemony[96] in Lebanon. Support for Nasrallah and Hizbullah extended to the Arab world where citizens in different capitals carried Nasrallah's image as an identity marker and as a symbol of Arab nationalism, provoking comparisons with the late Egyptian President Gamal Abdel-Nasser who wooed Arabs with his nationalist rhetoric in the late '60s and early '70s. The war and Hizbullah's self-proclaimed victory were the charismatic moments that emboldened Hizbullah to 'add to the recognition of the leader, endowing him with still further significance as author of the movement and their own fortunate condition, leading him to take evermore seriously the conception of himself as someone out-of-the-ordinary'.[97]

Within weeks of the end of the war, however, Hizbullah's ideological hegemony was destabilised as simmering domestic tension boiled over following the establishment of the Special Tribunal for Lebanon to investigate the assassination of Rafic Hariri.[98] With political tensions and challenges to Nasrallah's image escalating, Hizbullah began a new phase in its political communication strategy aimed at validating Nasrallah's standing in the public sphere and maintaining popular support for the group. Hizbullah's media platforms and spaces launched a coordinated marketing campaign to reclaim legitimacy focusing on aspects of Nasrallah's upbringing and personal life, his ethos, religious integrity, political credibility and extraordinary qualities. The campaign was marked with the publication of several books about his life history that included lengthy testimonies from his family and party members, as well as ordinary people.

Al-Manar, meanwhile, produced several new videos about Nasrallah's life and deeds. Among these was a highly stylised movie-like trailer with English translations that broadcast key quotes from Nasrallah's speeches, with Hizbullah and nationalist songs playing in the background.[99] In addition, the station continuously re-broadcast some of Nasrallah's most significant speeches, using a combination of visual effects and a variety of sound tracks. Some of these programmes played religious chants while others used nationalist songs reminiscent of the 1960s and 1970s Arab nationalist productions, reminding their audiences of Nasrallah's religious and national attributes.

In March and April 2010, the Hizbullah-sympathetic newspaper *al-Diyar* began a series of articles as part of a comprehensive file about Nasrallah, his life and his achievements, published in two instalments. In the first instalment, the writer Radwan al-Dheeb provided narrative after narrative of Nasrallah's life history, sacrifices and credibility. The second was a handwritten statement by Nasrallah telling his life story which was first published on 12 May 2006 in the Tehran-based magazine *Risalat al-Hussein* (the Letter of Hussein). There were lengthy testimonies from members of his family (including his father, sister, mother and wife) and supporters as well as other Hizbullah leaders reciting and repeating his extraordinary qualities, his dedication to the cause of resistance and his heroic deeds.[100] His dedication is amplified by the narratives of his upbringing, his devotion to religious pursuits, his charisma and leadership skills. Another shows Nasrallah's humane and sentimental side, particularly when referring to the death of his son Hadi[101] and the martyrs of Hizbullah while not mentioning the loss of his eldest son: 'I feel shy [when I meet] martyrs' families ... and those whose family members sacrificed their loves ones to protect the homeland and its honour.'[102] All tell the same story: that of a charismatic, eloquent religious–political ideologue and an inspirational leader whose charismatic deeds influenced the history of Lebanon as no other leader had done. One report, written by al-Dheeb, reads: 'He [Nasrallah] is a leader who looks to history with the future in perspective ... He acts on the basis of the belief that stems from the people's hopes and potential. He does not surrender or wait in resignation until helped by others.'[103] Another ponders Nasrallah's humane and sentimental side while emphasising his rootedness in Arab and Islamic history:

[He is] an inclusive and forgiving leader, the defender of Arab civilisation and culture ... a feat he achieved through his and his party's actions ... Nasrallah is the 'Khomeini' of the Arabs.[104]

Rising challenges to Nasrallah's charismatic image

The cultivation and mediation of Hassan Nasrallah's image of presence and charismatic authority produced powerful effects during an interrelated set of historically specific constellations of social, cultural and political and institutional forces, helping Nasrallah transcend political–ideological legacies in Lebanon. However, a challenging set of unprecedented historically specific constellations, such as the Arab uprisings that began in 2011, was bound to challenge Nasrallah's image as the ultimate Arab hero. Nasrallah expressed support for the uprisings in Tunisia, Egypt and particularly Bahrain, which has a large oppressed Shiite population. But Hizbullah's and Nasrallah's open support for the Syrian regime in its violent repression of opponents dented his credibility and image as an organic leader with support in mass culture. In order to legitimise his support for Bashar al-Assad, Nasrallah framed the uprising in Syria as an anti-nationalist and anti-resistance Israeli and American plot while warning of a 'counter-revolutionary' US plot to subvert the uprisings.[105]

Within two years, and as Sunni Islamist jihadi groups entered the conflict to fight against the Assad regime, Hizbullah's military involvement in support of the Syrian regime was made public. Nasrallah justified Hizbullah's intervention in the conflict as a fight against those *takfiris* (i.e. non-believers) using the same frame of resistance against Israel and its allies to defend the engagement of Hizbullah fighters in a battle outside Lebanese soil:

> We have entered a completely new phase. What is happening in Syria is very important and fateful, for Lebanon's present and future. Let us not bury our heads in the sand and act like we live in Djibouti, we are here on the border with Syria. ... to be honest, we didn't intervene until a month ago ... We used all our contacts with Islamic and national forces, as well as with states, to no avail; nothing but the downfall of the regime ... I will have three points to make. This is the first development, and that is the domination and control by the *takfiri* trend ... second, Syria is no longer an arena for popular revolution against a political system, but an arena for the imposition of a political project led by America and the West and its regional tools. And we all know that the American project is an Israeli project through and through. Third, Syria is the backbone of the resistance and support for the resistance and the resistance cannot sit idly while its back is being broken. We are not stupid. ... If Syria falls into the hands of America, Israel and the takfiris, and all of America's tools in the region, the resistance will find itself under siege, and Israel will invade Lebanon, in order to impose its terms on the Lebanese people ... Hizbullah can never belong to the same front which includes America ... it can never belong to a front which wants to destroy all our achievements and squander our sacrifices and make us slaves of America and Israel once again.[106]

But it was in his speech marking Jerusalem Day on 2 August 2013 that Nasrallah's rhetoric suggested the beginning of a new phase in Hizbullah's history and identity. The speech was particularly interesting for the absence of the ideological ambiguity that has characterised his language since the 1990s, as well as for its hard-line rhetoric against Israel and for invoking symbolic Shiite leaders to reclaim legitimacy for himself and his group. In the speech, in which Nasrallah appeared at the rally in person for the first time in about a year, he used the 'liberation of Palestine and Jerusalem' ideological frame to call for the annihilation of Israel, which, he said, would serve the national interests of Lebanon. 'Israel is a danger to Lebanon and its annihilation is a Lebanese national interest ...' But unlike in previous speeches in which he insisted Hizbullah was a Lebanese national party and had no sectarian roots or objectives, Nasrallah invoked the most significant religious figure in Shiite history to emphasise Hizbullah's Shiite and resistance identity: 'We are the Shiites of 'Ali bin Talib who will not give up Palestine' or the resistance.[107]

In the past, Nasrallah's religious–political populist discourse had mobilised diverse publics, brought together by the powerful tropes of resistance, power and individual empowerment. However, Nasrallah's rhetoric in reference to Syria, contrasting with the flow of visual and material evidence from Syria attesting to the brutality of the regime against its people, served to dent his image as a 'genuine' charismatic leader who reiterates, and speaks to, ordinary people's grievances and concerns. It would be premature to suggest that Hassan Nasrallah's role in Lebanese and regional politics is over or that he has lost his populist appeal—in fact, he remains revered by a large number of Lebanese Shiites and other sectors of society. Yet as this chapter has shown, the story of his transformation from a humble cleric into the Arab world's foremost populist leader at the start of the twentieth-first century showed that whatever charisma and skills he has were continuously amplified, worked on and manifested in vivid and visible forms to consolidate power. However, it has also shown the limits of charismatic authority and the transitory and contested nature of his mediated image of presence, underlining the symbiotic relationship between image and historical contexts.

CONCLUSION: HIZBULLAH AT A CROSSROADS

Lina Khatib and Dina Matar

The challenge of the Syrian crisis

At the beginning of 2013 Hizbullah found itself at a crossroads. The Syrian rebellion against President Bashar al-Assad's regime that began in March 2011 presented the group with a serious conundrum. Syria is Hizbullah's strategic ally, the country through which the group's weapons are smuggled from Iran and where its troops train, and the nation is considered part of the anti-Israeli triangle of resistance in the Middle East. At the same time, Hizbullah's ongoing 'war of position' with rival political forces in Lebanon, particularly the March 14 coalition, had entered a new and more confrontational stage as diverse forces began to speak out against Hizbullah's increased power in the public sphere.

Hizbullah's open alliance with the Assad regime, coupled with the indictment of four of its members by the UN Special Tribunal for Lebanon over their alleged involvement in the assassination of Rafic Harri, had seriously dented the group's credibility. Yet Hizbullah, at least on paper, had never been stronger—it had replenished its arsenal in the period since the 2006 war with Israel and had emerged as a majority partner in the Lebanese Cabinet under Prime Minister Najib Miqati.

THE HIZBULLAH PHENOMENON

The way in which Hizbullah chose to handle the Syrian crisis marked a change in its communication strategy: Hizbullah's public messages became firmly reactive, not proactive. Hizbullah was no longer setting the agenda, but seeking to limit the damage to its image and credibility. In doing so, Hizbullah resorted to familiar discursive frameworks: Lebanonisation and resistance. But Hizbullah struggled to maintain an anti-sectarian position when it sought to justify its military intervention in Syria by using the language of victimisation, arguing that the intervention was intended to confront the threat posed by Sunni *takfiri* jihadi groups to Lebanon.

When the Syrian protests began, Hizbullah continuously affirmed its support for the Assad regime, a stance that irked many Arab nationals who had previously supported Hizbullah in its resistance and operations against Israel. In a speech discussing the Arab uprisings on 25 May 2011, Hassan Nasrallah rationalised his opposition to the Syrian revolution in the following terms:

I will be very honest with you as the situation requires a clear responsibility ... we in Lebanon, particularly Hizbullah, harbour deep appreciation to Syria and its leadership, to the President Hafiz al-Assad and President Bashar al-Assad ... Syria helped strongly the unity of Lebanon ... it is a resistant and rejectionist country in its regime, leadership, army and people ... in Bahrain, there is 'a closed system'; Mubarak was closed, Qaddafi was closed, Zein al-'Abideen Bin Ali was closed; in Syria, the system is not closed.[1]

Following a series of violent incidents in Lebanon that were linked to the Syrian crisis, and which demonstrated the Lebanese political system's fragility while evoking memories of Lebanon's civil war,[2] Nasrallah issued a message of defiance, warning that any external involvement in the Syrian conflict could lead to a war with Israel, and would thus be 'very ... costly ... we can change the face of Israel'.[3] Invoking Israel to unite Arabs is a tool that has been used by many Arab leaders, and, in this sense, Nasrallah's words were certainly not new. However, given Hizbullah's history of defiance and resistance, the language was clearly designed to deflect attention from the group's support for the Syrian regime while emphasising Hizbullah's role in resisting Israeli aggression. Indeed, in a speech on 14 January 2012 to commemorate the fortieth day after the killing of Hussein, Nasrallah lambasted the Arab rulers who had gathered in Mecca to discuss the Syrian crisis, and argued that only

CONCLUSION

Hizbullah's model of resistance had succeeded in deterring Israel.[4] In addition, as has been shown throughout this book, by invoking and evoking Palestine in its discourse, Hizbullah has tried to suggest that the Arab governments have failed to help in the liberation of Palestine, and that it is only the model of Hizbullah, and by extension those of Iran and the Syrian regime, that can achieve this goal. Hizbullah has consistently argued that it is only through 'force', not statements, that Palestine will eventually be liberated and the suffering of its people alleviated.

Throughout 2011 and 2012 Hizbullah mobilised its various media platforms (and Hassan Nasrallah) to justify its stance towards the Syrian uprising, a position which it has sought to frame as consistent with the 'genuine' wishes of the Syrian people. In the autumn of 2011, as the violence in Syria escalated, al-Manar did not report the number of casualties that had resulted from the violence; nor did it even mention the fact that there were casualties. Instead, al-Manar simply emphasised that international criticism of the Syrian regime was part of a 'failing' international conspiracy led mainly by the United States and Israel, which aimed to break the alliance between Syria and Iran and weaken their role in the Middle East. This was followed by a reminder that the 'resistance' was ready to wage war against Israel again because of its hostile policies in the region. In its news bulletin on 31 October 2011, al-Manar quoted Assad as stating that the Western media had been subjective in their coverage of the Syria crisis, and that—in harmony with Nasrallah's position—any foreign interference in the region would lead to serious instability. This was followed by an announcement that Syria planned to implement a number of reforms that would be encapsulated in the new Syrian constitution, which was then being drafted.

Al-Manar continued its coverage the following day by emphasising the 'love' that the Syrians had for the Assad regime and its reforms, with a report on a rally supporting Assad in Deir Ezzor, during which Syria's citizens expressed gratitude to the pro-Assad Russian and Chinese positions regarding the situation. Al-Manar even used its cultural shows to reiterate this message. Episode 153 of the weekly show *Coloured Pages*, which was broadcast in the same week, showed Syrian filmmakers expressing support for the Syrian regime and their rejection of a petition signed by fellow artists in support of the revolution. The filmmakers claimed that they did not suffer from censorship, that they supported 'a unified Syria behind its president and government' and that 'there is a group of betrayers inside Syria who want to muddy the waters and lead the country to chaos'. As these examples illustrate, Hizbullah was trying to use the framework of victimisation that it had resurrected in the wake of the indictments by the Special Tribunal for Lebanon to justify its position towards its Syrian ally. But this kind of justification was now becoming much harder to 'sell' to Arab audiences as the flow of visual evidence from Syria attesting to the brutality of the regime against its people continued.

A year after the start of the Syrian uprising, Hizbullah's Lebanese political opponents were also speaking out loudly against Hizbullah's support for the Assad regime, with some comparing Hizbullah to the authoritarian regimes that were rapidly collapsing throughout the region.[5] Others argued that the party had blinded itself to the transformations taking place in the Arab world and that this would eventually result in a serious threat to its own power in Lebanon.[6] As the international community as well as Arab citizens across the region took the side of the Syrian protesters, Hizbullah's support for the Assad regime became, at best, a source of embarrassment for a party that seemed unable to adapt its political and communication strategies for the first time in its history.

As Hizbullah became more involved in the Syrian crisis, not only through its declared support for the Assad regime but also by sending its own men to fight alongside the Syrian army, the group embarked on a communication path designed to deflect attention from the violent reality of its on-the-ground engagement in Syria. At the start of 2013, following a period when the Hizbullah leader was markedly less prominent in the media—which sparked rumours that he was receiving cancer treatment in Iran (which he denied)—Nasrallah sought to divert attention away from Hizbullah and the Syrian crisis and back to local Lebanese politics. In response to suggestions that Hizbullah fighters were helping the Assad regime crush its opponents, Nasrallah emphasised Hizbullah's rootedness in Lebanon, its determination to avert sectarian strife and its involvement in the domestic electoral process. In a speech on 27 February 2013, he proposed a new electoral law based on proportional representation for the parliamentary elections scheduled for June 2013, noting that such a law would avert a division of the country along sectarian lines—mainly along a Sunni–Shiite axis—and force all sects and political parties to form alliances and work together. In a further speech on 6 March 2013, Nasrallah again emphasised Hizbullah's support for proportional representation, adding that it would exert every effort to support a system allowing all Lebanese groups and sects the opportunity for representation. Yet at the same time he returned to the discursive framework according to which Hizbullah is a Lebanese party that will continue to protect the country, while he also warned the group's enemies that they risked pushing the country towards a new conflict:

There are some elements in Lebanon that are pushing the country towards a sectarian conflict along Sunni–Shiite lines. All actualities point to this, but strife is not in anybody's interest, and a sectarian conflict is a dangerous issue … Hizbullah will not respond to those who are attacking it. We do not want to enter a house or a mosque to attack who is in it. We are busy day and night watching and preparing for what the Israeli enemy has in store for us … Lebanon is for all Lebanese.[7]

This emphasis on Lebanon began to dissipate when the country's political groups failed to reach a consensus on the electoral law to be implemented in the June 2013 elections. The talks on electoral reform were postponed indefinitely, an outcome that coincided with the biggest attack that Hizbullah has launched to date against the Syrian opposition within Syria itself. In June 2013, Hizbullah, alongside the Syrian army, successfully recaptured the strategic town of Qusair from the Syrian opposition after a battle that lasted over two weeks. As the bodies of dead Hizbullah fighters started arriving back in Lebanon, Hizbullah found it impossible to maintain the illusion of minimal involvement in the Syrian crisis. Consequently, Hizbullah once again framed the crisis as an existential battle against the United States and Israel, while adding a new dimension: the fight against Sunni *takfiri* jihadis. Such jihadi groups had indeed fought against the Assad regime and Hizbullah in Qusair and elsewhere in Syria, thereby lending a degree of credibility to Hizbullah's efforts to present its military involvement as being about staving off the *takfiri* threat before it reached Lebanese soil. In his speech on 25 May 2013, the day commemorating the liberation of the South, and at the height of the battle of Qusair, Nasrallah called *takfiris* a 'disease' that would spread to Lebanon if the group simply stood by and did nothing, and described the territories in Syria adjacent to Lebanon as a critical area whose control by Hizbullah would prevent jihadi groups from reaching Lebanon.[8]

Hizbullah, which is keenly aware of the dangers inherent in a Shiite movement clashing with Sunni groups, sought to deflect attention away from sectarianism. After al-Arabiya screened a YouTube video showing Hizbullah fighters raising a black flag, on which the words 'Oh Hussein' (*ya Hussein*) were written in red, on top of a mosque in Qusair, with the al-Arabiya report claiming that the mosque was a Sunni one, Nasrallah gave another speech on 14 June in which he claimed that the mosque was actually a Shiite mosque. However, it became harder for Hizbullah to avoid the issue of sectarianism after the Lebanese Sunni Salafist Imam Ahmad al-Assir, who had been threatening Hizbullah in the southern city of Sidon ever since the start of the Syrian crisis, led an attack against the Lebanese army and Hizbullah in the city in response to the throwing of rocks at al-Assir's brother by Hizbullah sympathisers. Al-Assir's provocation on 23 June 2013 escalated into a clash between his followers on the one hand and Hizbullah and the Lebanese army on the other. The deadly clashes eventually caused al-Assir to flee the city and provoked a renewed public affirmation by Hizbullah of the 'people, the army and the resistance' mantra, while the group also attempted to emphasise its role in 'protecting' the army. The clashes also gave Hizbullah another justification for framing its actions in Syria as essential for preventing a Sunni *takfiri* takeover of Lebanon, especially as al-Assir had recruited Syrians who fought alongside his Lebanese supporters in the Sidon clashes. These tropes were illustrated in an al-Manar programme broadcast in late June detailing an alleged 'plot' by al-Assir to cause '*fitna*' (discord) between Sunnis and Shiites in Lebanon as well as to undermine the Lebanese army.[9]

Hizbullah thus found elements in its external environment that enabled it to present a coherent story of the need for self-preservation in the face of its victimisation. The credibility of this narrative was enhanced by the European Union's decision to list Hizbullah's military wing as a terrorist organisation in July 2013—which Hizbullah framed as being part of a wider Western conspiracy led by the United States and Israel—and two attacks on Hizbullah's stronghold in Beirut's southern suburbs, the first in July and the second in August 2013. The second attack in particular, a major car bomb in a civilian area that resulted in the highest number of casualties since the days of the Lebanese civil war, was an occasion for Nasrallah to affirm the group's commitment to the protection of Lebanon against Sunni *takfiri* jihadis. However, in his reaction to both attacks, Nasrallah simultaneously rejected and affirmed sectarianism, thus using a discourse of ideological ambiguity that he had employed on many previous occasions. In his speech on 2 August 2013, three weeks after the first attack, for example, Nasrallah emphasised Hizbullah's Shiite identity. Yet in a speech on 16 August 2013, following the second attack, he criticised those who use sectarian rhetoric, saying that Sunni *takfiris* are a shared enemy of all sects. But Hizbullah's political opponents in Lebanon, mainly Saad Hariri and the Future Movement, responded by accusing Hizbullah of not matching words and deeds—of speaking against sectarianism yet escalating sectarian tension through its violent involvement in Syria. They also pointed out that Nasrallah's 16 August speech was marked by a contradictory stance towards the Lebanese state, at once accusing it of being weak—which necessitates Hizbullah's interference to 'protect' the country—and stating that Hizbullah wanted the state to be strong, while in practice Hizbullah was undermining the authority of the state by intervening in the Syrian crisis without being sanctioned to do so by the government.[10] The speech was also notable for its efforts to frame Hizbullah's involvement in Syria as being about the liberation of Palestine. As Nasrallah put it, 'If the battle against Takfiris required this, I will personally go fight in Syria, so will Hizbullah for the sake of the Syrian people and the country's cause, which is Palestine.'[11] Hizbullah's opponents responded by emphasising that it was Hizbullah's military intervention in aid of the Assad regime that caused jihadis to engage in terrorist attacks within Lebanon.

The trajectory of Hizbullah's political communication strategies

Hizbullah, as this book has shown, has used media and communication forms and spaces as discursive and symbolic realms in which identities and ideologies are performed and enacted, and as instrumental and material tools for realising its immediate and long-term goals. The group has proved remarkably adept at making use of institutional and organisational structures and different media spaces to construct and assemble a continuous and seamless repertoire of politics through which it represents itself, seeks to call diverse publics to action and deploys culturally significant frames to produce truth-claims about its role and identity. These discursive frameworks rest on an image of Hizbullah that is based on four interrelated pillars: Hizbullah as an ally of Iran; Hizbullah as a resistance group against Israel; Hizbullah's commitment to the liberation of Palestine; and Hizbullah's role as a religious party that is representative of the Shiite community in Lebanon.

Since its inception, Hizbullah has paid a remarkable degree of attention to ensuring that its self-image and identity reached out to its intended audiences. Its model of political communication meant that all its media products worked together simultaneously to produce the same narrative, and that the messages, images and symbols used in different media and spaces constantly reinforced each other. As Hizbullah expanded and as it managed to enhance its reach beyond its main constituency, the Shiites of Lebanon, the group's various media platforms themselves gained 'new political dimensions', particularly through their capacity to record information about Hizbullah, disseminate its worldview and construct a counter-narrative, constituting an archive of Hizbullah's 'story' from its own perspective. This archive, as suggested throughout the book, should be seen as a part of Hizbullah's efforts to construct and affirm a mediated regime of truth,[12] which refers to the discourses that societies use to denote truth. Hizbullah's articulation of its power intensified with the expansion of its institutional structures, media institutions and practices, allowing it to assert a 'visible and material presence' in Lebanon, and beyond that served as a visual and discursive representation of its power.

Hizbullah's communication strategy can be interpreted as a constant process of strategic communication based on 'developing a set of comprehensive messages and planning a series of symbolic events and photo opportunities to reinforce them'.[13] It is an example of Blumenthal's 'permanent campaign'. In his words, 'the permanent campaign is a process of continuing transformation. It never stops, but continues once its practitioners take power.'[14] The aim of the permanent campaign is to sustain legitimacy and credibility. To do so, Hizbullah has sought to act in a way that is consistent with Blumenthal's maxim that 'Credibility is verified by winning, staying in power. And legitimacy is confused with popularity.'[15]

At another level, Hizbullah's communication strategy can be seen as a traditional model of communication, or a one-to-many process of self- and image-mediation[16] that balances potential opportunities with structural constraints. As a group, Hizbullah focuses on its own media institutions and structures to disseminate information and announcements in order to summon its intended audiences as an engaged collective. Thus, mediation processes in Hizbullah's case reflect an asymmetric, rather than a dialectical, process of communication, a top-down model that centralises the dissemination of its messages and mirrors its hierarchical organisational structure. Such a model is intended to interpellate targeted populations as an imagined collective rather than allow for an open-ended and ongoing process of meaning-making, which is a feature of contemporary dialogical models of communication. Indeed, it is notable that Hizbullah, despite its heavy investment in media structures and institutions, has yet to embrace the digital media age entirely. Hizbullah has never had its own Facebook or Twitter page, although some of its media outlets do maintain a presence in social media. While, at the time of writing, al-'Ahd had Twitter, YouTube and Facebook accounts, al-Manar's Facebook page was removed in August 2012 in order to comply with US regulations concerning 'terrorist' organisations.[17] Al-'Ahd and al-Manar's YouTube channels disseminate their own programmes and news bulletins as well as Hassan Nasrallah's speeches.[18] Their Twitter accounts publicise news from their websites.[19] However, these Twitter feeds do not appear to include re-tweets of material from other sources or comments by users. Hizbullah's current use of social media therefore contrasts with these media's function, which is to allow multiple voices and points of view to be expressed without top-down, centralised control.

The trajectory of Hizbullah's communication strategy offers a number of important lessons for scholars of social movements, activism and political communication: first, communication strategy succeeds when a group can bridge the gap between the way it perceives itself and the way others perceive it, rather than remaining focused on the validity of its ideologies vis-à-vis those of others—the smaller the distance between these perceptions, the higher the degree of the communication strategy's success. Second, no communication strategy can succeed if it lacks credibility. Hizbullah has consistently relied on notions of justice and liberty to prove its legitimacy to its audiences, claiming to represent the voices of the people, to speak for the oppressed and to seek 'justice' for victims of Israeli aggression while branding itself as a 'liberator' and 'defender' of land and people. But this image was threatened when the Assad regime in Syria turned its weapons on its own people during the Arab Spring, as opposed to directing them towards the Israeli 'enemy' in the occupied Golan Heights. Finally, in order to be successful, there is a need for a dynamic relationship between communication strategy and changing political contexts. Hizbullah's evolving communication strategy is part of the party's place within a larger political opportunity structure[20] where 'fixed or permanent institutional features combine with more short-term, volatile, or conjectural factors to produce an overall particular opportunity structure'.[21] Before the Arab uprisings, particularly the Syrian revolt, Hizbullah had been largely successful at taking advantage of changes in the political environment to carve a favourable image and, simultaneously, to adapt its image according to changes in the environment. This highlights the fine balance that exists between political adaptability and reliability and between structure and agency. However, the uprisings, coupled with a significant shift in the visible performance of politics by ordinary citizens in the Arab world, thus far constitute the main impediments to maintaining the credibility of Hizbullah's familiar communication frames, and consequently its ability to capture the imagination of its intended audiences.

NOTES

INTRODUCTION

1. For a detailed history of Hizbullah see Amal Saad-Ghorayeb, *Hizbu'llah: Politics and Religion*, London: Pluto Press, 2002; Naim Qassem, *Hizbullah: The Story from Within*, Beirut: Dar al-Mahaja al-Baida', 1995, 2006 and 2010; Augustus Richard Norton, *Hezbollah*, Princeton: Princeton University Press, 2007; Fadil Abul al-Nassr, *Hizbullah: haqaeqwa-ab'ad*, Beirut: the International Company for Publishing, 2003; Judith Harik Palmer, *Hezbollah: The Changing Face of Terrorism*, London: I.B. Tauris, 2004; Thanassis Cambanis, *A Privilege to Die*, New York: Free Press, 2009; Joseph Al-Agha, *The Shifts in Hizbullah's Ideology: Religious Ideology, Political Ideology and Political Program*, Amsterdam: Amsterdam University Press, 2006; Lara Deeb, *An Enchanted Modern: Gender and Piety in Shi'i Lebanon*, Princeton: Princeton University Press, 2006.

2. Some scholars have even labelled Hizbullah the 'Khomeini' party. See, for example, Waddah Sharara, *Dawlat Hizbillah: Loubnan mojtama'an islamiyan*, Beirut: Dar An-Nahar, 2006.

3. Al-Sadr founded the Movement of the Deprived in Lebanon in 1974. He was an Iranian Shia cleric with Lebanese family ties who came to Lebanon in 1959 to replace the late clerical leader in the city of Tyre. In 1978 he mysteriously disappeared while on a trip to Libya, an event that catapulted him directly into the narrative of the Hidden Twelfth Imam al-Mahdi, or the hidden imam, who went into occultation in the eighth century and whose eventual return is seen as heralding the beginning of Islamic rule on earth.

4. Norton, *Hezbollah*.

5. Power in this sense is not something that rulers held over the ruled, but the result of complex and shifting interactions between various groups, particularly the dominant and the subordinate. Furthermore, power, according to Antonio Gramsci, is theorised as transactional without a fixed and permanent location, inherently unstable and constantly shifting. See Antonio Gramsci, *Selections*

191

from the Prison Notebook, trans. Quintin Hoare and Geoffrey Nowell-Smith, London: Lawrence and Wishart, 1970.

6. The political system set up at the end of the French Mandate was widely perceived to be the most useful way of representing the formally recognised religious sects in Lebanon. The gentlemen's agreement between two prominent Lebanese leaders, a Sunni and a Maronite, which came to be known as the National Pact, produced an arrangement whereby the most important government positions were determined on the basis of sect. In 1990, seats in parliament were determined on a presumed 50:50 ratio between Muslims and Christians.

7. The war of position, according to Gramsci, refers to the political struggle between hegemonic and would-be hegemonic forces fought in and across a variety of modern institutions, spaces and practices. See Gramsci, *Selections from the Prison Notebook*.

8. Iran's Ayatollah Ruhollah Khomeini postulated that the laws of a nation should be the laws of God, the sharia, and therefore those holding power should possess a full knowledge and understanding of the holy laws. The ruler of an Islamic state should be the preeminent *faqih* or jurist who surpasses all others in knowledge and whose ordinances must be obeyed.

9. In the manifesto, Hizbullah positioned itself as a force resisting the actions of Israel and the superpowers in order to free Lebanon from the manipulation of outside forces, but it left Hizbullah's aims for Lebanon vague. See Norton, *Hezbollah*, pp. 35–41, for further details of the manifesto.

10. See Saad-Ghorayeb, *Hizbu'llah*.

11. Palmer Harik, *Hezbollah*, p. 21.

12. Naim Qassem, *Ḥizb Allāh: al-manhaj, al-tajribah, al-mustaqbal*, Beirut: Dar al-Hadi, 2007.

13. Zahera Harb, *Channels of Resistance in Lebanon: Hizbullah and the Media*, London: I.B. Tauris, 2011.

14. Success, in this sense, refers to observable rather than concrete effects as it relates to the ways in which Hizbullah managed to boost its popularity and summon different publics in different contexts. The summoning of these publics does not mean that the reception of Hizbullah's practices and ideologies is uncontested.

15. Ahmad Nizar Hamzeh, *In the Path of Hizbullah*, Syracuse: Syracuse University Press, 2004, pp. 44–5.

16. See, e.g., Daniel Pipes, *Militant Islam Reaches America*, New York: W.W. Norton, 2003; Gilles Kepel, *Jihad: The Trail of Political Islam*, London: I.B. Tauris, 2004; and Bernard Lewis, *What Went Wrong? The Clash between Islam and Modernity in the Middle East*, New York: Harper Perennial, 2005.

17. See Chapter 5 for a history of Nasrallah's rise to power and charismatic authority.

18. For discussions on networks and Islamist movements, read Salwa Ismail, *Rethinking Islamist Politics: Culture, the State and Islamism*, London: I.B.

Tauris, 2006, and Sami Zubaida, *Islam, the People and the State: Political Ideas and Movements in the Middle East*, London: I.B. Tauris, 1993.

19. Manuel Castells, *The Network Society*, Amhurst: University of Massachusetts, 1997, p. 23.

20. Robert D. Benford and David A. Snow, 'Framing Processes and Social Movements: An Overview and Assessment', *Annual Review of Sociology*, 26 (2000), pp. 611–39.

21. Bert Klandermas, *The Social Psychology of Protest*, London: Wiley-Blackwell, 1997, p. 45.

22. See John Downing, *Radical Media: Rebellious Communication and Social Movements*, London: Sage, 2000.

23. Charles Tilly has proposed the concept 'the repertoire of collective action' as an analytical tool to address the logic of action and the logic of contexts. See Charles Tilly, 'Contentious Repertoires in Great Britain, 1758–1834', in Marth Traugott (ed.), *Repertories and Cycles of Collective Action*, Durham, NC: Duke University Press, 1995, pp. 15–42.

24. Talal Atrissi, 'What do the Shiites Want from their State?' *An-Nahar*, 25 Aug. 2010, http://www.annahar.com/content.php?priority=6&table=main&type=main&day=Wed (last accessed 15 Dec. 2012).

25. Atef Alshaer, 'Towards a Theory of Culture of Communication: The Fixed and the Dynamic in Hamas' Discourse', *Middle East Journal of Culture and Communication*, 1, 2 (2008), pp. 101–21.

26. A sophisticated body of revisionist anthropological and historical work that emerged in the 1980s challenged the view of culture as bounded, old and unified, shaped by internal logic, or packaged by certain ethnic, territorial or even civilisational space.

27. Amal Saad-Ghorayeb, interview with author. Beirut, 11 Nov. 2011.

28. Diane Singerman, for example, has provided a detailed analysis of informal networks in Cairo, thus giving guidelines for further studies on the role of families and institutions in contesting formal politics. See Diane Singerman, *Avenues of Participation: Family, Politics and Networks in Urban Quarters of Cairo*, Princeton, NJ: Princeton University Press, 1995.

29. The Palestine Liberation Organisation and Iran both used different popular cultural practices and spaces, such as symbols, flags and posters, to mobilise supporters.

30. Fritz Plasser with Gunda Plasser, *Global Political Campaigning: A Worldwide Analysis of Campaign Professionals and their Practices*, London: Praeger, 2002, p. 16.

31. Sharara, *Dawlat Hizbillah*.

32. The unit was responsible for all Hizbullah-affiliated media outlets until 1996, when it was restructured. The restructuring saw the television station al-Manar and the radio station al-Nour become controlled by an elected board of directors in accordance with the Lebanese Audio-Visual Law. See Harb, *Channels of Resistance*, pp. 173–228.

33. Hassan Nasrallah, interview with *Nida al-Watan*, 31 Aug. 1993, cited in Nicholas Noe (ed.), *Voice of Hezbollah: The Statements of Sayyed Hasan Nassrallah*, London: Verso, 2007.

34. Toby Harnden, 'Video Games Attract Young to Hizbollah', *Daily Telegraph*, 21 Feb. 2007.

1. HIZBULLAH'S POLITICAL STRATEGY

1. Amin Elias, 'Looking into the Manifestos of Future Movement and Hizbullah: The Obscure Nation' (Qira'a fi wathiqatayytayyar al-moustaqbalwahizbillah: al-watan al-ghamidh), *An-Nahar*, 25 Oct. 2010, http://www.annahar.com/content.php?priority=9&table=main&type=main&day=Mon(last accessed 1 Nov. 2010).

2. Hizbullah, '2009 Manifesto', reproduced in Ziad Majed, *Hezbollah and the Shiite Community: From Political Confessionalization to Confessional Specialization*, Washington, DC: The Aspen Institute, 2010, pp. 21–4, http://www.aspeninstitute.org/sites/default/files/content/docs/pubs/LRF_AW_digital_1122.pdf (last accessed 10 Jan. 2011).

3. Naim Qassem, *Hizballah: al-manhaj, al-tajribah, al-mustaqbal*, Beirut: Dar al-Hadi, 2008, p. 290.

4. Quoted in Nicholas Blanford, *Killing Mr Lebanon: The Assassination of Rafik Hariri and its Impact on the Middle East*, London: I.B. Tauris, 2009, p. 190.

5. Hizbullah, '2009 Manifesto', in Majed, *Hezbollah and the Shiite Community*.

6. Thanassis Cambanis, *A Privilege to Die: Inside Hezbollah's Legions and their Endless War Against Israel*, New York: Simon and Schuster, 2010.

7. Hizbullah, '2009 Manifesto', in Majed, *Hezbollah and the Shiite Community*.

8. Sheikh Abbas Shehadi, 'The Muslim and the Secularism of the State', *Al-'Ahd*, 26 Mar. 1999, p. 21 (the article's author is credited as writing from 'Holy Qom' in Iran).

9. Hizbullah, 'Identity and Goals', 2004, reproduced in Joseph Al-Agha, *The Shifts in Hizbullah's Ideology*, Amsterdam: University of Amsterdam Press, 2006, pp. 244–6, 245.

10. Naim Qassim, *Mujtama' al-muqawamah: Irādat al-shahādahwa-sinā'at al-intissār* (The Society of Resistance: The Will to Martyrdom and the Making of Victory), Beirut: Dar Al- Maaref Al-hijmiah, 2008, p. 79.

11. Gideon Rose, *How Wars End: Why We Always Fight the Last Battle*, New York: Simon and Schuster, 2010, p. 5.

12. Rami Olleik, *Tarik al-nahl: joumhouriyat Rami Olleik*, Beirut: Dar Al-Nahl, 2008, p. 96.

13. Cambanis, *A Privilege to Die*.

14. See Elizabeth Picard, 'The Political Economy of Civil War in Lebanon', in Steven Heydemann (ed.), *War, Institutions, and Social Change in the Middle East*, Berkeley: University of California Press, 2000, pp. 292–322.

15. The March 8 and March 14 coalitions were formed in 2005 shortly after the assassination of Hariri. The first group was formed by Hizbullah, Amal and the Free Patriotic Movement—a Maronite political party led by Michel Aoun, which signed a memorandum of understanding with Hizbullah—as well as a number of smaller groups. March 8 declared its loyalty to the Syrian regime in the face of popular anti-Syrian protests in Lebanon accusing Syria of being behind Hariri's assassination. The March 14 coalition was formed by Hariri's political party the Future Movement, the Maronite parties Kataeb and the Lebanese Forces, as well as the Progressive Socialist Party led by the Druze leader Walid Jumblat (who later detached himself from the group as an 'independent'). The two camps have been engaged in intense political rivalry since their formation, with March 14 taking a clear anti-Syrian stance and calling on Hizbullah to hand over its weapons to the Lebanese state.

16. David Hirst, *Beware of Small States: Lebanon, Battleground of the Middle East*, New York: Nation Books, 2010.

17. Blanford, *Killing Mr. Lebanon*. Hariri also created the Elyssar project that aimed to regenerate the Ouzai area along the coast between Beirut's airport and central Beirut. As the area is controlled by Hizbullah, being adjacent to the southern suburbs, and housing a significant number of Hizbullah supporters who were originally displaced to the area from the South during the Lebanese civil war, the Elyssar project was met with strong resistance and was never fully implemented. See http://www.elyssar.com/overview.html

18. Vali Nasr, *The Shia Revival: How Conflicts Within Islam Will Shape the Future*, New York: W.W. Norton, 2006, p. 260.

19. Rose, *How Wars End*, p. 240.

20. Abbas William Sami, 'A Stable Structure on Shifting Sands: Assessing the Hizbullah–Iran–Syria Relationship', *The Middle East Journal*, 62, 1 (2008), pp. 32–53.

21. Blanford, *Killing Mr. Lebanon*, p. 66.

22. 'Prime Minister Hariri and the "Useful Peace"', *Al-'Ahd*, 10 Sep. 1993, p. 8.

23. For an analysis of the impact of proportional representation, see Elias Muhanna, 'Who Would Benefit from Proportional Representation in Lebanon's 2013 Elections?' qifanabki.com, 21 Sep. 2011, http://qifanabki.com/2011/09/21/who-would-benefit-from-proportional-representation-in-lebanons-2013-elections/ (last accessed 8 Mar. 2013).

24. Hizbullah, 'Open Letter', 1985, reproduced in Fayez Qazzi, *Min Ḥasan NaṣrAllāh ilá Mīshāl Awn: qirā'ahsiyāsiyah li-ḤizbAllāh*, Beirut: Riyāḍ al-Rayyis lil-Kutubwa-al-Nashr, 2008, p. 186.

25. Hizbullah, 'Identity and Goals', p. 246.

26. Hirst, *Beware of Small States*, p. 179.

27. Hizbullah, '2009 Manifesto', in Majed, *Hezbollah and the Shiite Community*.

28. Cambanis, *A Privilege to Die*, p. 114.

29. Fareed Zakaria, *From Wealth to Power: The Unusual Origins of America's World Role*, Princeton, NJ: Princeton University Press, 1998.

30. Jeffrey W. Taliaferro, 'Neoclassical Realism and Resource Extraction: State Building for Future War', in Steven N. Lobell and Norrin M. Ripsman (eds), *Neoclassical Realism, the State and Foreign Policy*, pp. 194–226, Cambridge: Cambridge University Press, 2009, p. 216.

31. Rose, *How Wars End*, p. 278.

32. Sara Fregonese, 'Beyond the "Weak State": Hybrid Sovereignties in Beirut', *Environment and Planning D: Society and Space*, 30, 4 (2012), pp. 655–74.

33. Ahmad Nizar Hamzeh, *In the Path of Hizbullah*, Syracuse: Syracuse University Press, 2004.

34. Hirst, *Beware of Small States*, p. 314.

35. Quoted in Hirst, *Beware of Small States*, p. 313.

36. Blanford, *Killing Mr. Lebanon*, p. 191.

37. Al-Algha, *The Shifts in Hizbullah's Ideology*.

38. Quoted in Nir Rosen, *Aftermath: Following the Bloodshed of America's Wars in the Muslim World*, New York: Nation Books, 2010, p. 395.

39. Quoted in Qazzi, *Min Ḥasan NaṣrAllāh ilá Mīshāl Awn*, p. 85.

40. Hizbullah, '2009 Manifesto', in Majed, *Hezbollah and the Shiite Community*.

41. Augustus Richard Norton, 'Hizballah: From Radicalism to Pragmatism?' *Middle East Policy*, 5, 4 (1998), pp. 147–58; Magnus Ranstorp, 'The Strategy and Tactics of Hizballah's Current "Lebanonization Process"', *Mediterranean Politics*, 3, 1 (1998), pp. 103–34.

42. Tony Badran, 'Hezbollah's Agenda in Lebanon', *Current Trends in Islamist Ideology*, 8 (16 May 2009), http://www.currenttrends.org/research/detail/hezbollahs-agenda-in-lebanon (last accessed 31 July 2013); Blanford, *Killing Mr. Lebanon*.

43. Blanford, *Killing Mr. Lebanon*.

44. Hizbullah and its allies captured twelve seats in the first parliamentary election it contested in 1992; by 2009, Hizbullah alone had twelve parliamentary seats, with the March 8 coalition gaining fifty-eight seats to March 14's sixty in a parliament of 128 seats (if the Progressive Socialist Party is counted as an independent).

45. Al-Agha, *The Shifts in Hizbullah's Ideology*, p. 164.

46. Ibid., p. 165.

47. Qassim, *Hizballah*, p. 279.

48. Cambanis, *A Privilege to Die*.

49. Hirst, *Beware of Small States*, p. 315.

50. 'Hizbullah Imposes its Political Power at the Cost of its Military Power' (Hizbullah yafourdh qowwatahu al-siyasiya 'ala hisab qowatihi al-'askariya), *Elnashra*, Monday, 8 Nov. 2010, http://www.elnashra.com/papers-1-24067.html (last accessed 9 Nov. 2010).

51. Quoted in Hirst, *Beware of Small States*, p. 314.

52. Quoted in Rosen, *Aftermath*, p. 402.

53. It is interesting to observe how Nasrallah has capitalised on the existence of a Lebanese state seen as unable to defend itself against Israel in his speech of

2010, placing Hizbullah as the protector of the Lebanese army.

54. Quoted in Hirst, *Beware of Small States*, p. 384.

55. Quoted in Cambanis, *A Privilege to Die*, p. 140.

56. The text of the speech can be found in English on http://realisticbird. wordpress.com/2009/05/23/sayyed-nasrallah-execute-spies-starting-with-shiite-collaborators/ (last accessed 31 July 2013).

57. Of course, not all Lebanese Shiites support or follow Hizbullah, but the majority at least sympathises with Hizbullah.

58. Martin Rudner, 'Hizbullah Terrorism Finance: Fund-Raising and Money-Laundering', *Studies in Conflict and Terrorism*, 33, 8 (2010), pp. 700–15.

59. See Simon Haddad, 'The Origins of Popular Support for Lebanon's Hezbollah', *Studies in Conflict and Terrorism*, 29, 1 (2006), pp. 21–34.

60. Rose, *How Wars End*, p. 278.

61. Ibid., p. 279.

62. See Cynthia Sylva Hamieh and Roger MacGinty, 'A Very Political Reconstruction: Governance and Reconstruction in Lebanon after the 2006 War', *Disasters*, 34 (2010), pp. 103–23.

63. Hirst, *Beware of Small States*, p. 315; see also Blanford, *Killing Mr. Lebanon*, p. 168.

64. See Lara Deeb and Mona Harb, *Leisurely Islam: Negotiating Geography and Morality in Shi'ite South Beirut*, Princeton: Princeton University Press, 2013.

65. Cambanis, *A Privilege to Die*.

66. Fadi Toufic, *Bilad allah al-dhayiqa: al-dhahiya ahlan wa hizban*, Beirut: Dar al-Jadid, 2004.

67. Hirst, *Beware of Small States*.

68. A timeline of incidents against the Lebanese Option Gathering in 2009 can be found on http://licus.org/blog/2009/06/timeline-attacks-against-lebanese. html (last accessed 31 July 2013).

69. Raghida Bahnam, 'Ali al-Amin: Hizbullah Exercises Coercion on Lebanon's Shiites' (Ali al-Amin: Hizbullah youmaris al-tarheeb 'ala shiat loubnan), *Asharq Alawsat*, Thursday, 2 Dec. 2010, http://www.aawsat.com/details.asp?s ection=4&paper=597713&issueno=11692

70. The information presented here is based on in-depth interviews conducted by the author with several Shiite public figures who shall remain anonymous for security purposes.

71. Talal Atrissi, 'What do the Shiites Want from their State?' (Mathayourid al-shia min dawlatihim?), *An-Nahar*, 25 Aug. 2010, http://www.annahar.com/ content.php?priority=6&table=main&type=main&day=Wed (last accessed 30 Aug. 2010).

72. Hizbullah, '2009 Manifesto', in Majed, *Hezbollah and the Shiite Community*.

73. Hirst, *Beware of Small States*, p. 231.

74. Cambanis, *A Privilege to Die*, p. 226.

75. Ibid., p. 110.

76. Carl von Clausewitz, *Principles of War*, 1942 [1812], http://www.clausewitz.

com/readings/Principles/ (last accessed 10 Nov. 2010).

77. Carl von Clausewitz, *On War*, Digireads edition, 2008 [1832], http://books. google.com/books?id=qkj-gQGD5g8C&printsec=frontcover#v=onepage&q &f=false, p. 343 (last accessed 10 Nov. 2010).

78. See Bernedetta Berti, 'Armed Groups as Political Parties and their Role in Electoral Politics: The Case of Hizballah', *Studies in Conflict and Terrorism*, 34, 12 (2011), pp. 942–62.

79. Clausewitz, *On War*, p. 35.

80. Al-Agha, *The Shifts in Hizbullah's Ideology*.

81. Blanford reports that only 100,000 attended.

82. Blanford, *Killing Mr. Lebanon*, p. 117.

83. Clausewitz, *Principles of War*.

84. Quoted in Waddah Sharara, *Dawlat Hizbillah: Loubnan mojtama'an islamiyan*, Beirut: Dar An-Nahar, 2006, p. 401.

85. Hirst, *Beware of Small States*, p. 315.

86. Rose, *How Wars End*, p. 11.

87. Hamzeh, *In the Path of Hizbullah*, p. 29.

2. FROM THE INVASION TO THE LIBERATION: COMMUNICATING HIZBULLAH'S POLITICAL REPERTOIRE, 1982–2000

1. Ahmad Nizar Hamzeh, *In the Path of Hizbullah*, Syracuse: Syracuse University Press, 2004, p. 44

2. For further details of Hizbullah's structures and leadership, see Hamzeh, *In the Path of Hizbullah*.

3. See Salwa Ismail, *Rethinking Islamist Politics: Culture, the State and Islamism*, London: I.B. Tauris, 2004.

4. Diane Singerman, 'The Networked World of Islamist Social Movements', in Quintan Wiktorowicz (ed.), *Islamic Activism: A Social Movement Theory Approach*, Bloomington: Indiana University Press, 2004, p. 159.

5. Waddah Sharara, *Dalwat Hizbillah: Lubnan mujtama'an islamiyyan*, Beirut: Dar An-Nahar, 1996/2006.

6. The launch was timely as it coincided with the establishment of al-Muqawama al-Islamiyya (the Islamic Resistance in Lebanon), Hizbullah's military wing.

7. Judith Palmer Harik, *Hezbollah: The Changing Face of Terrorism*, New York: I.B. Tauris, 2007, p. 66.

8. See Chapter 1 for further details.

9. Iran's Ayatollah Ruhollah Khomeini postulated that the laws of a nation should be the laws of God, the sharia, and therefore those holding power should possess a full knowledge and understanding of the holy laws. The ruler of an Islamic state should be the preeminent *faqih*, or jurist who surpasses all others in knowledge and whose ordinances must be obeyed.

10. Maura Conway, 'Terror TV? An Exploration of Hizbullah's al-Manar Television', in James F. Forest (ed.), *Countering Terrorism and Insurgency in the 21st Century*, pp. 401–19, Westport, CT: Greenwood Publishing Group, 2007.

11. Naim Qassem, *Hizbullah, al-manhaj, al-tajriba, al-mustaqbal*, Beirut: Dar al-Mahajja al-Baida, 2010, p. 139.

12. The unit was responsible for all Hizbullah-affiliated media outlets until 1996, when it was restructured. The restructuring saw the television station al-Manar and the radio station al-Nour become controlled by an elected board of directors in accordance with the Lebanese Audio-Visual Law. See Zahera Harb, *Channels of Resistance in Lebanon: Liberation Propaganda, Hezbollah and the Media*, London: I.B. Tauris, 2011.

13. Hamzeh, *In the Path of Hizbullah*.

14. Ibid.

15. Cited in *al-'Ahd*, 7 June 1989.

16. Cited in *al-'Ahd*, 6 June 1989.

17. Cited in *al-'Ahd*, 7 June 1989.

18. Ibid.

19. Zeina Maasri, 'The Aesthetics of Belonging: Transformations in Hizbullah's Political Posters (1985–2006)', *Middle East Journal of Culture and Communication*, 5, 2 (2012), pp. 149–89.

20. The use of the language of Islam, in which Palestine was implicated by virtue of Jerusalem, was common during the rule of the Egyptian leader Gamal Abdel Nasser. Indeed, as Albert Hourani writes, 'the language of Islam was the natural language which the leaders used in appeals to the masses'. See his *A History of the Arab Peoples*, Cambridge: Cambridge University Press, 1991, p. 405.

21. Cited in *al-'Ahd*, 12 Oct. 1990.

22. *Al-'Ahd*, 28 June 1984, issue 1.

23. Ibid.

24. Quran, 17/8–4.

25. Walid El-Houri and Dima Saber, 'Filming Resistance: A Hezbollah Strategy', *Radical History Review*, 106 (2010), pp. 70–85.

26. Fernando Solanas and Octavio Getino, 'Towards a Third Cinema', *Cineaste*, 4, 3 (1970), pp. 1–10.

27. Boris Groys, *Art Power*, Cambridge, MA: The MIT Press, 2003.

28. Author interview with Amal Saad-Ghorayeb, Beirut, 11 Nov. 2011.

29. Ibid.

30. This discourse built on the doctrine of Sayyed Mohammad Hussein Fadlallah, who advocated abjuring power in favour of justice.

31. See Barbara Harlow, *Resistance Literature*, London: Routledge, 1987.

32. *Al-'Ahd*, 4 Sep. 1987, pp. 4–5, and also *al-'Ahd*, 14 Oct. 1988, p. 10.

33. *Safhat 'izz fi kitab al-ummah: 'ard wa-tawthiq li-'amliyyat al-muqawamah al-islamiyyah*, Beirut: Al-wihdah al-I'lamiyyah al-markazziyyah, 1996, p. 319.

34. Franz Fanon, *The Wretched of the Earth*, New York: Grove Press, 1963, p. 29.
35. In this context, Sayyed Abbas al-Musawwi states that 'this *umma* which does not possess the same material capacity as that of its opponents has nothing but to mobilise all forces of activity within it. Is there a power more powerful than that of an *umma* which has decided to choose martyrdom over humiliation?' See *Safhāt 'izz fi kitab al-ummah*, p. 5.
36. *Dirasat fi mithaq harakat amal, al-kitab al-awwal*, Beirut: Maktab al-'aqidah wal-thaqafah, n.d., pp. 99–100.
37. Jamal Sankari, *Fadlallah: The Making of a Radical Shiite Leader*, London: Saqi Books, 2008.
38. *Al-'Ahd*, 18 June 1984, p. 6.
39. Ibid., p. 1.
40. Talal Atrissi, 'What do the Shiites Want from their State?' *An-Nahar*, 25 Aug. 2010, http://www.annahar.com/content.php?priority=6&table=main&type=main&day=Wed (last accessed 12 Jan. 2011).
41. *Al-'Ahd*, 18 July 1984, p. 5.
42. Augustus Richard Norton, *Hezbollah*, Princeton: Princeton University Press, 2007.
43. Benedict Anderson, *Imagined Communities*, London: Verso, 1983.
44. See Harb, *Channels of Resistance*, p. 202.
45. Naim Qassem, *Hizb Allah: al-manhaj, al-tajribah, al-mustaqbal*, Beirut: Dar al-Hadi, 2005, p. 257.
46. Lucia Volk, *Memorials and Martyrs in Modern Lebanon*, Bloomington: Indiana University Press, 2010, p. 139.
47. See Lara Deeb, *An Enchanted Modern: Gender and Public Piety in Shi'i Lebanon*, Princeton: Princeton University Press, 2006.
48. Ibid.
49. Kamran Scot Aghaie, *The Martyrs of Karbala: Shi'i Symbols and Rituals in Modern Iran*, Seattle: University of Washington Press, 2004.
50. Joseph Alagha, *Hizbullah's Identity Construction*, Amsterdam: Amsterdam University Press, 2010, pp. 48–9.
51. Deeb, *An Enchanted Modern*, p. 138.
52. The enclosed structure incorporated a major road and adjacent lots.
53. Deeb, *An Enchanted Modern*, p. 15.
54. It is noteworthy to refer to Joseph Alagha, who writes about the Movement of the Deprived that 'Imam al-Sadr did not establish *Harakat Al-Mahrumin* (The Movement of the Deprived) on his own.' As he writes, in 1974 al-Sadr, together with Gregoire Haddad, a Greek Catholic archbishop, founded Harakat Al-Mahrumin in a bid to alleviate the suffering of the deprived people regardless of their sectarian or ethnic affiliations. As such it was open to all the 'downtrodden' from every sect, and not only restricted to the Shiites. However, this intercommunity openness did not last long enough, as the ruling elites were afraid this would undermine the community's patronage system. With the outbreak of the civil war, Harakat Al-Mahrumin

developed into a Shiite-based movement under the leadership of al-Sadr. See Alagha, *Hizbullah's Identity Construction*, pp. 205–6.

55. *Al-'Ahd*, 14 Feb. 1985, p. 5.
56. Ibid., p. 7.
57. *Al-'Ahd*, 9 Nov. 1990, p. 8.
58. Nasrallah's speech on 'the Day of the Martyr' in 2010. Available at http://www.moqawama.org/essaydetails.php?eid=17725&cid=142 (last accessed on 5 May 2012).
59. *Al-'Ahd*, 27 Oct. 1989, p. 1.
60. In fact, most of the Islamic-oriented parties in the Middle East, but particularly Hamas and Hizbullah, integrate nationalism within an Islamic framework, using references to the Quran and the Hadith. For example, they use phrases like '*hub al-watan min al-Imaan*' (the love of the homeland is part of belief).
61. Hizbullah's most prominent Lebanese political ally is Michel Aoun's Free Patriotic Movement. Though Aoun has long called for Hizbullah's disarmament, he reached an accord with Hizbullah in Feb. 2006 that reflects his movement's positioning as a relative outsider in the country's political system and his frustration with the domination of the Sunni and Christian urban bourgeoisie. The agreement was also a result of his long-standing rivalry with the more traditional Christian leadership. See Heiko Wimmen, 'Rallying around the Renegade', *Middle East Report*, 27 Aug. 2007, http://www.merip.org/mero/mero082707 (last accessed 12 Mar. 2013).
62. See Palmer Harik, *Hezbollah*.
63. Alagha, *The Shifts in Hizbullah's Ideology*, pp. 38–41.
64. Ibid., pp. 55–9.
65. Ibid.
66. See Chapter 5 for a detailed history of Nasrallah's rise in Hizbullah's structures.
67. See Chapter 3 for a detailed discussion of Hizbullah's visual media.
68. See Chapter 5 on Nasrallah's mediated image.
69. *Al-'Ahd*, 7 July 1992, p. 4.
70. Ibid.
71. Ibid., p. 21.
72. Ibid.
73. Ibid., p. 22.
74. Ibid.
75. Avi Jorisch, 'Al-Manar: Hizbullah TV, 24/7', *Middle East Quarterly*, XI, 1(2004), pp. 17–31, http://www.meforum.org/583/al-manar-hizbullah-tv-24-7
76. 'The Experience of al-Manar is One of Openness towards the Other', *As-Safir*, 4 Aug. 1993.
77. Robert Fisk, 'Television News is Secret Weapon of the Intifada', *The Independent*, 2 Dec. 2000.

78. See Chapter 5.

79. Laleh Khalili, *Heroes and Martyrs of Palestine: The Politics of National Commemoration*, Cambridge: Cambridge University Press, 2007, pp. 73, 177.

80. Sune Haugbolle, *War and Memory in Lebanon*, Cambridge: Cambridge University Press, 2010, p. 189.

81. Hala Jaber, *Hezbollah, Born with a Vengeance*, New York: Columbia University Press, 1997, p. 196.

82. *As-Safir*, 16 Apr. 1996.

83. Harb, *Channels of Resistance in Lebanon*, pp. 177–8.

84. Ibid., p. 174.

85. Nicolas Blanford, *Warriors of God: Inside Hezbollah's Thirty-Year Struggle against Israel*, New York: Random House, 2012, p. 196.

86. Ibid., p. 182.

87. See Volk, *Memorials and Martyrs in Modern Lebanon*, 2010.

88. Ibid.

89. *Al-'Ahd*, 23 Apr. 1999, p. 5.

90. See Harb, *Channels of Resistance*, pp. 190–91.

91. Hassan Nasrallah, 'Speech about the Martyrdom of Hadi Nasrallah', *Al-Manar*, 13 Sep. 1997, http://www.youtube.com/watch?v=l3A0IwDL_M0 (last accessed 10 Aug. 2011).

92. Nasrallah used his demeanour, popularity and religious credentials to attract more followers, and did not seem to mind a cult forming around him, as evident in the banners, photos, oil paintings and other memorabilia dedicated to him and about him in shops and public spaces in the southern suburbs of Beirut and elsewhere in Lebanon.

93. Cited in *As-Safir*, 11 Apr. 1997.

94. *Al-'Ahd*, 26 Oct. 1999, p. 21.

95. Lisa Wedeen, *Ambiguities of Domination: Politics, Rhetoric and Symbols in Contemporary Syria*, Chicago: University of Chicago Press, 1999.

96. The concept of the archive has been broadly used by cultural studies scholars as a paradigmatic concept to interpret the production and consumption of popular media, particularly when it is used by various groups and parties for identity construction and to undermine authoritarian power.

97. Mark Poster, *The Mode of Information: Poststructuralism and Social Context*, Cambridge: Polity Press in association with Basil Blackwell, 1990, pp. 73–98.

3. HIZBULLAH IN THE TWENTY-FIRST CENTURY: THE STRUGGLE FOR POLITICAL SURVIVAL, 2000–12

1. Augustus Richard Norton, 'Hizballah and the Israeli Withdrawal from Southern Lebanon', *Journal of Palestine Studies*, 30, 1 (2000), pp. 22–35;

Augustus Richard Norton, *Hezbollah: A Short History*, Princeton, NJ: Princeton University Press, 2009.

2. Hassan Nasrallah, 'Speech about the Liberation of South Lebanon', Al-Manar, 25 May 2000, http://www.youtube.com/watch?v=V_EAmIzqtu8 (last accessed 20 July 2012).

3. Ibid.

4. See Chapter 5 for a discussion of Nasrallah as a Hizbullah leader.

5. *Al-'Ahd*, 2 June 2000, no. 852, p. 1.

6. Zahera Harb, *Channels of Resistance in Lebanon: Liberation Propaganda, Hezbollah and the Media*, London: I.B Tauris, 2011, p. 221.

7. *Al-'Ahd*, 28 June 2000, no. 852, p. 1.

8. Victoria Firmo-Fontan, 'Power, NGO's and Lebanese Television: A Case Study of Al-Manar TV and the Hizbullah's Women's Association', in Naomi Sakr (ed.), *Women and Media in the Middle East: Power through Self-Expression*, pp. 138–62, London: I.B. Tauris, 2004.

9. Nayef Krayyem, 'Al-Manar', *As-Safir*, 28 Dec. 2004.

10. Ibid.

11. Robert Fisk, 'Television News is Secret Weapon of the Intifada', *The Independent*, 2 Dec. 2000.

12. Krayyem, 'Al-Manar'.

13. Joseph Elie Al-Agha, *The Shifts in Hizbullah's Ideology: Religious Ideology, Political Ideology, and Political Program*, Amsterdam: Amsterdam University Press, 2006, p. 90.

14. For example, see Ja'far Atrisi, *Hizbullah: al-khaiar al-as'ab wa-damanat al-watan al-kubra, qira'ah fi Lubnaan: Sykes-Picot wa Balfour wa al-qaraar 1559* (The Most difficult Choice, the Grandest Pledge of the Homeland, a Reading of Lebanon, Sykes-Picot, Balfour Declaration and Resolution 1559), Beirut: Dar al-mahajjah al-baida', 2005.

15. Anne Marie Baylouny, *Al-Manar and Alhurra: Competing Satellite Stations and Ideologies*, DTIC Document, 2006, http://www.dtic.mil/cgibin/GetTR Doc?AD=ADA478865&Location=U2&doc=GetTRDoc.pdf (last accessed 20 July 2012).

16. 'Hezbollah's Unconventional Quiz', BBC News, 20 Apr. 2004, http://news.bbc.co.uk/2/hi/middle_east/3640551.stm (last accessed 8 Mar. 2013).

17. Osama Safa, 'Lebanon Springs Forward', *Journal of Democracy*, 17, 1 (2006), pp. 22–37.

18. *Al-'Intiqad*, photo spread on Hariri, 18 Feb. 2005, no. 1097, p. 10.

19. *Al-'Intiqad*, 'Washington and Paris Push for Internationalising the Lebanese Situation', 18 Feb. 2005, no. 1097, p. 9.

20. Ibid.

21. Lina Khatib, 'Television and Public Action in the Beirut Spring', in Naomi Sakr (ed.), *Arab Media and Political Renewal: Community, Legitimacy and Public Life*, pp. 28–43, London: I.B. Tauris, 2007.

22. Lisa Wedeen, *Ambiguities of Domination: Politics, Rhetoric, and Symbols in*

Contemporary Syria, Chicago: University of Chicago Press, 2009, p. 13.
23. Ibid.
24. Ibid.
25. Ibid.
26. Khatib, 'Television and Public Action in the Beirut Spring'.
27. March 14 won sixty-nine out of 128 seats in this election.
28. 'Atrisi, Hizbullah, pp. 99–100.
29. Judith Palmer Harik, Hezbollah: The Changing Face of Terrorism, London: I.B. Tauris, 2005.
30. See al-Intiqad, 1 July 2005, no. 1116, p. 9.
31. Ibid., p. 1.
32. Ibid.
33. Baylouny, Al-Manar and Alhurra.
34. Augustus Richard Norton, 'Lebanon: Securing a Lasting Cease-Fire', opening statement (updated) of testimony for a hearing of the US Senate Foreign Relations Committee 13, 2006, http://www.globalsecurity.org/military/library/congress/2006_hr/060913-norton.pdf, last accessed 20 Jan. 2012.
35. Marvin Kalb and Carol Saivetz, 'The Israeli–Hezbollah War of 2006: The Media as a Weapon in Asymmetrical Conflict', The Harvard International Journal of Press/Politics, 12, 3 (2007), pp. 43–66.
36. Peter Ajemian, 'Resistance Beyond Time and Space: Hezbollah's Media Campaigns', Arab Media & Society, 5 (Spring 2008), pp. 1–17.
37. David M. Rosen, 'Leadership in World Cultures', in Barbara Kellerman (ed.), Leadership: Multidisciplinary Perspectives, pp. 39–62, Englewood Cliffs, NJ: Prentice-Hall, 1984.
38. See Chapter 5 for further discussion.
39. Ajemian, 'Resistance Beyond Time and Space'.
40. Gabriel Weimann, 'Hezbollah Dot Com: Hezbollah's Online Campaign', in Dan Caspi and Tal Samuel-Azran (eds), New Media and Innovative Technologies, pp. 17–38, Beer-Sheva, Israel: Ben-Gurion University Press, 2008.
41. Quoted in David Aaker, Building Strong Brands, New York: The Free Press, 1995, p. 303.
42. Peter van Ham, 'The Rise of the Brand State: The Postmodern Politics of Image and Reputation', Foreign Affairs, 10 Oct. 2001.
43. Weimann, 'Hezbollah Dot Com'.
44. 'Hezbollah Launches Another Anti-Israel Computer Game', Tayyar.org, 15 Aug. 2007, http://www.tayyar.org/tayyar/articles.php?type=news&article_id=32018 (last accessed 21 June 2012).
45. Andrzej Falkowski and Wojciech Cwalina, 'Methodology of Constructing Effective Political Advertising: An Empirical Study of the Polish Presidential Election in 1995', in Bruce I. Newman (ed.), Handbook of Political Marketing, Thousand Oaks, CA: Sage, 1999, p. 286.

46. Ibid.
47. David Aaker, *Building Strong Brands*, New York: The Free Press, 2005.
48. Jim Quilty and Lysanda Ohrstrom, 'The Second Time as Farce: Stories of Another Lebanese Reconstruction', *Middle East Report*, 243 (2007), pp. 31–48.
49. Claus Mueller, *The Politics of Communication: A Study in the Political Sociology of Language, Socialization, and Legitimation*, New York: Oxford University Press, 1973, p. 129.
50. Kalb and Saivetz, 'The Israeli–Hezbollah War of 2006'.
51. Anthony Shadid, 'Israel, Hizbollah Vow Wider War', *The Washington Post*, 15 July 2006, p. A01, http://www.washingtonpost.com/wp-dyn/content/article/2006/07/14/AR2006071400385.html (last accessed 8 June 2011).
52. Knut Bergmann and Wolfram Wickert, 'Selected Aspects of Communication in German Election Campaigns', in Bruce I. Newman (ed.), *Handbook of Political Marketing*, pp. 455–84, London: Sage, 1999, p. 458.
53. Peter Radunski, *Wahlkämpfe: Moderne wahlkampfführung als politische Kommunikation*, Munich: Olzog, 1980, p. 9.
54. Peter Grafe, *Wahlkampf: Die Olympiade der Demokratie*, Frankfurt: Eichborn, 1994, p. 155.
55. Arthur Schweitzer, *The Age of Charisma*, Chicago: Nelson-Hall, 1984.
56. Hackman and Johnson, *Leadership*, p. 113.
57. David Douglas Belt, 'Global Islamism: Understanding and Strategy', *Connections*, 4 (2006), p. 47.
58. Lawrence Pintak, 'The Role of the Media as Watchdogs, Agenda-Setters and Gate-Keepers in Arab States', paper 5.3, the Role of the News Media in the Governance Reform Agenda, World Bank/Harvard Kennedy School, 2008.
59. *Al-'Abaya*, Dir. Reda Qashmar, 2006.
60. Ajemian, 'Resistance Beyond Time and Space'.
61. Pels, 'Aesthetic Representation and Political Style', p. 59.
62. Hizbullah named its 2006 operation 'The Truthful Pledge' in reference to Nasrallah's pledge to return detainees in Israeli prisons.
63. Pels, 'Aesthetic Representation and Political Style'.
64. Weber, *Economy and Society*.
65. Boris Groys, *Art Power*, Cambridge, MA: The MIT Press, 2008, p. 131.
66. James Stanyer, *Modern Political Communications: National Political Communication Systems in an Uncertain, Fragmented and Unequal Age*, Cambridge: Polity Press, 2007.
67. Bruce I. Newman, 'A Predictive Model of Voter Behavior: The Repositioning of Bill Clinton', in Bruce I. Newman (ed.), *Handbook of Political Marketing*, Thousand Oaks, CA: Sage, 1999, p. 261.
68. Newman, 'A Predictive Model of Voter Behavior', p. 278.
69. William M. Arkin, 'Divining Victory: Airpower in the 2006 Israel–Hezbollah War', *Strategic Studies Quarterly*, 1, 2 (2007), pp. 98–141.
70. Kevin Peraino, 'Winning Hearts and Minds', *Newsweek*, 2 Oct. 2006, http://

www.newsweek.com/2006/10/01/winning-hearts-and-minds.html (last accessed 10 July 2011).

71. Ibid.
72. Ibid.
73. Ibid., emphasis added.
74. See http://july2006.moqawama.org/aggression/index.php.
75. See http://www.moqawama.org/uploaded1/flashes/infograph/30years2013/index.html
76. Maryam Ali Jum'a, *Rusul al-muhibbeen*, in *Qalam Rassas*, Beirut: Risalaat, 2010, pp. 229–35.
77. Arwa Mahmoud, *Qitaal Hizbullah, ad-deen fi muwaajahat Israel: kaifa intasara Hizbullah fii harb tammuuz 2006*, Beirut: Daar al-Ameer, 2008, p. 20.
78. Hayden White, 'The Value of Narrativity in the Representation of Reality', *Critical Inquiry*, 7, 1 (Autumn 1980), pp. 5–27.
79. Georg Wilhelm Friedrich Hegel, *The Philosophy of History*, New York: Dover, 1956, p. 61.
80. White, 'The Value of Narrativity in the Representation of Reality', p. 23.
81. Ibid.
82. Scott McCloud, *Understanding Comics: The Invisible Art*, New York: Harper Paperbacks, 1993.
83. The full press release was published in *As-Safir*, 25 Nov. 2006.
84. Michael Shaw, 'Cracking the Cedar: How Hezbollah Re-Envisioned the Democracy Movement (and the West Hardly Noticed)', *Bag News*, 16 Dec. 2006, http://www.bagnewsnotes.com/2006/12/cracking-the-cedar-how-hezbollah-re-envisioned-the-democracy-movement-and-the-west-hardly-noticed/ (last accessed 10 July 2010).
85. Quoted in Michael J. Totten, *The Road to Fatima Gate: The Beirut Spring, the Rise of Hezbollah, and the Iranian War Against Israel*, New York: Encounter Books, 2011, p. 180.
86. See www.lebanon-ilovelife.com (last accessed 10 July 2010), emphasis in original.
87. Naim Qassem, *Mujtama' al-muqawamah: Irādat al-shahādah wa-sinā'at al-intissār* (The Society of Resistance: The Will to Martyrdom and the Making of Victory), Beirut: Dar Al-Maaref Al-Hijmiah, 2008, p. 13.
88. See http://www.english.moqawama.org/essaydetails.php?eid=10211&cid=257, published 15 Feb. 2010.
89. See Chapter 2.
90. Laleh Khalili, *Heroes and Martyrs of Palestine: The Politics of National Commemoration*, Cambridge: Cambridge University Press, 2007.
91. Patrick Fuery and Kelli Fuery, *Visual Cultures and Critical Theory*, London: Arnold, 2003, p. 121.
92. Ibid., p. 122.
93. Jean Baudrillard, *Simulacra and Simulation*, Ann Arbor: The University of

Michigan Press, 1999.

94. Ibid., p. 3.
95. Ajemian, 'Resistance Beyond Time and Space', p. 6.
96. Walter Benjamin, *The Work of Art in the Age of Mechanical Reproduction*, London: Penguin, 2008, p. 12.
97. Hamid Mowlana, *Global Information and World Communication*, London: Sage, 1997.
98. Michel Foucault, *Power/Knowledge: Selected Interviews and Other Writings*, New York: Pantheon Books, 1980.
99. Groys, *Art Power*, p. 127.
100. Edmund Burke, *A Philosophical Enquiry into the Origin of Our Ideas of the Sublime and Beautiful*, London: J. Dodsley, 1756.
101. Quoted in Benjamin, *The Work of Art in the Age of Mechanical Reproduction*, pp. 36–7.
102. Mowlana, *Global Information and World Communication*.
103. Robert Jervis, *The Logic of Image in International Relations*, Princeton, NJ: Princeton University Press, 1970, p. 8.
104. See Chapter 2.
105. Hanin Ghaddar, presentation at 'The Messages of Hizbullah' conference, SOAS, University of London, 25 May 2011.
106. See Majed Nasser Al-Zubaidi, *Karamaat al-wa'd al-sadeq* (Honours of the Truthful Pledge), Beirut: Dar al-Mahaja al-Baidha', 2007, pp. 150–205.
107. Mark C. Suchman, 'Managing Legitimacy: Strategic and Institutional Approaches', *The Academy of Management Review*, 20, 3 (1995), p. 574.
108. Ibrahim Al-Amin, speech on 15 May 2008, Al-Manar, http://www.almanar. com.lb/NewsSite/NewsDetails.aspx?id=43820&language=ar (last accessed 30 July 2011).
109. Quoted in Ibrahim Bairam, 'What is Hizbullah's Roadmap to Face the STL "War" On It?' *An-Nahar*, 24 July 2010.
110. 'Hizbullah Continues its Campaign', *Al-Hayat*, 31 July 2010.
111. Hassan Nasrallah, 'Speech Accusing Israel of Assassinating Rafic Hariri', Press TV, 9 Aug. 2010, http://www.youtube.com/watch?v=5odeTwU2zjw (last accessed 20 July 2011).
112. Bairam, 'What is Hizbullah's Roadmap to Face the STL "War" On It?'
113. 'Hizbullah Sticks to Information about Hariri Transmitted by Nasrallah about the Indictments', *An-Nahar*, 25 July 2010.
114. 'Hizbullah Continues its Campaign'.
115. 'Hizbullah Questions STL Credibility', *As-Safir*, 3 Aug. 2010.
116. 'Hizbullah: We are not Responsible for Searching for Accused or Present Evidence to STL', *As-Safir*, 17 Aug. 2010.
117. Lina Khatib, 'Hezbollah's Mobilization of Multitudes', *Foreign Policy Middle East Channel*, 29 Oct. 2010, http://mideast.foreignpolicy. com/posts/2010/10/29/hizbullah_s_mobilization_of_the_ multitudes?showcomments=yes (last accessed 7 Mar. 2013).

118. See *al-Intiqad*, 31 Dec. 2010, no. 1431, p. 4.

119. Quoted on Al-Arabiya website, 23 May 2012, http://www.alarabiya.net/articles/2012/05/23/215870.html (last accessed 23 May 2012).

120. Hassan Nasrallah, 'Speech on the Lesson of the Tunisia Revolution', Orange TV, 16 Jan. 2011, http://mrzine.monthlyreview.org/2011/nasrallah170111.html

121. 'Hezbollah Hails Egypt Revolution', Press TV website, 11 Feb. 2011, http://www.presstv.ir/detail/164799.html (last accessed 11 Mar. 2011).

122. 'Hezbollah Confirms Egypt Arrest', BBC News, 10 Apr. 2009, http://news.bbc.co.uk/2/hi/7994304.stm

123. 'MP Moussawi Condemns Ugly Massacres Conducted by Qaddafi against the Libyan People', *Al-Intiqad* website, 23 Feb. 2011, http://www.alintiqad.com/essaydetails.php?eid=41095&cid=75&st=%E1%ED%C8%ED%C7 (last accessed 7 Mar. 2011).

124. Quoted in Ali Matar, 'Echoes of Nasrallah's Speech on the Egyptian Street', *Al-'Ahd*, 11 Feb. 2011.

125. 'Revolution of the Egyptian People Equivalent to the Resistance Victory in 2006 and Gaza's Steadfastness in 2008', *Al-Intiqad*, 11 Feb. 2011, pp. 4–5.

126. Text of Khamenei's speech, *Al-Intiqad*, 11 Feb. 2011, no. 1437, pp. 2–3.

127. See http://www.almanar.com.lb/main.php (last accessed 15 Aug. 2012).

128. Naziha Saleh, 'Will Syria be the Key of the "New Middle East" Map?' Moqawama.org, 28 June 2011, http://www.english.moqawama.org/essaydetails.php?eid=14367&cid=269 (last accessed 18 July 2012).

129. Hizbullah has used the term '*takfiri*' in reference to the Sunni jihadist groups that have aligned themselves against the regime in Syria. The choice of the word '*takfiri*' (from *kafir*, meaning apostate) is to emphasise that such groups, according to Hizbullah, regard Shiites and Alawites as apostates.

130. W. Sean McLaughlin, 'The Use of the Internet for Political Action by Non-State Dissident Actors in the Middle East', *First Monday*, 8, 11, 3 Nov. 2003, http://firstmonday.org/htbin/cgiwrap/bin/ojs/index.php/fm/article/view/1096/1016 (last accessed 10 July 2011).

131. Suchman, 'Managing Legitimacy', p. 574.

132. Peter van Ham, 'The Rise of the Brand State', p. 2.

133. Schweitzer, *The Age of Charisma*.

134. Michael Z. Hackman and Craig E. Johnson, *Leadership: A Communication Perspective*, Long Grove, IL: Waveland Press, 2004.

4. THE POETRY OF HIZBULLAH

1.   This chapter draws mainly on poetry and other materials written in Arabic. All the translations are the author's unless otherwise indicated.

2.   See Saleh Said Agha, 'Of Verse, Poetry, Great Poetry, and History', in Ramzi Baalbaki, Saleh Said Agha and Tarif Khalidi (eds), *Poetry and History: The*

Value of Poetry in Reconstructing Arab History, Beirut: American University of Beirut Press, 2011, p. 7.

3. Salma Jayyusi, *Modern Arabic Poetry: An Anthology*, New York, Guildford: Columbia University Press, 1987; and Paul Starkey, 'Commitment', in *Encyclopaedia of Arabic Literature*, vol. 1, pp. 175–6, London and New York: Routledge, 1998.

4. See Bassam Frangieh, 'Modern Arabic Poetry: Vision and Reality', in Khamis Nassar and Najat Rahman (eds), *Mahmoud Darwish: Exile's Poet*, pp. 11–41, Northampton, MA: Olive Branch Press, 2008.

5. See Salma Jayyusi, *Anthology of Modern Palestinian Literature*, New York: Columbia University Press, 1992.

6. The idea of the poetry of Resistance was first articulated by the Palestinian novelist Ghassan Kanafani (1936–73). He was referring to the Palestinian poets who were then (the 1960s) in the occupied Palestinian territories, such as Mahmoud Darwish, Samih al-Qasim, Tawfiq Ziad and others.

7. Refer to Chapter 2 in this book for the argument on Hizbullah's acceptance of popular 'creation' but not 'curation'.

8. See Yasir Suleiman, 'Introduction: Literature and Nation in the Middle East: An Overview', in Yasir Suleiman and Ibrahim Muhawi (eds), *Literature and Nation in the Middle East*, pp. 1–16, Edinburgh: Edinburgh University Press, 2006.

9. I have argued in an earlier paper that authenticity is paramount in any culture of communication rooted in past convictions. See Atef Alshaer, 'The Poetry of Hamas', *Middle East Journal of Culture and Communication*, 2, 4 (2009), pp. 214–30. Similarly, Arshin Adib-Moghaddam writes, 'I have argued that Islamisms advocate authenticity; they define autonomy as a virtue', see *A Metahistory of the Clash of Civilisations: Us and Them beyond Orientalism*, London: Hurst, 2011, p. 248.

10. See Mohammad Mahdi Shams ad-Din, '*Khitab al-imam al-Sadr al-thaqafi*' (The Cultural Discourse of Imam Musa al-Sadr), in *Al-hawiyya al-thaqafiyya: qir'aat fi al-bu'ud ath-qafi limasirat al-imam as-sayyed Musa al-Sadr*, Beirut: Markaz al-Imām al-Sadr lil-abhath wa-dirasat, 2000, p. 43.

11. See Joseph Alagha, *Hizbullah's Identity Construction*, Amsterdam: Amsterdam University Press, 2011, pp. 178–81.

12. See Ahmad Abu-Haqqa, *Al-iltizam fi al-shi'r al-'Arabi*, Beirut: Dar al-'ilm lil-malayeen, 1979.

13. As mentioned in the text, the dictatorial Iraqi leader Saddam Hussein was such an example who found many poets to praise and adulate him. In return, he lavished them with gifts and honours. One such poet was Abd al-Razzaq Abd al-Wahid who wrote several poems in praise of Saddam Hussein. See Stephan Milich, 'The Positioning of Baathist Intellectuals and Writers Before and After 2003: The Case of the Iraqi Poet Abd al-Razzaq Abd al-Wahid', *Middle East Journal of Culture and Communication*, 4, 3 (2001), pp. 298–338.

14. See Michel Foucault, *The Archaeology of Knowledge*, London and New York: Routledge, 1972, pp. 24–33.

15. There are other oaths to Hizbullah, but the ones mentioned are the most widespread. One noteworthy oath to highlight, which evokes several past and present Shiite figures and ends with Hizbullah, is the following: 'We have pledged our allegiance, O Khomeini … in the name of al-Mahdi … the soul of God … of Sayyed Abbas … the martyr of God … and Khamenai … the shadow of God … we will continue to honour the pledge, O Nasrallah …'

16. See Laurence Louër, *Transnational Shia Politics: Religious and Political Networks in the Gulf*, London: Hurst, 2011, pp. 204–5.

17. Ibid., p. 9.

18. See Alagha, *Hizbullah's Identity Construction*, pp. 93–112.

19. See Naim Qassem, *Mujtama' al-muqawamah: iradat al-shahadah wa-sina'at al-intisar*, Beirut: Dār al-ma'arif al-hakmiyya, 2008.

20. See *al-'Ahd*, 3 Sep. 1993 supplement, issue 482, pp. 17–24, where there is a discussion of the Prophet Muhammad's life and meaning to Muslims from cultural, existential and political perspectives. See also 26 Mar. 1999, issue 790, pp. 12, 14, 16, with references on the life of Hassan and Hussein and other role models of the Shiites.

21. The poetry of this era represents a break from the past of the Shiites of Lebanon, who did not link themselves so organically (through Hizbullah in particular) in their culture in general (poetry included) to the Iranian system before the Iranian Revolution in 1979. Instead, the poetry that emerges from South Lebanon includes themes such as the beauty of nature, particularly that of al-Shaam (Syria, Lebanon and Palestine), the Arab heritage, valour, nobility, loyalty and generosity. The latter are aspects which are generally associated with the classical period in Arabic literature. If there are references to Shiite figures or places, they are often to Iraq, where there are seminal Shiite places and historical memories, such as Najaf and Karbala respectively (see Hassan al-Amin, *'asir Hamad al-Mahmuud wa al-haiyaah al-shi'riyyah fii jabal 'Amil*, Beirut: Daar al-Turaath al-Islami, 1974).

22. See *al-'Ahd*, 15 Feb. 1985, issue 34, p. 1.

23. Ibid., p. 7.

24. See the undated *al-'Ahd* newspaper special edition from June 1989, entitled, 'Farewell the Imam of the Umma', p. 4.

25. See Kamran Scot Aghaie, *The Martyrs of Karbala: Shi'i Symbols and Rituals in Modern Iran*, Seattle: University of Washington Press, 2004.

26. The quoted poems above of Mohammad al-Qabisi were recited to me by a Lebanese citizen who agreed for his name to be mentioned, namely Khalil Ahmad Issa from the village of Ramiyyah in South Lebanon. Khalil Issa confirmed that the poems in question were widespread in South Lebanon. Though he did not know the poet in question very well, he referred to his poetry as an important part of what he called, 'the poetry of resistance'.

27. There are a number of choral singers and singing teams affiliated with Hizbullah. They have become particularly important after 2006 as they perform at several functions, such as social occasions like weddings or political rallies. These include Firqat al-Fajr, Firqat al-Isra', al-Mahdi, etc.

28. See Augustus Richard Norton, *Hizbullah: A Short History*, Princeton and Oxford: Princeton University Press, 2007, p. 80.

29. *Al-'Ahd*, 2 June 2000, issue 852, p. 8.

30. Ibid.

31. Ibid., p. 19.

32. Ibid.

33. Ibid., p. 31.

34. The poem 'Rijal Allah' was one of the poems that al-Farra recited to a packed audience of Hizbullah supporters in his poetry reading evening at the International Arab Book Fair in Beirut on 10 May 2007.

35. Omar Al-Farra, *Umsiyya* (DVD), Dar al-Manar lil-intaaj al-fani wa-tawzii', 2007.

36. Barbara Harlow, *Resistance Literature*, New York and London: Methuen, 1987.

37. Clifford Geertz, *The Interpretation of Cultures*, New York: Basic Books, 1983, p. 220.

38. See Norton, *Hizbullah*.

39. Poem by Rida Shu'ayb and the choral group al-Fajr. The poem was adapted by Tarik Sharifa and produced by Hizbullah's Dar al-Manar, 2006.

40. Norton, *Hizbullah*, p. 285.

41. Atef Alshaer, 'Towards a Theory of Culture of Communication: The Fixed and the Dynamic in Hamas's Communicated Discourse', *Middle East Journal of Culture and Communication*, 1, 2 (2008), pp. 101–21.

42. Hamid Mavani, 'Ayatullah Khomeni's Concept of Governance (*wilayat al-faqih*) and the Classical Shi'i Doctrine of Imamate', *Middle Eastern Studies*, 47, 5 (2001), pp. 807–24.

43. Ibid.

44. It merits attention to quote Amal Saad-Ghorayeb on the concept and institution of the *wilayat al-faqih* and Hizbullah's relationship to it, in the sense that the *faqih* (the one on whom religious authority is invested, in this case, Khomeini) recognises 'the national boundaries dividing the umma and the consequent limits of his Wilayat. Hizbullah's claim that it is "enlightened enough to decide for itself" on other political issues which are not religiously problematic, such as its vote of confidence in the government or its promulgation of laws, further limits the scope of the Faqih's political authority. Thus, the party is able to balance its intellectual commitment to the concept of the Wilayat with its allegiance to the Lebanese state.' See Amal Saad-Ghorayeb, *Hizbullah: Politics and Religion*, London: Pluto Press, 2002, p. 68.

45. Adeed Dawisha, *Rise and Fall of Arab Nationalism*, Princeton: Princeton

University Press, 2003, pp. 24–41.

46. Ibid.
47. Ibid.
48. Philip Hitti, *History of the Arabs: From the Earliest Times to the Present*, London and New York: Palgrave Macmillan, 1937 [2002].
49. Jayyusi, *Modern Arabic Poetry.*
50. See Dina Matar, 'The Power of Conviction: Nassrallah's Rhetoric and Mediated Charisma in the Context of 2006 July War', *Middle East Journal of Culture and Communication*, 1, 2 (2008), pp. 122–37.
51. Atef Alshaer, 'The Poetry of Hamas', *Middle East Journal of Culture and Communication*, 2, 4 (2009), pp. 214–30.
52. Haidar (lion in classical Arabic) is one of the titles of Imam Ali to evoke his courage and powerful leadership.
53. An example of this is to be found in an interview with the Palestinian poet Mahmoud Darwish, as he refers to the tenth-century Arab poet Al-Mutanabbi as 'my grandfather of poetry', *jaddi al-shi'ri* (see Wazan Abdu, *Al-gharib yaqa'u 'ala nafsihi*, Beirut: Riad El-Rayyes Books, 2006, p. 93).
54. For the poem in question, see http://alorobanews.com/vb/showthread. php?t=503 (last accessed 3 Mar. 2013).
55. See http://www.jebchit.com/article.php?arid=18 (last accessed 25 Sep. 2012).
56. See Chapter 3 for a discussion of Hizbullah as a brand.
57. The German philosopher Heidegger quotes the German poet Holderlin who wrote, 'that is why language, the most dangerous of goods, has been given to man … so that he may bear witness to what he is …' (IV, 246). On poetry as the essence of language and humanity, see the beautiful essay of Heidegger, *Holderlin and the Essence of Poetry*, New York: Prometheus Books, 1981, pp. 5–65; see also Adonis, *An Introduction to Arab Poetics*, Beirut: Saqi Books, 2003, pp. 55–75.
58. See Matar, 'The Power of Conviction'.
59. For the entire words of the letter and the song itself see: http://lachyab. jeeran.com/archive/2006/10/106267.html (last accessed 13 Sep. 2012).
60. Al-Farra, *Umsiyya.*
61. See the following video, where the remarks of Najm appeared: http://www. youtube.com/watch?v=jhUVXG12j1c (last accessed 12 Jan. 2013).
62. Lila Abu-Lughod, *Veiled Sentiments: Honour and Poetry in a Bedouin Society*, Berkeley: University of California Press, 1989 [2000].

5. HASSAN NASRALLAH: THE CENTRAL ACTOR IN HIZBULLAH'S POLITICAL COMMUNICATION STRATEGIES

1. See Max Weber, *Economy and Society*, ed. Guenther Roth and Claus Wittich, New York: Bedminster Press, 1968.
2. Michel Foucault has argued that Western societies have internalised patterns

of authority and relations of control, resulting in what he calls carceral societies in which obedience is normal and controlled. See Michel Foucault, *Discipline and Punish: The Birth of the Prison*, trans. Alan Sheridan, New York: Vintage Books, 1979.

3. Lisa Wedeen, *Ambiguities of Domination: Politics, Rhetoric and Symbols in Contemporary Syria*, Chicago: University of Chicago Press, pp. 19–20, 199.

4. Dick Pels, 'Aesthetic Representation and Political Style', in John Corner and Dick Pels (eds), *Media and the Restyling of Politics*, London: Sage, 2003, p. 59.

5. Compulsion in this sense refers to the emotional and affective bonds between the leader and the led, and is thus different from obedience.

6. Such a structuralist notion of ideologies interpellating or summoning identities does not mean that actions are accepted by the target populations.

7. Roger Silverstone, 'Complicity and Collusion in the Mediation of Everyday Life', *New Literary History*, 33, 4 (2002), pp. 761–80.

8. Hassan Nasrallah, interview with *Nida al-Watan*, 31 Aug. 1993, 'Who is Sayyed Hassan Nasrallah', in Nicolas Noe (ed.), *Voice of Hezbollah: The Statements of Sayyed Hassan Nasrallah*, London: Verso, 2007, pp. 116–43.

9. Abdel-Karim Nasrallah, interview published in *Al-Diyar*, 21 Mar. 2010.

10. Ibid.

11. *Al-Diyar*, 19 Mar. 2010.

12. Ibid.

13. See *From al-Sadr to Nasrallah: The March of the Resistance and the Lives of the Two Men*, Beirut: Al-Rida publications, 2007.

14. Hassan Nasrallah, interview in *Al-Diyar*, 19 Mar. 2010.

15. Nicholas Blanford, 'Introduction', in Nicholas Noe (ed.), *Voice of Hezbollah: The Statements of Sayyed Hassan Nasrallah*, London: Verso, 2007, p. 3.

16. Babak Dehghanpisheh and Christopher Dickey, 'The Real Nasrallah', *Newsweek*, 20 Aug. 2006, http://www.newsweek.com/id/46415 (last accessed 12 Nov. 2011).

17. The religious title *sayyed* is used to refer to people believed to be descendants of Imam Hussein, the revered Shiite leader. The title *ayatollah* is a higher-ranking title given to the Twelver Imams in Shiite history.

18. As presented earlier in this book, al-Sadr was an Iranian Shiite cleric with Lebanese family ties who came to Lebanon in 1959 to replace a deceased clerical leader in the city of Tyre. In 1978 he mysteriously disappeared while on a trip to Libya, an event that catapulted him directly into the narrative of the Hidden Twelfth Imam, or the hidden imam, who went into occultation in the eighth century and whose eventual return is seen as heralding the beginning of Islamic rule on earth.

19. Not much else is known of Nasrallah's intimate and personal life other than the fact that he has been married to Fatemah Yassin since 1978 and has four children, the eldest of whom, Hadi, was martyred in an Israeli attack in 1997.

20. Hassan Nasrallah, 'Who is Sayyed Hassan Nasrallah', in *Voice of Hezbollah*, pp. 116–43.

21. The manifesto detailed Hizbullah's objectives and aims, including ending Israel's occupation of parts of Lebanon, a commitment to Iran and its leaders and a preference for Islamic rule in Lebanon. Soon afterwards, the group began its campaign to attract recruits, forming what was known as the *tabi'a* (mobilisation), units composed of part-time fighters whose job was to hang posters, banners and flags and distribute the party's paper *al-'Ahd*.

22. See Thansasis Cambanis, *A Privilege to Die: Inside Hezbollah's Legions and their Endless War against Israel*, New York: Free Press, 2009.

23. Blanford, 'Introduction', p. 7.

24. Tufaili opposed any participation in a confession-based system, in accordance with Hizbullah's 1985 manifesto. Nasrallah and Mussawi did not see this participation as going against Hizbullah's interests and ideologies, but as maintaining it.

25. The divisions continued to haunt the party, though the pragmatist stance taken by Nasrallah and Mussawi prevailed and continued to define Hizbullah's political strategies and dealings within and outside Lebanon.

26. Nasrallah, 'Who is Sayyed Hassan Nasrallah'.

27. Hizbullah gave financial assistance to families to rebuild poverty-stricken areas in Shiite neighbourhoods and subsidised housing in the South after the Israeli withdrawal in 2000. Much of this money was reported to have come from Iran. After 2000 Hizbullah began to raise funds on its own. See Chapters 3 and 4 for further details.

28. Norton, *Hezbollah*.

29. For details of the changes in Hizbullah's media strategies since 1996, read Zahera Harb, *Channels of Resistance in Lebanon: Liberation Propaganda— Hezbollah and the Media*, London: I.B. Tauris, 2011, pp. 173–227.

30. See Chapter 2 for details of Hizbullah's communication strategies following the Qana massacre.

31. Nasrallah would later use the trope of victory to describe other significant moments in Hizbullah's history of conflict with Israel, including the 2000 liberation of the South and the 2006 war.

32. Hassan Nasrallah, 'The April Understanding', interview with *as-Safir*, 30 Apr. 1996. Cited in *Voices of Hezbollah*, p. 155.

33. Hassan Nasrallah speech, n.d., available at http://www.youtube.com/ watch?v=6yqZTues0-g&feature=related (last accessed 21 Dec. 2012).

34. See Elihu Katz and Daniel Dayan, *Media Events: The Live Broadcasting of History*, Cambridge, MA: Harvard University Press, 1994.

35. Talal Salman, cited in Harb, *Channels of Resistance*, p. 194.

36. Sayyed Ahmed Rif'at et al., *Al-tha'er al-'amili*, Beirut: Dar al-Mizan, 2009, p. 89.

37. Ahmad Hussein Magdi, *As-Shaab*, 23 Sep. 1997, cited in Rif'at et al., *Al-tha'er al-'amili*, p. 163.

38. Quoted in *Al-Kifah Al-Arabi*, 18 Mar. 1998, cited in Harb, *Channels of Resistance*, p. 195.

39. Hassan Nasrallah, 'Speech on the Liberation of South Lebanon', Al-Manar, 25 May 2000, http://www.youtube.com/watch?v=V_EAmIzqtu8 (accessed 12 Nov. 2012).

40. Hassan Nasrallah, 'The Second *Intifada*', interview with *Al-Rai al-Aam*, 5 Oct. 2000, cited in *Voice of Hezbollah*, pp. 244–55.

41. Judith Palmer Harik, *Hezbollah: The Changing Face of Terrorism*, London: I.B. Tauris, 2007.

42. *As-Safir*, 9 Mar. 2005.

43. Blanford, 'Introduction'.

44. Available at http://www.youtube.com/watch?v=1gJqggKzPb4&feature=related (last accessed 5 Jan. 2013).

45. In some of the contemporary literature on celebrity politicians, Max Weber's account of charismatic leadership has been reduced to discussing the personal characteristics of leaders. In the original formulation, however, Weber argued that pure charisma was a feature of ancient societies, particularly of small religious communities in which charismatic leaders literally exuded the divine power of charisma. The basis of genuine charisma lay in conceptions that it is the duty of those subject to charismatic authority to recognise its authenticity, and that this recognition is a matter of complete personal devotion to the possessor of the quality. For more details see Weber, *Economy and Society*.

46. *Al-fares al-'arabi: sirat hayat assayed Hassan Nasrallah mina al-wilada hatta al-qiyada* (The Arab Knight: The Life Story of Hassan Nasrallah from Birth until Leadership), arranged by Ballouq, Lana Hussein, Beirut: Dar al-Mahajja al-Baida', n.d.

47. Critics of Weber's argument note that charisma, as a form of power, played a role when the church and state were inseparable, but that it has no analytical potential in rationalised political environments. Since charisma depends on personal contact and primary group involvement, it is of little analytical value in explaining its relevance in the era of impersonal mass and mediated politics. Loyalties in the media age have therefore been described as based on perceptions of political efficacy, planned propaganda and political mobilisation as much as on ideas, interests and ideologies.

48. Weber, *Economy and Society*, pp. 122–3.

49. Ibid.

50. Ann Ruth Willner, *The Spellbinders: Charismatic Political Leadership*, New Haven and London: Yale University Press, 1985, pp. 5–8.

51. Ibid., p. 14.

52. Ibid.

53. Ibid., pp. 16–17.

54. *Al-Diyar* is owned by Charles Ayoub, a well-known supporter of the Assad regime.

55. Cited in *al-Diyar*, 10 Apr. 2010.

56. Author interview with Suha Dabbagh, Beirut, 11 Nov. 2011.

57. Author interview with Amal Saad-Ghrorayeb, Beirut, 9 Nov. 2011.

58. Simon Coleman, 'Transgressing the Self: Making Charismatic Saints', *Critical Inquiry*, 35, 3 (2009), pp. 417–39.

59. Atef Alshaer, 'Towards a Theory of Culture of Communication: The Fixed and the Dynamic in Hamas' Communicated Discourse', *The Middle East Journal of Culture and Communication*, 1, 2 (2008), pp. 101–21.

60. Antonio Gramsci, *Selections from the Prison Notebooks*, New York: Columbia University Press, pp. 276–77. In his articulation, Gramsci did not use the Marxist concept of false consciousness, but distinguished between organic and arbitrary ideology. The former generally had a constituency and served collective aims and the latter had no constituency, but depended on its creator.

61. Roy Wallis, 'The Social Construction of Charisma', *Social Compass*, 29, 1 (1984), pp. 25–39.

62. Hamzeh writes that the organisational structure of Hizbullah assumes the shape of a hierarchical pyramid that corresponds to the territorial division of Lebanon's governorates, in particular the ones that have a majority of Shiites, such as Beirut, the Bekaa and South Lebanon. The party has leadership, political and administrative, and military and security organs, along with a number of service subunits within each apparatus. See Ahmad Nizar Hamzeh, *In the Path of Hizbullah*, Syracuse: Syracuse University Press, 2004.

63. Hizbullah is secretive about its organisational structure, which is mainly made up of a clerical leadership whose members are seen to be closer to and more understanding of the meaning of Islam than average Muslims. The party's *shura* (consultative) council is made up of six clerics and one lay, or non-*'ulama* member. Decisions are taken collectively. See Hamzeh, *In the Path of Hizbullah*, for more details.

64. Ibid., p. 48.

65. Nasrallah alludes to the same procedures in another interview with the Lebanese journalist Ibrahim al-Amin in *as-Safir* newspaper published on 27 Feb. 1992. Here he says: 'From a religious point of view, we have a tenet that says that a legitimate leader is a hard-working and religious scholar who enjoys many relevant attributes. These are, among other things, ability, knowledge, a sense of justice, experience, historical awareness, good management skills ... and faith.' See 'After the Assassination' in *Voice of Hezbollah*, p. 70.

66. Hassan Nasrallah, interview with *Nida' al-Watan*, cited in *Voice of Hezbollah*, pp. 116–43. Though Nasrallah was one of the more visible leaders of Hizbullah at the time, his appointment came as a surprise to some veteran leaders of the Shiite community, notably Nabih Berri, the leader of the Amal movement and twenty-two years Nasrallah's senior.

67. Available at http://www.youtube.com/watch?v=yIGxYa_-59w (last accessed

12 Nov. 2012).

68. Read Annabelle Mohammadi-Sreberny and Ali Mohammadi, *Small Media, Big Revolution: Communication, Culture and the Iranian Revolution*, Minneapolis: Minnesota University Press, 1994, for a discussion of the use of cassette recorders by the Iranian revolutionary leaders, Khomeini and other clerics in Iran's Islamic Revolution of 1979.

69. Ibid., p. 110.

70. Hassan Nasrallah, 'Civil War and Resistance', interview with *Al-Khaleej*, 11 Mar. 1986, cited in *Voice of Hezbollah*, pp. 23–33.

71. Ibid.

72. In fact, most of the Islamist parties in the Middle East, but particularly Hamas and Hizbullah, integrate their nationalist discourse within an Islamic framework, using references from the Quran. For example, such parties regularly use phrases like '*hub al-watan mina al-iman*' (the love of the homeland is part of belief) to make the link between Islam and the nation.

73. Hassan Nasrallah, quoted in *al-'Ahd*, 7 June 1992.

74. Hassan Nasrallah, quoted in a*l-'Ahd*, 25 May 1995.

75. Roland Barthes, 'The Photographic Message', in Susan Sontag (ed.), *A Roland Barthes Reader*, London: Vintage, 2000, p. 200.

76. Historically, a majority of Muslims considered the *khalifa* (caliph ruler) elected through a council of elders as the legitimate heir. The Shiite imams were considered, in contrast to caliphs, to possess charismatic authority over all aspects of life. For a historical account of Islam's earliest charismatic movements and their maintenance, see Hamid Dabashi, *Authority in Islam: From the Rise of Mohammed to the Establishment of the Umayyads*, New Brunswick, NJ: Transaction Publishers, 1989.

77. Hassan Nasrallah, cited in *As-Safir*, 3 June 1992.

78. Hassan Nasrallah, cited in *al-'Ahd*, 7 June 1992.

79. John Corner and Dick Pels have argued that the increasing informality of public address and the resulting closer articulations of the personal and the political bring about a secondary orality in which a theatre of voices has partly displaced the written accounts of the press. See 'Introduction', in John Corner and Dick Pels (eds), *Media and the Restyling of Politics*, London: Sage, 2003, pp. 1–13.

80. John Corner, 'Mediated Persona and Political Culture', in *Media and the Restyling of Politics*, p. 69.

81. Jacques Rancière, *The Politics of the Aesthetics*, trans. Gabriell Rockhill, New York: Continuum, 2004, p. 12.

82. Dina Matar, 'The Power of Conviction: Nassrallah's Rhetoric and Mediated Charisma in the Context of the 2006 War', *Middle East Journal of Culture and Communication*, 1, 2 (2008), pp. 122–37.

83. See *al-tha'er al-'amili* for a thorough discussion of the strategies and themes in Nasrallah's speeches.

84. Matar, 'The Power of Conviction'.

85. Palmer Harik, *Hezbollah*, pp. 57–8.

86. Lisa Wedeen, *Ambiguities of Domination: Politics, Rhetoric and Symbols in Contemporary Syria*, Chicago: University of Chicago Press: pp. 19–20, 199.

87. Media events, as Katz and Dayan have argued, serve to bring publics together as a collective.

88. See Chapter 4 for a discussion of Hizbullah's poetry.

89. See Chapter 4 for a detailed discussion of such poetry.

90. This is a reference to the heirs of the Prophet Muhammad.

91. Imam Hussein offers a powerful symbol, if not a paradigm, of Shiite martyrdom. He was killed in Karbala in AD 680 with a small band of followers in a battle with the army sent by the then Damascus-based Caliph Yazid. His readiness to sacrifice himself in battle against the oppressor has become a source of emulation for future generations of Shiite warriors.

92. *Ahiba'i*, available at http://www.youtube.com/watch?v=JTuRHvnGJSI (last accessed 20 Aug. 2012).

93. See Chapter 3 for a discussion of an example, the programme *Al-'Abaya*.

94. Portraits of *sayyeds* and sheikhs cannot solely be seen as religious images. Rather, they must also be seen as part of the popular practice of plastering public surfaces with the images of prominent political figures that is common in Lebanon and other parts of the Middle East.

95. Barthes, 'The Photographic Message', p. 203.

96. See Gramsci, *Selections from the Prison Notebook*.

97. Roy Wallis, 'The Social Construction of Charisma', *Social Compass*, 29, 1 (1984), pp. 25–39.

98. See Chapter 3 for details of the STL and the events of May 2008.

99. See http://www.youtube.com/watch?v=P_AA6uQiD9I (last accessed 12 Dec. 2012).

100. The testimonies of his parents, as well as his own statements, are cited in the sections above.

101. In this interview, titled 'I and my Family Lost our Precious Son who we Love, but Will Meet in Paradise', the author Radwan al-Deeb praises Nasrallah and his knowledge. Al-Diyar, 10 Mar. 2010, p. 2.

102. Nasrallah, interview with Radwan al-Deeb, cited under the title 'A Comprehensive File on Hizbullah's Secretary-General … the Parents' Longing', Al-Diyar, 21 Mar. 2010, p. 3.

103. Radwan Al-Dheeb, cited in *Al-Diyar*, 20 Mar. 2010.

104. Ibid., p. 4.

105. See http://www.almanar.com.lb/main.php (last accessed 4 Mar. 2013).

106. http://www.youtube.com/watch?v=H8UG1ktd_EY

107. http://www.youtube.com/watch?v=USNGvn98xbo

CONCLUSION: HIZBULLAH AT A CROSSROADS

1. Read Hassan Nasrallah's speech regarding Syria on 25 May 2011 at: http://www.moqawama.org/essaydetails.php?eid=20819&cid=142 (last accessed 28 Nov. 2012).

2. See Lina Khatib's article in the *Guardian*, 'The Crisis in Syria is Reopening Lebanon's Old War Divisions', 9 June 2012, http://www.guardian.co.uk/commentisfree/2012/jun/09/crisis-syria-lebanon-clashes (last accessed 15 Aug. 2012).

3. See http://www.almanar.com.lb/adetails.php?eid=288131&cid=21&fromval=1&frid=21&seccatid=19&s1=1 (last accessed 18 Aug. 2012). For Nasrallah's entire speech see http://www.almanar.com.lb/adetails.php?fromval=1&cid=21&frid=21&eid=288691

4. See the following link for Nasrallah's speech: http://www.youtube.com/watch?v=wxEoQG3c_lA (last accessed 14 Jan. 2012).

5. Ziad Majed, 'The Hizbullah Regime', Ziad Majed blog, 28 Feb. 2012, www.ziadmajed.net (last accessed 28 Jan. 2011).

6. Hanin Ghaddar, 'Adieu, Hezbollah', Now Lebanon, 19 Mar. 2012, http://www.nowlebanon.com/NewsArticleDetails.aspx?ID=377701 (last accessed 20 Mar. 2012).

7. The text of the speech was posted on Hizbullah's website: http://www.moqawama.org/essaydetails.php?eid=26966&cid=199 (last accessed 7 Mar. 2013).

8. See http://www.youtube.com/watch?v=wHHnYwr2044

9. See http://www.almanar.com.lb/english/adetails.php?eid=99319&cid=23&fromval=1

10. See http://www.nna-leb.gov.lb/ar/show-news/49730/

11. http://www.naharnet.com/stories/en/94378

12. Mark Poster, *The Mode of Information: Poststructuralism and Social Context*, Cambridge: Polity Press in association with Basil Blackwell, 1990, pp. 73–98.

13. Mark Leonard, 'Diplomacy by Other Means', *Foreign Policy*, 132 (Sep.–Oct. 2002), p. 51.

14. Sidney Blumenthal, *The Permanent Campaign: Inside the World of Elite Political Operatives*, Boston: Beacon, 1980, p. 8.

15. Ibid., p. 7.

16. Mediation is a useful concept to capture diverging articulations between media, communication, protest and activism. See Jesús Martin-Barbero, *Communication, Culture and Hegemony: From Media to Mediation*, London: Sage, 1993, and Roger Silverstone, 'Complicity and Collusion in the Mediation of Everyday Life', *New Literary History*, 33, 4 (2002), pp. 761–80.

17. https://www.facebook.com/Alahednews

18. http://www.youtube.com/user/channelalmanar2?feature=watch; http://www.youtube.com/alahednews

19. https://twitter.com/almanarnews; https://twitter.com/alahednews

20. Cliff Staten, 'From Terrorism to Legitimacy: Political Opportunity Structures and the Case of Hezbollah', *The Online Journal of Peace and Conflict Resolution*, 8, 1 (2008), pp. 32–49.

21. Kai Arzheimer and Elisabeth Carter, 'Political Opportunity Structures and the Extreme Right', *European Journal of Political Research*, 45, 3 (2006), p. 422.

INDEX

Aaker, David: 84–5

Abbas: family of, 139

Abdel-Nasser, Gamal: 83, 88; death of (1970), 88; nationalisation of Suez Canal (1956), 88; political rhetoric of, 176–7; speeches of, 46

Abu-Lughod, Lila: 152

'Adnan: cultural significance of, 141–2

Adonis: 120; speeches of, 130–1

Aflaq, Michel: 141

Afwaj al-muqawama al-lubnaniya (Brigades of the Lebanese Resistance) (Amal): 19, 23, 50, 66, 98; defeat of (1998), 31; founding of (1975), 2; member of Lebanese National Opposition, 98; members of, 156–8

al-Agha, Joseph: 54, 76, 119, 121

Agres, Stuart: definition of 'brand', 84

Ahibba'i (My Beloved) (song): 145–6; lyrical meaning of, 146

Um Ahmad, Hajjeh: 55

Ahmadinejad, Mahmoud: electoral victory of (2005), 82

bin Ali, al-Abbas: 78–9

Ali, Imam: 140; depictions of, 108, 126, 130; descendants of, 140; family of, 125, 143

Alshaer, Atef: 166

al-Amin, Ibrahim: 171; Hizbullah political bureau chief, 109

Aoun, Michel: leader of Free Patriotic Movement, 18, 25

Aql, Saeed: Qadmus, 138

Arab-Israeli War (1948): 73, 120

Arab Spring: 72, 113, 115, 118, 151, 190; Bahraini Uprising (2011–), 22, 113, 115–16, 178; Egyptian Revolution (2011), 22, 113–15, 118, 151, 178; Libyan Civil War (2011), 22, 113–15; Syrian Civil War (2011–), 5, 11, 20, 22, 32, 35, 38, 112, 116–18, 155, 179, 181–4, 190; Tunisian Revolution (2010–11), 22, 113, 115, 118, 178; use of social media in, 35–6, 186; Yemeni Revolution (2011–12), 114

Arabic (language): 74, 91, 101, 110, 119; 'ammiyya, 173; fus'ha, 169; poetry, 120; rural, 147; use in broadcasts of Political Propaganda Unit, 64–5

Argentina: Buenos Aires, 100

al-Ass'ad, Ahmad: founder of Lebanese Option Gathering, 31–2

al-Assad, Bashar: 88, 183; regime of, 5, 7, 35, 37, 116–17, 151, 155, 178–9, 181–2, 184, 187, 190

al-Assad, Hafez: 154

al-Assir, Imam Ahmad: 186

Atrisi, Ja'far: *Hizbullah: The Most Difficult Choice*, 81–2

INDEX

Baath Party (Iraq): 157
Baath Party (Syria): 100, 151
Bahrain: 30, 88; Uprising (2011–), 22, 113, 115–16, 178
al-Barghouti, Tamim: *Sha'ir al-malyun'* (The Poet of the Million), 144
Battle of Karbala (AD 680): 138–9; capture of Zeinab during, 143; significance of for Shiites, 53–4, 125
Battle of Khaibar (AD 629): 93
al-Bayati, Abd al-Wahab: 120
Bedouin: 133
Belt, David: 88
Ben Ali, Zine El Abidine: regime of, 113; removed from power (2011), 118
Benjamin, Walter: 103
Bergmann, Knut: 87
Blanford, Nicholas: 20, 25
Burke, Edmund: concept of 'political sublime', 105

Cambanis, Thanassis: 33
Christianity: 4, 22, 25, 38, 41, 58, 98, 117, 155; Bible, 142; imagery of, 137
von Clausewitz, Carl: theories of, 33–5
Clinton, Bill: presidential election campaign of (2006), 91
Coleman, Simon: 166
collective action framing: concept of, 6
colonialism: 50, 136
Consultative Centre for Studies and Documentation: personnel of, 29
Corner, John: 172
Cwalina, Wojciech: 84

Dar al-Amir: publications of, 164
Dar al-Mahajja al-Baida': publications of, 164

Darwish, Mahmoud: 120; speeches of, 130–1
al-Dheeb, Radwan: 177–8
dhimmis: concept of, 25
ad-Din, Mohammad Ali Shams: *Blood of Hussein Coined the Dawn, The*, 131–2
Doha Accord (2008): 100; brokering of, 18; provisions of, 18, 26, 100; significance of, 18–19

Egypt: 30, 88, 114; Cairo, 95, 114; Revolution (2011), 22, 113–15, 118, 151, 178; Suez Canal, 88
Elnashra: 28
European Union (EU): listing of Hizbullah's military wing as terrorist organisation (2013), 186

Facebook: 189
Fadlallah, Mohammad Hussein: poetry of, 132
Fadlallah, Sheikh Mohammed Hussain: 32, 51; mobilisation efforts of, 6
al-fajr, Firqat: songs released by, 143
Falkowski, Andrzej: 84
al-Farra, Omar: 147, 150–1, 175; background of, 133; Hamida, 133–4; Men of God, The, 134–7
Fayyad, Ali: Director of Consultative Centre for Studies and Documentation, 29
First Barbary War (1801–5): 60
fitna: concept of, 186
France: 81, 113; colonies of, 2, 7; Paris, 79
Free Patriotic Movement: 98; alliance with Hizbullah, 81; member of Lebanese National Opposition, 98; members of, 18, 25

INDEX

Fuery, Kelli: 102
Fuery, Patrick: 102
Future Movement: 187; members of,
   18

Gramsci, Antonio: concept of
   'hegemony', 8, 76, 167
Groys, Boris: 48
Guevara, Che: 176

Haidar, Reem: media depictions of, 89
van Ham, Peter: 84, 117
Hamas: political rhetoric of, 47
Hamzeh, Ahamd Nizar: 5, 24, 37, 167
Harb, Sheikh Ragheb: 68; assassination
   of (1984), 41, 55, 86, 101, 114,
   127; media depictions of, 86
Harb, Zahera: 64, 74
Harik, Judith Palmer: 162
Hariri, Rafic: 20–1, 34, 82; assassina-
   tion of (2005), 4–5, 14, 21, 31, 36,
   71–2, 79–80, 97, 109–10, 116–17,
   162, 177, 181; economic policies of,
   19; family of, 18
Hariri, Saad: 99, 112, 187; family of,
   18; leader of Future Movement, 18;
   media companies of, 99–100; role in
   March 14 coalition, 35
Hebrew (language): 91; use in
   broadcasts of Political Propaganda
   Unit, 64–5
Hegel, Georg Wilhelm Friedrich: 96
Hirst, David: observations of Hizbullah activity, 22, 24, 27–8, 33
Hizbullah: 2–4, 12–13, 17–19, 27–8,
   34, 37–40, 57–8, 61–2, 73–5,
   79–80, 84–5, 93–5, 98, 112,
   118–19, 131, 148–9, 151–2, 154,
   163–4, 168, 173–4, 176–7, 185–6,
   190; al-'Ahd (The Pledge), 9–10,
   20–1, 40, 43–4, 46, 49, 51, 53–4,
   56–7, 59–62, 66, 68, 74–5, 79, 122,
   125–7, 133–4, 171–2; alliance with
   Free Patriotic Movement, 81; Ahl
   al-thugour (The People of the
   Outpost), 9; 'Arabisation', 137;
   al-Bilad, 42; Central Information
   Unit, 10, 42; Central Media Unit,
   65; communication strategy of, 4–5,
   7–11, 13, 20, 35, 42, 48–9, 82, 85,
   88–91, 106–10, 115–16, 188–9;
   connections to Iran, 1, 8, 11, 20,
   22, 30, 34, 44–5, 94, 106–7, 123,
   128, 139–42, 167, 176, 181;
   connections to Syria, 8, 20, 34, 94,
   142, 151; 'Divine Victory' campaign, 4, 36, 72, 85, 90–2, 96–7,
   101–3, 146, 163, 175; electoral
   performance of (2000), 4; Executive
   Council (al-majlis al-tanfithi), 10,
   42; formation of (1982), 1–2, 5, 7;
   Hebrew Monitoring Unit, 65;
   'Identity and Goals' declaration
   (2004), 15, 22, 32; ideology of,
   25–7, 43, 45–6, 106, 120–1, 124,
   136, 141, 147, 150, 161–2, 170,
   187–8; infitah (opening up) policy,
   10, 42, 45, 58, 170; initiation rites
   of, 123–4; al-Intiqad, 79, 82–3,
   109, 111, 114–16, 174; al-Ismailiya,
   42; Jihad al-bina' (Struggle for
   Construction), 52; Lajnat imdad
   al-Khomeini (Khomeini Support
   Committee), 52; 'Lebanonisation'
   of, 25–6, 67, 137, 139, 170, 182;
   al-Mahdi scouts, 52, 63, 111;
   al-Manar (The Beacon), 10, 40, 42,
   53, 60–1, 64–7, 73–8, 83, 86, 89,
   100, 107, 114–15, 122, 162,
   174–7, 183, 186, 189; manifesto
   (2009), 14–16, 22–3, 25–6; Media
   Department, 93; Media Relations

INDEX

Unit, 65; member of Lebanese National Opposition, 98; members of, 3–4, 6–7, 10–11, 14–15, 17, 25, 28–9, 32, 41, 45, 53, 56, 59, 63, 67–8, 72, 76–8, 86, 95, 97, 100, 102, 105, 109, 111, 114, 116–17, 123, 125, 134–6, 138–9, 142–3, 149–50, 153, 157–8, 167, 176, 179, 184; Military Media Unit, 65; mobilisation strategies of, 6–9; Mo'assasat al-shahid (Martyrs' Foundation), 45; *al-Mujtahid* (The Struggler), 9, 40; al-muqawama al-islamiya (Islamic Resistance), 174; Mu'assassat al-jarha (Wounded Foundation), 52; al-Nour, 53, 60, 64–5; 'Open Letter' (1985), 3, 14, 22, 24–5, 33, 41, 158; 'Operation Radwan', 104; organisational structure of, 17; poetry festivals organised by, 122; poetry focusing on, 120–6, 146–7, 149; political strategy of, 13, 18, 30–1, 37–8, 47–50, 53, 55, 67–9, 82–3, 85, 93; public rallies organised by, 103–4; publications of, 94–6, 108; Al-qard al-hassan, 52; Qism al-di'ayah al-siyassiyah (Political Propaganda Unit), 64–5; Resistance Department, 65; al-Risalaat, 94; al-Saraya al-lubnaniya li-muqawamat al-ihtital (Lebanese Brigade to Resist the Occupation), 67–8; shura council of, 158; suicide bombing campaigns of, 56, 78, 93; supporters of, 29, 81, 84, 87, 145, 159, 171, 173; Al-ta'bia' al-tarbawiya (Educational Enforcement Office), 52; territory controlled by, 4, 23, 109; use of social media, 189; Waad programme, 106–7; al-Wihda, 42

al-Husari, Sati': 141
Hussein, Imam: 175; death of, 54, 182; depictions of, 108, 126, 133, 138–9; family of, 125, 139; followers of, 53, 55, 130
Hussein, Magdi: 160–1
Hussein, Saddam: 124

Idea Creation: personnel of, 91–2; role in Hizbullah Divine Victory campaign (2006), 10, 91–2
Iran: 8, 38, 48, 80, 82, 123, 127–8, 130, 152–3, 169, 183; Bonyad-e shahid, 45; Clerics of, 17; Green Movement (2009), 37, 116; Islamic Revolution (1979), 2–3, 40, 43–4, 54–5, 115, 141; political connections to Hizbullah, 1, 8, 11, 20, 22, 30, 44–5, 94, 106–7, 123, 128, 139–42, 167, 176, 181; Qom, 115, 158; Revolutionary Guards, 158; Tehran, 20, 55, 177; *wilayat al-faqih* (Guardianship of the Jurisprudence), 3, 15–17, 24, 41, 44, 58, 140–1, 157, 168
Iraq: 156; Kufa, 138; Najaf, 168; Operation Iraqi Freedom (2003–11), 4
Islam: 3, 12, 14, 22, 27, 37, 39, 46, 88, 119, 130; 'Ashoura, 54–5, 62, 110, 122; political, 5; Quran, 43, 47, 86, 114, 142, 152, 169, 173; Ramadan, 62, 111; Shaaban, 111; Shiite, 2, 4, 6, 8–9, 16, 19, 22, 26, 29–31, 33, 38–9, 42–3, 50–5, 57–60, 73, 81–3, 102, 106–8, 112–13, 115, 117, 120–1, 123, 125–6, 137–40, 143, 145, 153, 155, 157, 159, 169–70, 173, 175–6, 179–80, 184, 187–8; Sunni,

INDEX

4, 22–3, 35–6, 38, 112, 115, 117, 182, 184, 186

Islamic Jihad: political rhetoric of, 47

Islamism: 2–3, 6, 10, 26, 42–3, 47, 74, 124, 136, 142, 159, 161, 178; jihadi, 39; poetry, 143; Shiite, 155, 157

Israel: 11, 19–20, 28, 38, 47, 60–1, 64, 77, 79–80, 86, 93, 95–6, 109, 116, 134, 137, 142, 144, 152, 161, 169–70, 175, 179, 185, 187–8; borders of, 91, 94; creation of (1948), 46, 73; Haifa, 94; Invasion of Lebanon (1982), 2, 7, 9, 22, 40, 42, 55, 126, 157; Israeli Defence Force (IDF), 20, 56, 65, 73, 83–4, 86–7, 97, 105, 108, 149–50, 159, 162; prison system of, 89, 92, 103–4, 106–7; settlements of, 107; territory occupied by, 78, 190; withdrawal from Lebanon (2000), 4, 10, 35, 117, 130, 143, 152

Ivory Coast: 112

Al-Jazeera: coverage of July War (2006), 85, 162

Jervis, Robert: 106

Jesus Christ: 127, 132; crucifixion of, 136

jihadism: 55, 62, 68; Sunni, 117, 186–7; takfiri, 182, 187

Jraisati, Saleem: 111

Judaism: 142

July War (2006): 7, 29–30, 42, 122, 130, 134, 139, 141–2, 145, 147, 181; casualties of, 4, 83, 92; depictions of, 95; Hizbullah media responses to, 10–11, 27, 35–6, 72, 82–92, 94, 97, 103, 107–8, 164, 174; media coverage of, 85, 162–3; Operation Truthful Pledge (2006),

20, 34, 83, 92, 149–50; outbreak of, 20, 34, 71

Jum, Maryam Ali: Messengers of the Beloved, The, 95

Kawtharani, Mohammad: 91–2

Khalili, Laleh: 102

Khamenei, Ayatollah Ali: 24, 43, 75; influence of, 102, 167, 176; speeches of, 115

Khomeini, Ayatollah Ruhollah: 22, 62–3, 67, 115, 127–8; death of (1989), 44, 127; depictions of, 107, 127, 140; influence of, 43–5, 102, 153, 157; writings of, 43–4

Khuttar (The Uninvited Guests) (poem): 147–50; lyrical content of, 149

al-kifah al-mussallah (armed struggle): use by political groups, 49

Lahd, General Anton: leader of South Lebanese Army, 133

latmiyaat': concept of, 127

Lebanese Civil War (1975–90): 1–2, 7–8, 138, 156, 170, 182, 186–7; expulsion of PLO from Lebanon (1982), 22; Israeli Invasion of Lebanon (1982), 2, 7, 9, 22, 40, 42, 55, 126, 157; Ta'if Accord (1989), 3, 34, 56–7, 158; War of the Camps (1985–8), 23, 31, 61

Lebanese Communist Party: 48; supporters of, 156

Lebanese Option Gathering (Option Party): founding of (2007), 31–2

Lebanese Supreme Shiite Council: members of, 2

Lebanon: 1, 13, 16, 24, 27, 37, 39–40, 56, 69, 71, 110, 121, 128, 131, 136, 139, 142, 152, 160, 185–6;

INDEX

Alawite population of, 112; Ansarieh, 65; Audio-Visual Law, 65; Bazouriyeh, 155–6; Beirut, 2, 4, 18, 23, 26, 30, 34, 43, 45, 48, 54, 56, 61–2, 80, 83, 86, 88–91, 93, 97–101, 103, 107–9, 111–13, 146, 155, 158, 162, 166, 186; Bint Jbeil, 73, 161; borders of, 20; Cedar Revolution (2005), 4, 79, 82, 98; Christian population of, 4, 25, 38, 41, 58, 98, 117, 155; coup d'état (2011), 111–12; electoral system of, 21–2; government of, 3, 26, 112–13; Hermel, 111; Hosh, 111; Independence of (1943), 7; Israeli withdrawal from (2000), 4, 10, 17, 35, 71, 73–6, 82, 117, 130, 143, 152; Khiam, 74–5; Maroun al-Ras, 107; military of, 28–9, 73, 159–60; Ministry of Tourism, 75; Nabati-yyeh, 29, 102; National Pact (1943), 2, 57; Shiite population of, 2, 8–9, 16, 22, 26, 29, 31, 38–9, 42–3, 50–5, 57–60, 82–3, 106–8, 112, 117, 121, 128, 137, 145, 153, 159, 170, 173, 188; South Lebanon security belt (1985–2000), 17, 19, 49–50; Sunni population of, 38, 112, 117; Sur (Tyre), 56, 155; Syrian occupation of (1976–2005), 21, 25–6, 79

Libya: 157; Civil War (2011), 22, 113–15; Tripoli, 113

Mahdi: prophecies regarding, 75, 175
al-Mahdi, Imam: 108, 143; ancestors of, 140
Mahmoud, Arwah: 95–6
majalis: use in commemoration of Battle of Karbala, 54
majalis al-'aza: use of poetry in, 122

al-Manar, Dar: 137–8
March 14 coalition: 79, 82, 112, 181; accusation of support for Mubarak regime, 114; billboard campaigns of, 99; key figures of, 35; opposition to Hizbullah, 79–80; rallies organised by, 80–1, 98; response to Iranian elections (2005), 82; shortcomings of, 19
March 8 coalition (Lebanese National Opposition): 98–9; anti-government sit-ins organised by, 98; members of, 98; public image of, 98
Marinetti, Filippo Tommaso: Futurist Manifesto (1909), 106
Martyrs' Association: 53
Marxism: 142
Miqati, Najib: administration of, 181
Mleeta: 104–6; establishment of (2010), 103–4; military vehicles displayed at, 36; Spider's Web (exhibition), 11, 36, 103
Mohammadi, Ali: 168
Moses: 127
Movement of the Deprived: 106; founding of (1974), 2, 55; members of, 55, 156
Mu'assassat al-shaheed (Martyrs' Foundation): 45; aims of, 52
Mu'awiyah: death of (AD 680), 138; family of, 143
Mubarak, Hosni: 114; removed from power (2011), 113, 118
Mueller, Claus: 85
Mughniyeh, Imad (Haj Radwan): 102, 158; assassination of (2008), 100, 114; head of external operations for Hizbullah, 100; public image of, 100–4
Muhammad, Prophet: 127, 142, 144; death of (AD 632), 44, 140;

descendants of, 168, 173; military campaigns of, 93

Mukhs, Musa: poetry of, 126–7

al-Mussawi, Abbas: 45, 68, 101–2; assassination of, 59, 101, 114; family of, 59; Secretary General of Hizbullah, 158

Musawi, Nawaf: 25

Muslim Brotherhood: ideology of, 2

Nasr, Vali: 19

Nasrallah, Abdelkarim: family of, 155

Nasrallah, Hadi: family of, 160, 178; martyrdom of, 160, 178

Nasrallah, Hassan: death of (1997), 67–8; family of, 67–8

Nasrallah, Sheikh Hassan: 15–16, 23, 33, 35, 45, 61, 67–8, 72, 74–5, 84–7, 89, 99, 103–4, 111, 115–16, 151, 157, 160, 162–4, 180; as subject matter of poetry, 133, 139, 144–6; background of, 155–7, 167; family of, 67–8, 155–6, 160, 178; political rhetoric of, 168–70, 172–4, 178–80, 182, 185; public image of, 86–9, 91–2, 98, 100, 104, 118, 143–4, 153–6, 160–3, 165–7, 171–4, 177–8; Secretary General of Hizbullah, 3–4, 6–7, 10–11, 15, 142, 153, 158; speeches of, 11, 28, 59, 73, 77, 83, 88–9, 92, 108–10, 113–14, 116, 146, 168, 170, 174–6, 179–80, 182, 184–5, 187, 189

nationalism: 4, 48, 57–8, 116, 163, 170, 177; Arab, 47; Lebanese, 81, 138; *muqawama* (resistance), 48–9, 60; pan-Arab, 141, 176

Negm, Ahmad Fouad: poetry of, 151; role in Egyptian Revolution (2011), 151

Newman, Bruce: theories on components of political marketing, 90–1

Palestine: 38, 43–6, 48, 73, 78, 142, 147, 150, 183; al-Aqsa Mosque, 46, 62; Dome of the Rock, 176; Jerusalem (al-Quds), 46–7, 76–8, 101, 124–5, 129, 150, 179; Ramallah, 76; Occupied Territories, 78; Second Intifada (2000–5), 4, 76, 161–2

Palestinian Liberation Organisation (PLO): expulsion from Lebanon (1982), 22, 157; influence of, 48

Palestinian Television: bombing of Ramallah building, 76

poetry: 121, 127, 129–31, 137, 139–40, 144, 147; Arabic, 120; festivals, 122; focus on martyrdom in, 132–3; Hizbullah as subject matter, 120–6, 146–7, 149; ideology within, 135–9, 143, 152; Islamic cultural value of, 119–20, 122; Islamist, 143; love, 149; publication of, 125–7, 133; ritual use of, 123–4, 133; use in majalis al-ʿaza, 122

Qabani, Nizar: 120

Qaddafi, Muammar: opponents of, 114; speeches of, 114

Qahtan: cultural significance of, 141–2

al-Qasim, Samih: 120

Qassem, Naim: 26–7, 99, 125; Deputy Secretary General of Hizbullah, 14, 41, 53, 59, 76–7, 95, 158; speeches of, 109

Qassir, Ahmad: martyrdom of, 41, 56, 101

Qatar: 18

INDEX

al-Qubasi, Mohammad: background of, 128; poetry of, 128–9
Quntar, Samir: 104

Raad, Mohammad: 14
Rafsanjani, Hashemi: electoral defeat of (2005), 82
Rancière, Jacques: 172
Rice, Condoleeza: speeches of, 97
Rose, Gideon: 17, 19–20, 36

Saad-Ghorayeb, Amal: 8, 49
al-Sadr, Imam Musa: 50–1, 114, 121; as subject matter of poetry, 124, 129; disappearance of (1982), 157; founder of Amal, 2; founder of Movement of the Deprived, 2, 106, 156; head of Lebanese Supreme Shiite Council, 2; influence of, 153
al-Sadr, Sayyed Mohammed Baqir: execution of (1978), 157; influence of, 156
As-Safir: 171; Arab Documentation Centre, 94
Salafism: Sunni, 186
Saleh, Naziha: 116
Saudi Arabia: 112, 142; Mecca, 124, 182
Sharon, Ariel: 65
Shu'ayb, Rida: poetry of, 137–8
al-Sifar: 41
Silverstone, Roger: 154–5
Siniora, Fouad: 98; administration of, 25, 29
Six-Day War (1967): 120
South Lebanese Army: 66; members of, 133
South Lebanon Conflict (1982–2000): 65, 71, 73–6, 82, 101, 117, 126, 132, 143, 159, 161; April Understanding (1996), 159–60; Operation

Grapes of Wrath (1996), 63, 66, 159; Qana Massacre (1996), 64–6
Sreberny-Mohammadi, Annabelle: 168
Suchman, Mark: 108
Syria: 1, 20, 79–80, 142, 160, 180, 183; Civil War (2011–), 5, 11, 20, 22, 32, 35, 38, 112, 116–18, 155, 179, 181–5, 190; Damascus, 100; Golan Heights, 190; military of, 79; Palmyra, 133; political connections to Hizbullah, 8, 20, 34, 94, 142, 151, 178–9; Qusair, 185
Syrian Social Nationalist Party: 48

takfiri: 117
Tele Liban: 64, 74
Third Cinema: influence of, 48
al-Tufaili, Subhi: Secretary General of Hizbullah, 17, 32, 158
Tunisia: 151; Revolution (2010–11), 22, 113, 115, 118, 178
Twitter: 189; use in Arab Spring, 35–6

umma: 44, 77
United Arab Emirates (UAE): 169
United Nations (UN): 63; Interim Force in Lebanon (UNIFIL), 111; Resolution 1559 (2004), 21, 23, 25–6, 34, 98; Special Tribunal for Lebanon (STL), 14, 21, 26, 28–9, 33–5, 72, 97–8, 100, 109–12, 116–18, 177, 181, 184
United States of America (USA): 4, 20, 28, 76, 79–81, 96–7, 109, 113, 152, 170, 173, 179, 185; 9/11 attacks, 76–7; State Department, 112; Washington DC, 79

Wallis, Roy: 167
War on Terror: 4, 76

INDEX

Weber, Max: theory of charisma, 90,
    164–5
Wedeen, Lisa: 80–1, 154, 174
Wickert, Wolfram: 87
WikiLeaks: diplomatic cables released
    by, 112
Wilner, Ruth: 165

Yahiya, Ahmad: martyrdom of, 132
Yazid: army of, 53, 143; family of, 143
Yemen: Revolution (2011–12), 114
YouTube: 168; channels, 189; use in
    Arab Spring, 186

Zakaria, Fareed: 23–4
Zeinab: capture of (AD 680), 143;
    family of, 143
Zionism: 45, 48, 55, 147